A wide-eyed South African conscript relates his small share of the war in Angola and Namibia in the 1980s. This is not the usual military history, written by a commander armed with facts, nor a researched story of a war or campaign. It is a personal experience.

Being brutally honest, it will resonate not only with readers of all things military, but also with a wider literary audience for its poetic prose and subtle sentiments, as well as for its entertaining narrative – thus, it may be of interest not only to the South African men who were there, but also to their women who were left behind, and to all men and women anywhere. It is a book by a non-warrior dumped into a war which, nevertheless, provides vivid and alternative first-hand accounts whose validity cannot simply be brushed aside by professional historians.

Descriptive writing takes readers right into the colourful past, into the action and into personal interactions. Notes made at the time preserve intimate details of what it was like to be a white South African during Apartheid, and the surprisingly humane culture within its small but effective white-led army. Dialogue is remembered verbatim, as is the unique jargon and profanity of the time, with English translations where Afrikaans is spoken.

After a brief life-based background, the narrative moves chronologically through two years of military training, deployment, combat and demobilisation, with comments on the human effect of these experiences. The result is a compelling time capsule: the South African Defence Force ceased to exist in 1994 when South Africa began its non-racial democracy.

Surprisingly, because it was a humane army, it was a good one, but this is not just a liberal attitude: it meant that when a thing needed doing, it was done conscientiously and thoroughly, with thought for secondary effects. It was a dangerous opponent to have – inflicting maximum casualties where this was necessary – but when the need passed, it switched easily to a humanitarian purpose. There was much lost that being unique (and laudable) in the Old South African culture – and in its army's approach and attitude – is fascinating today.

After his compulsory military service, Evan Davies qualified as an architect at the University of Port Elizabeth, and thereafter studied Urban Design at the University of Cape Town. Several years behind a drawing board convinced him that instead, he should go farming in the Klein Karoo – an arid, pristine South African hinterland. While financially unrewarding (or at times even intimidating), this allowed him to shoo baboons out of his house, ride horses, be charged by lions, wrestle pigs to the ground and grow olives trees. He could also wear shorts, shave infrequently and develop a permanent farmer's suntan, while writing poetry in the evenings or watching the stars.

Currently, he is in Cape Town with custody of his two talented teenaged sons. Here, he cooks well enough because he has to, reads a lot of History and Science, writes the odd poem and annoys everyone on Facebook, while also pursuing his new main professional interest, which is forging Iron Age-type swords. He has a suburban forge with all the smoke and hammer noise necessary to annoy the neighbours properly, but the physical demands, the creativity, the applied technical knowledge and the parenting all combine in a satisfying life experience.

TEENAGE SAFARI

A SOUTH AFRICAN CONSCRIPT IN THE BORDER WAR IN ANGOLA AND NAMIBIA

Evan Davies

Helion & Company

Helion & Company Limited
26 Willow Road
Solihull
West Midlands
B91 1UE
England
Tel. 0121 705 3393
Fax 0121 711 4075
Email: info@helion.co.uk
Website: www.helion.co.uk
Twitter: @helionbooks
Visit our blog at http://blog.helion.co.uk/

Published by Helion & Company 2017
Designed and typeset by Farr out Publications, Wokingham, Berkshire
Cover designed by Paul Hewitt, Battlefield Design (www.battlefield-design.co.uk)
Printed by Hobbs The Printers Ltd, Totton, Hampshire

Text © Evan Davies 2017
Photographs © Evan Davies unless otherwise credited
Map © Evan Davies 2017

Cover: The author (closest) and 2nd Lt De Jager in a Puma helicopter en route to the 4 August 1982 ambush near Cuvelai. (Pierre De Jager)

Every reasonable effort has been made to trace copyright holders and to obtain their permission for the use of copyright material. The author and publisher apologise for any errors or omissions in this work, and would be grateful if notified of any corrections that should be incorporated in future reprints or editions of this book.

ISBN 978-1-911512-93-6

British Library Cataloguing-in-Publication Data.
A catalogue record for this book is available from the British Library.

All rights reserved. No part of this publication may be reproduced, stored in a retrieval system, or transmitted, in any form, or by any means, electronic, mechanical, photocopying, recording or otherwise, without the express written consent of Helion & Company Limited.

For details of other military history titles published by Helion & Company Limited, contact the above address, or visit our website: http://www.helion.co.uk

We always welcome receiving book proposals from prospective authors.

Contents

List of Illustrations		vi
Foreword		ix
Author's Preface		xii
List of Terms, Acronyms and Common Afrikaans Words		xv
Map of Operational Areas		
1	Origins	25
2	1 SAI: Basics	34
3	Separating the Wheat from the Chaff	44
4	The Plains of De Brug: Infantry and Mortars	54
5	Ratels: Mechanised Infantry	63
6	The Captain	73
7	Chosen for Action	81
8	Black Breasts	88
9	"Gemeenskap gehou met 'n koei"	95
10	Omuthiya	103
11	Into Angola: Operation Meebos 1	112
12	Operation Yahoo!	117
13	Tracks	125
14	Outpost Life	134
15	Into Angola: Operation Meebos 2	143
16	Cuvelai Road	151
17	Shot Down!	159
18	Marking Time Until Uitklaar	169
Epilogue		177
Appendices		
I	A Brief History of the Border War and the War in Angola	182
II	The 15 April 1982 Ambush in Operation Yahoo!	186
III	The 4 August 1982 Ambush in Operation Meebos	193

List of Illustrations

Training at Bloemfontein and De Brug, 1981
Training at Bloemfontein and De Brug, 1981
Bombing up for training at Rooi Hoenderhaan – the future crew of
    12A. Left to right: Pienaar, unknown, Scheepers, Cruywagen in
    the gunner's hatch.   i
A Ratel in the Koeikamp with 1 SAI and the Feeshuis in the background.   i
F Company's Rooi Hoenderhaan training base at De Brug as seen from the hill.   i
Me taking a break at Rooi Hoenderhaan with Marie Biscuits.   ii
Me multitasking on the go-kart toilets at Rooi Hoenderhaan. No
    National Servicemen failed to have this photo taken.   ii

Oshivello Training Base in the Operational Area, January-February 1982
Ready for night patrol at Oshivello. These were real combat patrols.   iii
Keeping an arrowhead formation in thick bush near Oshivello. Left
    to right: Marais, 2nd Lt De Jager, Hoy.   iii
Platoon 1 resting between platoon attack exercises at Oshivello.   iii
The 61 Mech Base at Omuthiya
The Everite Hotel.   iv
Platoon 1 HQ at a stalparade. Left to right: (standing) Van
    Schalkwyk, Cpl Mielmann, 2nd Lt De Jager, Cpl Robinson, Piek,
    Waite, Marais; (kneeling) Weterall, Davies, Singleton. (Pierre De Jager)   iv

Operation Yahoo!, April-May 1982
On the Bravo cutline.   v
Ratel cleaning inside the earth wall at the Tsintsabis army base.   v
Klaus Mais-Rische's farmhouse at Onderra.   v
Rushing to newly found tracks in the Etosha Game Reserve.   vi
Breakfast at Onderra. Left to right: Marais, Waite, Singleton, 2nd Lt
    De Jager, Hoy.   vi
The python at Otavi. Left to right: Piek, Cpl Mielmann, Davies, Wetherall.   vi
A Ratel in line abreast chasing insurgents through Etosha.   vii
Koevoet Casspirs arrive minutes before contact to steal our kills in Etosha.   vii

LIST OF ILLUSTRATIONS vii

61 Mech Training at the Bloubaan, June 1982

Advancing in convoy at dawn (that's a 140mm artillery gun ahead of the Ratel). viii

Forming into attack formation; a Ratel 90 tankbuster is seen
    integrating with the line of Ratel 20s from behind. viii

Ratel 90s begin the attack at a range of 1km. viii

Wetherall and I on the 60mm patrol mortar target deep defence
    positions. We were in trouble for not having camouflaged our helmets. ix

Troops debussed for a mechanised infantry fire-and-movement
    advance through the base. The haze is cordite. ix

The base overrun, with destroyed trucks and trees. ix

Operation Meebos, July-August 1982

Alpha Company during Operation Meebos near the Cuvelai
    River. Cpt Malan (with beard) is in front, below the flag aerial.
    (www.61mech.org.za) x

Maintaining weapons and ammunition in a Helicopter
    Administration Area. (Pierre De Jager) x

The spaghetti-carrying Ural truck having just been hit by an RPG-7. xi

An Alouette helicopter gunship victim. xi

The Ural truck that died in the killing ground on the Cuvelai Road
    on August 4 1982; note some remaining 122mm GRAD-P shells
    at the rear of the flatbed. xi

We each took an identically damaged note as a souvenir of this day. xii

Washing in the Cuvelai River. (Pierre De Jager) xii

Journal Entries

A recording the 15 April 1982 ambush. xiii

A sketch of the recovered Ratel 12A destroyed on 15 April 1982,
    Tsumeb Airport. xiii

A sketch of a SWAPO insurgent killed in April; note the AKM, the
    rice pattern camo and the knitted jersey. xiii

An air leaflet, Operation Yahoo! xiv

A record of the 4 August 1982 ambush near Cuvelai. xiv

A sketch of a FAPLA soldier hit by 20mm HE shells from an
    Alouette gunship, Operation Meebos xiv

People

Captain Jan Malan, CO Alpha Company. (www.61mech.org.za)	xv
Commandant Roland de Vries, CO 61 Mech. (www.61mech.org.za)	xv
The author (closest) and 2nd Lt De Jager in a Puma helicopter en route to the 4 August 1982 ambush near Cuvelai. (Pierre De Jager)	xvi
61 Mech Regimental Sergeant Major H.G. Smit (Killer Smit). (www.61mech.org.za)	xvi

Foreword

As commander of the renowned 61 Mechanised Battalion Group (61 Mech) in 1981-1982, I remember my brave young conscript soldiers particularly well. Many of them, like Evan Davies, were only 19 years old at the time. They had what it took as young national servicemen of the former South African Defence Force (SADF) and I was proud to have served with them in military operations such as Meebos and Yahoo.

The Border War, or bush war as it was also referred to, which Evan Davies writes about, lasted from 1966 until 1989, a total of 23 years, making it one of Africa's longest military conflicts. It was fought intermittently across the South West Africa/Angola border, and the insurgency war effectively ended on 1 November 1988, when South Africa and the South West Africa People's Organisation (SWAPO) called it even. Similarly a peace accord was signed between South Africa, Angola and Cuba in New York on 22 December 1988, ending the semi-conventional side of the war in southern Angola.

When the bush war reached its peak during the 1980s, the international perception was that South Africa had one of the toughest armies in the world, honed and sharpened by 20 years of anti-terrorist bush war on its northern borders. The SADF had also learned from the ways the Portuguese and Rhodesians had fought their respective bush wars, from their positive as well as negative experiences. Evan Davies became part of this fighting machine, all muscle and bone. From his military training and operational exploits he soon realised that solid military doctrine, esprit de corps and superb training were crucial for survival in a harsh combat environment accentuated by the darkness and denseness of the African bush.

Evan Davies was trained at 1 South African Infantry Battalion in Bloemfontein before he became a fully-fledged mechanised infantryman at 61 Mechanised Battalion Group in South West Africa, now called Namibia. It was one of the finest combat forces in the military history of South Africa. The Ratel six-wheeled armoured fighting vehicle became the tool of 61 Mech's fighting trade. It also became the epitome of the long-standing cavalry dictum, namely, that strength lies in mobility, that swiftness is an elemental factor of warfare, making up for numbers on the battlefield by the quickness of marches, and that an aptitude for warfare is an aptitude for movement. This aptitude is an inborn trait that South African soldiers have excelled at since their earliest pioneering days.

61 Mech formed an essential element of South Africa's mobile conventional forces as its first-ever multi-arms fighting unit. The unit was the designated mobile reserve for the South West Africa Territorial Force because of its unique fighting capabilities and its ability to be combat ready at all times. Another attribute of 61 Mech was that the unit could swiftly mount either conventional-type operations, or switch over to counterinsurgency.

Military operations took place in that one vast and almost trackless area which straddled both sides of the border between South West Africa/Namibia and Angola. It was a place of great distances, unforgiving terrain and frequently dreadful weather conditions, and it was populated by enemies ranging from artful, tenacious insurgents to conventional soldiers with tanks, artillery and fighter aircraft. The official SADF designation for this area of operations was the Western Sub-Theatre of War, although everybody, soldiers and civilians alike, called it by a simpler name, but one that said it all: 'The Border'.

The unit fought both a counterinsurgency war against the People's Liberation Army of Namibia (PLAN), SWAPO's armed wing, and a conventional war against the Angolan Army (FAPLA) and its Cuban allies. For this reason 61 Mech saw action in all the well-known large-scale operations formally recorded in history, such as Operation Reindeer in May 1978, Sceptic in June 1980, Protea in August 1981, Yahoo in April-May 1982, Meebos in July-August 1982 and Askari in December 1983-January 1984.

Additionally 61 Mech fought with distinction in the high-intensity conventional operations which followed in southern Angola from August 1987 until August 1988 – referred to by the SADF as Operations Modular, Hooper, Packer, Hilti and Prone. These conventional battles were fought by the SADF in alliance with UNITA (the National Union for the Total Independence of Angola) against a numerically overwhelming Angolan-Cuban coalition force, at a time when South Africa's politics became intertwined with the Angolan Civil War.

During cross-border operations in Angola it was expected of combat groups to fight independently or as part of larger combat groupings, such as brigade-sized task forces. 61 Mech was the crucible in which South Africa's modern mechanised army was forged, with a distinctive fighting culture that sprang from a combination of a finely tuned doctrinal synthesis and hands-on experience of conventional and semi-conventional African bush campaigning.

It is interesting to note that 61 Mech extraordinaire was commended by the Cubans for its superb fighting work in southern Angola under the direst of operational circumstances, a testament to the unit's widely recognised military professionalism and highly regarded operational standing. Politics aside, for this was during those turbulent years of Apartheid, the particular legacy of our pioneering spirit is revealed in the blending of tactics from different military cultures, the tradition of a citizen army rather than a large regular force, and an emphasis on keeping casualties to the minimum. This produced a military ethos that accentuated effectiveness rather than sacrifice.

Teenage Safari is Evan Davies' epic account of his youthful experience in the harsh military world outlined above and about his share of the task in defending South Africa. His adventurous exploits are well worth reading and I am justly proud of him.

Our young national servicemen were warriors – and in 61 Mechanised Battalion Group, every man counted!

Roland de Vries, Plettenberg Bay, South Africa,
6 November 2015
Major General (Retired) Roland de Vries was a former commander of 61 Mechanised Battalion Group (1981-1982) and a former deputy chief of the South African Army. He has also recently published his book, *Eye of the Firestorm* (Naledi, 2013, UK edition Helion).

Author's Preface

I drove in 2014 with my teenage son from Tsintsabis to Omuthiya on the D3001, dusty-white, wide and unfenced. He was four years younger than I had been when last here. I was a little shocked at the shabby rural squatting the SWAPO government is subsidising, enabling unsustainable donkey farming in marginal areas, leading to exponential growth of the majority Ovambo electorate. Then, lion and elephant roamed in pristine wilderness. No more. Still, the warm fragrant air, the stands of makalani palms, and the occasional lilac-breasted-roller, were powerful cues for my nostalgia. We passed the farms Koedoesvlei, the old home of Tannie Pompie, and Ondera, now a government project. It looked unchanged, with the same stand of maize as you drive to the farmhouse. We found Omuthiya quite easily, in spite of the new railway line and the well-trodden, littered sand. Wandering among disordered corrugated iron cucas, we found the ordered ruins of the mess, the hangar parks, the monument. Near this, I even found the concrete slab for my tent, my home for almost a year, where I wrote letters, cleaned my weapons, and heard Joan Jett and Rodrigues for the first time, as the moon was hanging in a purple sky. It was at the end of the second row of tents as you walked east from the monument. We took photos there.

It was not always fun: my old army photos suggest this. We look like we were having a whale of a time, always laughing. In the journal I kept it's a different story, one of angry tension between national servicemen and Permanent Force members. A desperation to go home, and when we did, it was to emptiness. It was a tough time. Today, everyone remembers the good things, so this book may re-awaken some uncomfortable controversies. Well, so be it. Strangely, I nevertheless I look back on my time at Omuthiya as the most carefree, happy time of my life. This is hard to explain, but perhaps the absence of bills, tax forms, or any possessions at all, provides the answer. And although our challenges seemed overbearing, we overcame them and felt fulfillment. Further, despite the tensions, we had loyalty and admiration for our combat leaders.

This is my personal account of army training in South Africa in 1981, and combat duty in Namibia and Angola in 1982 with 61 Mechanised Battalion, at the height of Apartheid. Having had journalistic pretensions, I kept a journal and wrote down many intimate details that would have been forgotten. This record, including

AUTHOR'S PREFACE   xiii

sketches, formed the basis for the story, which I wrote nine years later in 1991 to an imaginary receptive audience, when none were prepared to hear about the bottled-up experience. Some of the journal entries are immature or prejudiced and do not reflect my current views. I leave them here unchanged as a faithful record of the times, as well as our unique jargon and filthy language, plus a few things of a personal nature that are commonly thought improper to record. I would like no one today to feel aggrieved by resentments, insults, or accusations, regarding individuals or groups, expressed in the text. These were the opinion of a nineteen-year-old, 33 years ago. We are grown up and have moved on. In re-editing in 2015 I have added a balancing layer of historically accurate retrospect, so one might say this account has been written three times, by three different people.

This is the tale of a teenage excursion rather than contextualized facts: an 'adventure story for boys'. It does not claim historical authority. While some events have been described by others, the differences in my journal version remain uncorrected, as there is authentic value in a first-hand account no matter its faults. Certain memories may indeed be more accurate and detailed, having been put to writing immediately. For the sake of balance, and to let the reader decide, I include other first-hand accounts in the appendices, along with a brief overview of the war. This book simplifies the journal, forming a narrative of my choice. Many more situations, anecdotes and people complicated those two years than can fit in these pages.

Many white South African boys went off to 'the border' during the 1970s and 1980s, a long conflict, complicated to unravel. It has been my preoccupation to seek out facts and understand what happened, and the 1991 writing was my first step in this process. While, simplistically speaking, South Africans fought as proxies for the USA against the Soviet Union and Cuba, we also had our own interlocking regional agendas. We were involved at various levels with various players in the context of the Angolan Civil War, and the struggle for independence for South West Africa/Namibia. There are historical, narrative and fictionalised accounts, as well as politically inspired myths, all contributing to a swirling debate. But for we who were there, it was neither complicated nor mysterious, but simple and real.

The moral environment for us teenagers was a jangling discord. While right wing views called loud in the army, liberal thinking remained a steadfast undercurrent. Discourse was healthy. Our speech was never unfree. I don't think any of our beliefs were concrete, nor could they rightly be expected to be. We were sometimes certain, sometimes confused: as any teenagers would, we followed the direction of the dominant elders in our society. A clear thread though, central to the turbulent polemic, was actual SADF doctrine, which was pragmatic and did not respond to political emotions. Right wing fire was certainly taken advantage of to feed the will to fight, but at the same time cool liberal conscience restrained excesses. In retrospect, the SADF's two-fold mandate, to keep peace in South West Africa for democracy to emerge, and to sweep the Soviet and Cuban imperialists from our subcontinent, was fulfilled, a noble moral cause to have been part of. If anyone wants to debate this, ask, why did SWAPO, who vowed to overthrow the state by force of arms, instead submit to the democratic process, and why did the Cubans leave?

In South Africa, the 'Border War' and the 'War in Angola' have been difficult to discuss in politically correct or constructive debate, due to the bold propaganda disinformation of a 'Marxist victory' versus a 'Racist defeat'. We endure the same boring lies being dug up and repeated. Now, it seems, things are changing, and the shroud on a more nuanced and exciting truth is lifting. Recently, there has been a revival of the esprit de corps of SADF units, with the founding of veterans' associations based on social media. Ironically these are warmly regarded by our ex-Soviet opponents.

Into this miasma I cast my two cents' worth. As an insignificant passenger, once, amid the restless heat and wild smells of diesel, dust and torn vegetation, I tell a little-heard story, the story of a teenage safari. It is neither *very* exciting nor *very* significant, but it is a *true* story, and I hope, an entertaining one.

List of Terms, Acronyms and Common Afrikaans Words

1IC	First in Command.
1 Mil	1 Military Hospital.
1 SAI	1 South African Infantry Battalion.
2IC	Second in Command.
2 MOB	2 Mobilisation Depot.
4 SAI	4 South African Infantry Battalion.
31 Battalion	Unconventional light infantry unit made up of Angolan Bushmen led by South African officers.
32 Battalion	Unconventional light infantry unit made up of Angolan blacks led by South African officers.
61 Mech	61 Mechanised Battalion.
201 Battalion	Formerly 31 Battalion, Bushmen.
AK-47	Soviet assault rifle, 7.62 calibre.
Alouette	French-manufactured helicopter.
ANC	African National Congress, a South African liberation movement.
Anhara	Open river floodplain, Angola.
AP	Armour Piercing, penetration shells.
Armscor	South African armament manufacturer.
AWOL	Absent Without Official Leave.
Baie	Very, much, many (Afrikaans).
Bakkie	Pick-up truck (Afrikaans).
Balkie	Bar decoration.
Balsak	Duffel bag, literally 'ball bag' (Afrikaans).
Base-bleed	Gas generator in some artillery shells filling the aft vacuum, reducing drag.
Basics	Basic training.
Bedford	Outdated British Army truck.
Berede	Horse-mounted (Afrikaans).
Bergie	Homeless person, tramp (Afrikaans).

Bidparade	Prayer parade (Afrikaans).
Bivvy	Waterproof shelter sheet (derived from 'bivouac').
Black Widow	Nickname for a Soviet anti-personnel landmine.
Bloubaan	Blue (shooting) range (Afrikaans).
Boerewors	Literally 'farmer's sausage' (Afrikaans).
Bokbaaivygie	Succulent South African plant.
Bolyn	Capie slang for a homosexual (derived from 'Bollie Konyn', a rabbit cartoon character).
Bosbus	Punishment PT, literally 'bush bus' (Afrikaans).
Bossies	Mad from being in the bush, and combat stress (Afrikaans).
Botha, Pik	The South African Foreign Minister.
Braai	Barbecue, literally 'grill' (Afrikaans).
Brei	Afrikaans speech characteristic of certain regions of South Africa.
Breker	Bully, tough guy, literally 'breaker' (Afrikaans).
BRDM	Soviet armoured personnel carrier with a heavy machine gun.
Browning	A mounted machine gun.
BTR	Soviet armoured personnel carrier.
Buffel	South African open-topped mine-resistant troop carrier, literally 'buffalo' (Afrikaans).
Bunny chow	Hollowed-out loaf of bread filled with curry from Durban.
C130	Heavy freight aircraft.
Cape Corps	Second World War coloured infantry unit.
Casevac	Casualty evacuation (by helicopter).
Casspir	Police armoured vehicle.
China!	South African slang for 'mate'!
Cicada	Insect that makes a loud whining sound.
Claymore	Shrapnel mine with a horizontal blast.
Commandant	Equivalent rank of Lieutenant Colonel in the SADF.
CSM	Company Sergeant-Major.
Cuca	Traditional circular settlement, Namibia and Angola.
Curry Cup	Annual South African inter-province rugby tournament.
Cutline	Strip of soft soil originally used for disease control of cattle ('kaplyn' in Afrikaans).
Dagga	Marijuana.
DB	Detention Barracks.

De La Rey	A Boer War Boer general.
Death Triangle	Area between the towns Tsumeb, Otavi and Grootfontein.
Die Stem	National Anthem, literally 'The Voice' (Afrikaans).
Dixie	Aluminium cooking and eating pan.
Donder, foeter	To beat up (Afrikaans).
Doos	Cunt, idiot in semi-polite dialogue, literally 'box' (Afrikaans).
Doppie	Spent cartridge (Afrikaans).
Doybie	Plastic helmet inner liner.
DTA	Democratic Turnhalle Alliance, South African-initiated democratic process for South West Africa.
Dutchmen	English nickname for Afrikaners, insulting.
Eland	French armoured car, literally 'a type of large antelope'.
ELNA	Armed wing of the FNLA.
ENT	Ears, Nose and Throat specialist.
Esbit	Fuel tablet for cooking in the bush.
FALA	Armed wing of UNITA.
FAPLA	Armed wing of the Angolan Government (MPLA).
Feeshuis	Festival hall (Afrikaans).
FNLA	Pro-Western Angolan Resistance Movement.
Fok, fokken	Fuck, fucking (expletive, adjective or adverb only, not a verb) (Afrikaans).
G3	German assault rifle.
Geweer	Rifle (Afrikaans).
Grensvegter	Literally 'border fighter', a popular photo-comic character (Afrikaans).
Gunship	An Alouette helicopter armed with a 20mm cannon.
Gyppo	To sneak out of a duty.
Gyppogat	Truant (Afrikaans).
Gyppoguts	Diarrhoea (derived from British Army slang in Egypt).
HAA	Helicopter Administration Area (see HAG).
Haak-en-Steek	Certain types of thorny acacia bush, literally 'hook-and-stab' (Afrikaans).
HAG	Helikopter Administrasie Gebied (Afrikaans).
HE	High Explosive, shrapnel shells or bombs.
HF radio	High Frequency radio.
HNP	Herstigte Nasionale Party, right wing political party.
HQ	Headquarters.

Huisgenoot	Afrikaans print magazine.
Impala	Italian jet trainer converted for a combat role in South Africa, literally 'a type of antelope'.
Jacaranda	Blue-flowering tree.
Kaffir, kaffer	Insulting term applied to blacks, literally 'infidel' (Arabic).
Kafferboom	Red-flowering tree, 'coral tree' post-Apartheid (Afrikaans).
Kak, kakker	Shit, shitter (Afrikaans).
Karoo	An arid interior region of South Africa.
Kas	Military holding cell, literally 'cupboard' (Afrikaans).
Katyusha	Soviet 122mm artillery rocket (see Stalin Organ).
Kerkparade	Church parade (Afrikaans).
Khoisan	Anthropologically correct term for peoples formerly known as Hottentots and Bushmen.
Klaar out	Clear out (of the army) (Afrikaans).
Koevoet	Counterinsurgency unit of the South West Africa Police, literally 'crowbar' (Afrikaans).
Kompanie	Company (Afrikaans).
Koppie	Small hill (Afrikaans).
Korporaal	Corporal (Afrikaans).
Kraal	Cattle pen, traditional African village (Afrikaans).
Kudu	A large type of antelope.
Kurper	Tilapia fish (Afrikaans).
Kwanza	Angolan currency.
Kwêvoël	Mine-resistant off-road truck, literally 'grey lourie', which is a bird (Afrikaans)
Laer	Modern word for laager, a defensible enclosure made up of vehicles (Afrikaans).
Lariam	Malaria prophylactic.
Leguaan	Monitor lizard.
Lesingkaserne	Lecture hall (Afrikaans).
Lieut	Short for Lieutenant, pronounced 'Loot'.
LMG	Light Machine Gun.
Luitenant	Lieutenant (Afrikaans).
MAG	Belgian light machine gun.
Magsvertoning	Show of strength (Afrikaans).
Mamba	A deadly snake.
MAOT	Mobile Air Operations Team.

Mealie	Maize (Afrikaans).
Mirage	French supersonic jet-fighter bomber.
Mopani	A tree.
MP	Military Police.
MPLA	Marxist Angolan Resistance Movement (and later, government).
Muhangu	Traditional grain beer.
Napalm	Inflammable petroleum compound.
NCO	Non-Commissioned Officer.
Nek	Saddle between hills (Afrikaans).
Net Blankes	Whites only, non-whites only (Afrikaans).
Net Nie Blankes	Non-whites only (Afrikaans).
NP	National Party, the South African ruling party.
NSM	National Serviceman.
Olifant	South Africa main battle tank, literally 'elephant' (Afrikaans).
OP	Observation Post.
Opfok	Punishment PT, literally 'a fucking-up' (Afrikaans).
Opleiding	Training (Afrikaans).
Opsbalkie	Operation bar, a chest decoration (Afrikaans).
Oumanne	Old hands, veterans (Afrikaans).
Ovambo	Namibian black nation.
Parabats	Parachute Battalion members.
Patmor	Patrol mortar.
PB	Plaaslike Bevolking, literally 'local population' (Afrikaans).
Peleton	Platoon (Afrikaans).
PF	Permanent Force.
Pieletjies	Little pricks (Afrikaans).
Pikstel	Army issue table cutlery, literally 'pickaxe set' (Afrikaans).
Piss lily	Camp urinal.
PLAN	Armed wing of SWAPO.
Poes	Cunt (Afrikaans).
Poesboekie	Soft porn magazine, literally 'cunt book' (Afrikaans).
Poesplaas	Literally 'cunt farm' (Afrikaans).
Pom-zed	A Soviet mine that jumps and explodes at head height
Potjie	A traditional stew in a cast-iron three-legged pot made on a fire.
Puma	French troop-carrying helicopter.

QM	Quartermaster.
R1	Belgian FN-FAL assault rifle made in South Africa.
R4	Israeli Galil assault rifle made in South Africa.
Ratel	South African armoured personnel carrier, literally a 'honey badger'.
Ratpack	Ration pack.
Recces	South African Reconnaissance Commandos.
Rooi hoenderhaan	Red rooster (Afrikaans).
Rooigras	Long red-tinted grass from the Orange Free State (Afrikaans).
Rooinek	A derogatory term for English speakers, literally 'redneck' from the Boer War Battle of Magersfontein, where the Black Watch suffered chronic sunburn while pinned down by Boer marksmen (Afrikaans).
Rooitee	Rooibos tea, an herb endemic to Clanwilliam, literally 'red tea' (Afrikaans).
Rower	Slang for new recruits (Afrikaans).
RPG-7, RPG	Soviet hand-held anti-tank rocket.
RSM	Regimental Sergeant-Major.
Rugridder	Slang for a homosexual, literally 'back rider' (Afrikaans).
Russians	Smoked pork sausages.
SA-7	Soviet hand-held anti-aircraft heat seeking missile, commonly known as the SAM7.
SADF	South African Defence Force.
Samajoor	Sergeant-Major (Afrikaans).
SAMIL	South African Military Truck.
Samp and beans	Traditional South African maize and bean stew.
Scania	Swedish truck.
Scope	English actuality magazine.
Sersant	Sergeant (Afrikaans).
Shona	Flat pan with water in the rainy season (Namibia and Angola).
Sieltiffie	Slang for an army chaplain, literally 'soul mechanic' (Afrikaans).
Sifseun	Syphilitic boy, slang (Afrikaans).
Sitrep	Situation report.
Skaapwagter	Shepherd (Afrikaans).
Skrapnelhoender	Literally 'shrapnel chicken,' an almost inedible army dish (Afrikaans).

Skrapnelvis	Literally 'shrapnel fish', a totally inedible army dish (Afrikaans).
Skrik	Get a fright (Afrikaans).
SKS	Soviet rifle.
Slagyster	Gin trap, literally 'slaughter iron' (Afrikaans).
Snoek	South African sea fish.
Snotneus	American grenade launcher made in South Africa, literally 'snot nose' (Afrikaans).
SOP	Standard Operating Procedure.
Sorghum	African grain.
Soutpiel	A derogatory term for English speakers, literally 'salt-prick' from having a foot in Britain, a foot in South Africa and your penis hanging in the sea (Afrikaans).
Spaarpiel	Spare penis – a pun on 'spaarwiel', or 'spare wheel' (Afrikaans).
Springhaas	Spring hare (Afrikaans).
Staak vuur	Cease fire (Afrikaans).
Staaldak	Steel helmet (Afrikaans).
Stalin Organ	Soviet 122mm artillery rocket (see Katyusha).
Stalparade	Literally 'stable parade', originating with cavalry (Afrikaans).
STOL	Short Take Off and Landing.
Suiderkruisfonds	Southern Cross Fund (Afrikaans).
SWAPO	South West Africa People's Organisation, a liberation movement.
SWAPOL	South West Africa Police.
SWATF	South West Africa Territory Force, which was established to regionalise the conflict, like 'Vietnamisation', the creation of the ARVN by the United States.
T54, T55	Soviet main battle tank.
Tac HQ	Tactical Headquarters.
Tannie	Auntie (Afrikaans).
Tempe	A military suburb of Bloemfontein.
Tiet	Firing button, literally 'tit' (Afrikaans).
Tiffie	Army slang for a mechanic.
Total Onslaught	A propaganda concept created by the South African government to mobilise whites to fight.
Trommel	Steel trunk or box (Afrikaans).
Tsetse fly	Insect, a carrier of sleeping sickness.

UCT	University of Cape Town.
Uitpakinspeksie	Unpacked inspection (Afrikaans).
Unimog	A small and versatile 4x4 truck.
UNITA	Pro-Western Angolan Resistance Movement.
Ural	Soviet military truck.
Valgroep	Stick of paratroopers, literally 'fall group' (Afrikaans).
Varkpan	Stainless steel food tray, literally 'pig pan' (Afrikaans).
Veggroep	Integrated contact group, literally 'fight group' (Afrikaans).
Veld	Natural open country (Afrikaans).
Verkrampte	Right wing, Conservative (Afrikaans).
Vetkoek	Deep-fried bread rolls (unsweetened doughnuts) filled with mince, literally 'fat cake' (Afrikaans).
Vlaktes	Plains (Afrikaans).
Vloek	Curse, cuss (Afrikaans).
Voertuie	Vehicles (Afrikaans).
Vuil slet	Dirty slut (Afrikaans).
Weermag	Army (Afrikaans).
Werf	Farmyard (Afrikaans).
Werfetter	Farmyard pus, an insult (Afrikaans).
Widow bird	A black long-tailed bird found in open grassland.
Winkel	Shop (Afrikaans).
Wit olifante	Large white trucks, literally 'white elephants' (Afrikaans).
WO1	Warrant Officer First Class (sergeant-major).
Xhosa	South African black nation.
Zol	Marijuana (Afrikaans).
ZU23	Soviet anti-aircraft cannon.
Zulu	South African black nation.

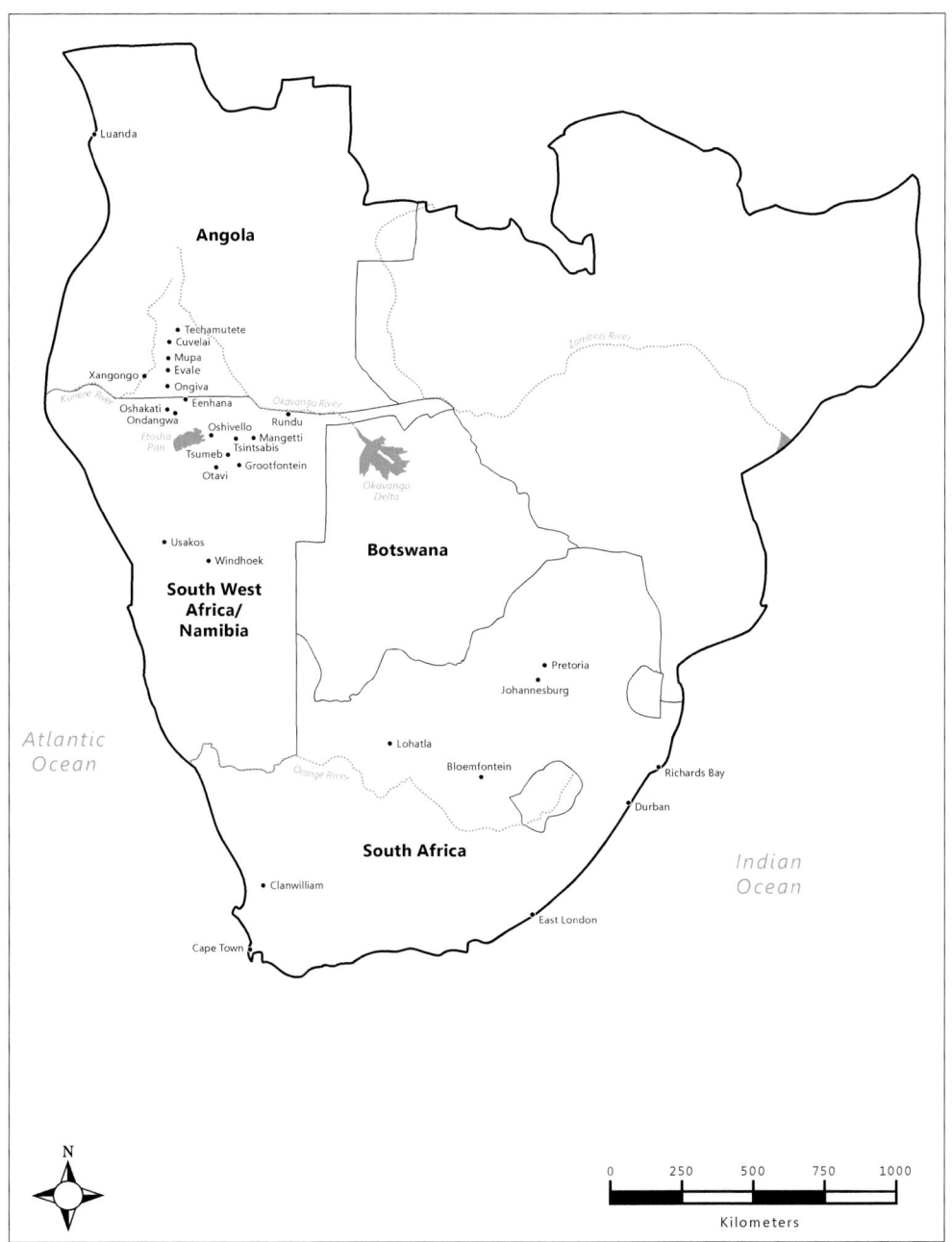

Map of operational areas

1
Origins

1965. I saw the land crab when I was about three, and it's probably my most vivid memory that survives the anthology of dreamscapes we keep from when we first come into the world. It was red and huge and terrifying, and it sidled out of the bokbaaivygies. I think I refused to go outside until after lunch, when the sun came out of the clouds, favouring me not the crab. There were crocodiles in my bedroom at night. They swarmed like Battlestar Galacticas in the 7.30pm darkness, curtains still luminous from direct sunlight, avoiding dust motes in warm, paper-thin sunbeams. My mother said she also saw them, just like Mrs McLeman, who saw leguaans in the street storm water drains and told me and her son Ross not to go near them. They were even bigger than my bedtime crocodiles. Mrs McLeman kept a catapult on her kitchen window sill, for the vervet monkeys that came up from the Buffalo River and raided the mealies in her vegetable garden.

1966. It's impossible to remember Edward's face or voice, or anything we said to each other. But I do remember him washing the dark earth off his calloused hands, at the tap outside my bedroom window, under the kafferboom. He called it a kafferboom too. Everyone did. He was the headman of a clan near East London, and it was 1966. The kafferboom had thorns on its thicker parts, so it was not a good tree to climb. A Mirage jet flew by during one of my excursions into the kafferboom. It didn't whoosh. There was a single shattering explosion and I remember seeing a dark blur through the leaves, not at all high in the air. My mother explained to me, Edward and the housemaid (of whom I remember little besides eating samp and beans in her quarters and listening to – learning – the Xhosa talk), who had rushed terrified from the kitchen, what a Mirage was and why it went bang.

My mother's aura is mostly yellow. Under her influence, all my early memories have a yellow tinge like sepia. My room was yellow. Mornings and evenings were yellow and warm. So were the flowers in our garden. Me and my Dad lived in this bright yellow environment that was light-filled and fresh.

1973. The faint line of whitish smoke was visible across 10 brown and grey miles of dry Clanwilliam veld, and would have been missed had it not been searched for every morning, along the skyline of the distant mountains, by my uncle Dennis, for the past weeks. Faint it was, yet meaningful to him alone. Calling for old Camel, once a Cape Corps batman during the Desert War, he took his morning tea before fetching his time-honoured .303 Lee Enfield rifle, and moving towards the open grey Series 3 Land Rover. At this point my mother's intercession placed me firmly in the passenger seat. My brother was too young. With Camel on the back, we bumped an hour's worth of rocky tracks to the summit.

Finally, through an acre of dead dorper sheep, we reached the fire that was still smoking, and next to it sat the skaapwagter (whose name might have been *Tol*, or *Jas*, or *Laan*), a wizened Bushman in ageless felt hat, drinking rooitee from a blackened tin. The conversation was strongly washed in the Khoisan brei, accent and idiom still heard in the Afrikaans in those parts, unintelligible to outsiders.

"Jáwas hysogiebult."

"Is hy nog fris?"

"Jáwas! Disse wyfietierg."

As we four picked our way down the rocky slope into the shade of the south side, between gharrabos and kanniedood (in front the skaapwagter, then my uncle, then Camel followed by small me), grunting barks and roars became audible from below and increased in ferocity as we drew nearer, every bit a mythologically dangerous foe of men. Then I saw it.

I believe that in some distant age, Man and Leopard faced each other across a merciless front, and that we are genetically imprinted in each other's memories as that most feared, most hated. It is one of the darkest of fears, being eaten. That is why I, a Western child, sat down at the sight of it and shook in a nightmare of terror. It communicated directly with me, and I cried. And through the tears, between the two retainers, on past my tall motionless aiming uncle, leaped and thrashed the yellow cat. Spitting and growling, showing every white tooth to the rooted audience, the report dropped it, a suddenly motionless and silent cushion of beautiful soft warm fur. The bullet had knocked out a fang. Oom het die vel heel gekry.

I came warily from hiding, too young for a hunter's initiation, wide-eyed. The skaapwagter and Camel trod open the slagyster and trussed the feet of the bundle with wire, small and light when dead. Then the skaapwagter thrust his kierie between the legs and swung it onto his shoulder. Later, watching the skinning and seeing the glossy pink interior of a leopard, defined and muscular, I finally understood that we were strong, and it was weak. And I never lost all of the awe I felt for Dennis Bergh on that mountain, and leopard dreams have visited me all my life.

The sad seventies. Everything, from hairstyles to politics, was misguided, and it was hard to express myself using the material available to me, as there were no teen media cultures to join. The South African English were sunk in a complex self-loathing. To us, hopelessness and hatred infected the Cape streets, the people and our homes. We understood in some mysterious unspoken way that English speakers were sinners and degenerates. That post-war Commonwealth pride had mostly evaporated, and the crude propaganda that flowed when SATV was born, enjoyed jibing at the English. My own extended family was largely Afrikaans, and as the minor English offshoot the projection of Afrikanerdom's willpower into our homes shocked us. Words like 'donder', 'foeter' and even 'kaffer' on TV news smacked into our cringing ears and I despised the smug, granitic, passionless faces of the politicians who interpreted our world, night after night.

Time is slow for 14-year-olds with their blinkered vision in times of darkness. The world was spiraling towards disaster – bad things happened constantly and the future looked to be worse. Amongst the features of the cold Cold War – the nuclear threat, hijackings, terrorism, bombings, and global Soviet aggression, a colourful thing for me was Purdey. A friend had worked with Joanna Lumley in London a few years earlier and this personalised her for me, and Purdey was (and still is) a great representation of what I wanted to find in the world. But in my environment this fantasy, and little else, could be expressed. We were definitely anal retentive. There were unsolved prison murders, riots, cruel African wars, denial and censorship, hatred and awful authoritarianism. Furthermore there was Military Service for school-leavers, which because of growing revolutionary activity in southern Africa, was lengthened in the 1970s to two long years. For this dreamy, wistful child, the present and the future were a soul-death, for powerful evils were advancing across the globe. Did anyone stop to think how Total Onslaughts, Uhurus and Evil Empires were alive and seething in the fragile minds of children?

My parents were both lawyers and my mother also worked hard for the South African Institute of Race Relations. At the same time she helped many black people steer their way through the legal mazes of Apartheid, using her skills at a volunteer legal advice service. Her mother was the sister of Victorianesque English capitalists cast in the mode of Rhodes, and her father was a Boer farmer from the Clanwilliam district. According to some versions he was descended from a union between the Swedish-born Governor of the Cape-become-embezzler-become-convict of the Dutch East India Company, Oloff Bergh, and the illegitimate daughter of Jan van Riebeeck and his mistress, the Malay woman Anna van Bengal. My father, who died unnecessarily during a spinal operation in 1972, came from solid turn-of-the-century Celtic immigrants who produced his Irish mother, born on a De Aar sheep farm, and his Welsh father, Colonel Owen Glynn Davies, from Port Elizabeth. He was a man who cast a large shadow, and I spent a lot of my time trying to make him proud of me. He had been a well-known and respected Mosquito pilot, and was the Safety Officer after the war for South African Airways, and the founder of Air Cape and Owenair. 'Lovely Lady', the Mosquito he flew, now hangs in the War Museum in Johannesburg. So there was a layering of perceptions in our strong family that produced subtle minds. We were troubled and divided by the fracturing of South African society and its moral flexibility during the seventies.

Oppressed by a hard stepfather, I think I went a bit mad, even for a teenager. I certainly escaped to a bygone age. On full-moon nights, I slipped out of the house and followed the Diep River up onto the southern slopes of Table Mountain, trusting my own stealth and the darkness for safety. I climbed Nursery Ravine alone, at midnight, and gazed across the moonlit land at the Hottentot's Holland mountains. I prayed to wild pagan gods to make the beauty of the Earth enter my soul. I went on stealthy hunting sorties with my 54lb bow into the surrounding vineyards and forests, seeking francolin and guinea fowl. I drew blood several times, bringing home supper to the table. I made my own soft-soled leather shoes for these excursions into the wild, and I knew more about the finer details of wild bird behaviour than anyone I met. I concealed myself motionless for hours and when I moved, birds did not see me.

My mother employed Julius Rwodzi, a Rhodesian, as a gardener who, as a young man, had hunted game with traps and spears in Mashonaland, and he taught me to set a trap that had a springy stick, which upon release would snap a noose round an unsuspecting prey's legs or neck. I can still do this and impress my friends. With him I took wild honey from hollow trees in the ancient way, getting stung sometimes by the confused and drugged bees. Julius was the first of my elected surrogate father figures, from whom I learned simple African dignity.

My keen escapist dream was to create, in a wild beautiful place, a self-contained domain where I could hunt honestly, and build dwellings of my own devising. I had scant respect for conventional wisdom, but learned it anyway, and made use of it, in my strange double life. The school and my mother sent me to a psychiatrist, in a last-ditch attempt to snatch me back from the deep valley within, and redirect me onto a future professional career-path, and to some extent this balanced me, and let me face some of my darker fears, though the process, being confrontational, was traumatic with often hysterical consequences. Later, the psychiatrist was cast from his profession for academic fraud – how's that for my perspective on trusting authority.

In 1978 I quickly learned to ride horses and this fulfilled an inner need. From being a bookish child who shirked school sports, I suddenly revelled in extreme physical effort and coordination. The pounding of wildly urged hoofs and bareback sprints either through sunlight or in dripping forests, fingers entwined in drenched mane to keep grip on the slipping reins – that pain and timeless brilliance was real, and made me alive and arrogant in short moments between the drudgery of school and other hopelessness. So the inner world did not die. Merely, it found a more comfortable context in which to exist and grow with me. And riding brought friends who thought my weirdness was cool.

Wet except for warm oval patches under my thighs where I grip Shari the Arab mare's bare steaming sides like a vice, I turn trotting into the long dripping avenue of Silverhurst's winter-black oaks, grasp the knots set in the slippery reins, talk to the horse and she heaves like a racehorse, and I slide back slightly until the flat-out gallop is stabilised. The rain whips my face when we prance splashing in three bouncing strides to a stop, at the far end, at the paddock gate.

The Land Rover parked amid the shambles of the old Silverhurst farmyard gives me a flood of joy. Mary, still dressed for the model agency, with a lustrous spread of blonde waves, strides around the corner of the stable with a grain bag. "Hail, Ivanovitch!" confidently called, and her tall proud carriage, musical voice and blue eyes infatuate me.

Shari ran loose into the field and picked her way through the mud like an old lady, while the two of us mixed food. In between the crooning that always passes from women to horses, Mary spoke of one day having a farm. And giving me a lift home in her trundling Land Rover in the cold, rainy dark, she sang folk songs from the sixties that I thought belonged to a chapter of ancient history, in a voice as sweetly melodic as a man could want. I went in the house by the back door, through the steaming kitchen full of cooking done by Eugenia the Xhosa maid, making my entry as inconspicuous as possible, stripped my wet things in the bathroom, and warmed up in the bath.

Our supper was a formal chess board prepared by Eugenia. Poor brave bighearted soul-eyed Eugenia, keeper of my secrets – my dirty underpants, my sneaking of a girl out of the house at dawn (this came later), now dead from a painful cancer for which radiology was refused and the inyanga failed. We didn't go to the funeral in dangerous Khayelitsha. Yes, her, shuffling in at the colonial sound of a little silver bell, clearing and bringing the next course, and returning to her Xhosa radio serial droning away in the kitchen. I was usually silent at the table. I turned inward throughout my stepfather's monologue about his day's frustrations, until he said stiffly, "Your mother tells me you didn't do your maths homework again."

"Yar I know." Stare at my scraped plate.

"Apparently Mr Lister says you should be beaten and I can only agree with him."

"Well I don't."

"And you bunked hockey to go riding."

"I hate hockey."

And it would go on until cornered by Victorian scholastic rhetoric and disdain becoming anger, and the threat of 'a thick ear', or 'you're going to get a clip' I would either be silenced seething with impotent hatred, or with ringing ear I would retire, cast out, to my room. On this occasion I was not accused of 'dumb insolence', a Rubicon in the cycle of our arguments, for then there was no reply ('answering back'), and as often as not petty violence would erupt at the dinner table. There were two men in the house, one much bigger than the other, with irreconcilable differences.

But this time we filed into the playroom, to watch the 8 o'clock news with coffee, and were united in stifled annoyance, as aggressive NPs argued with ugly HNPs in a studio squabble. After this, four troepe were reported dead in the Operational Area, as against 38 SWAPO terrorists killed over the past month. This meant a victory for May. The names of the dead scrolled over a shot of a bronze unknown soldier, FN rifle at the ready. Great celebrations were expected the next day for Republic Day and thereafter, in Die Weer, the weather was to repeat itself by being cold and wet. English entertainment followed for the rest of the night and my stepfather and I stared at it dispassionately, including the Epilogue in which a shiny minister said a bit about Republic Day and what the Lord meant us to understand of it. Then the colour pattern came on.

School began in the dark on winter Wednesdays, with Singing Practice, an extraordinary ritual. The entire school, minus teachers, was convened in the Chapel by Mr Hyslop the music master, to learn the following week's hymns and psalms. He was despised by one and all for being a pompous little bald-headed wanker. He struggled to keep control, for we hissed or hummed as one to annoy him or if he got into a tizz. Prefects patrolled the aisles handing out bicolours, a time-wasting punishment where you wrote out a length of text alternating the colour of each consecutive letter, but they were just as guilty, because humming was undetectable.

Some Singing Practices were real gems. Mr Hyslop would explode apoplectically and scream vain falsetto threats, at which the humming or hissing would rise to an echoing crescendo. Once he left in tears from a Chapel that was roaring with unrestrained laughter. In the winter, Singing Practice was mediaeval – humidity of rainy clothing, pale yellow lights, the cold, rattling portals, and echoes.

Like this Republic Day, when later in the morning we trooped onto the Main Field to sing the National Anthem in Afrikaans. The melody died in the grey outdoors as more than half the school refused to sing. Most of us forgot the words to Die Stem in those years. This was superlative classical colonial schooling, which kept us children for longer than is natural. I hated it. Of course, it had its moments because all the teachers were eccentrics. Oddjob, the Afrikaans teacher, came up with unselfconscious masterpieces like 'open the window and let the klarmit come in' and 'you thrrree at the back therrre make a fine pairrr'. Boot the art master would throw his false leg at inattentive new boys, or in an oft-repeated yarn, would graphically relate the experience of having one's leg blown off by a Jerry hand grenade. Tank was watched screwing his wife by 20 boarders perched in a tree outside his window, and Knob the headmaster, Nick Mallet's dad, was frequently heard to hot-potato at rugby matches, and this has become legend, "A little more pressure in the REAR, Bishops!" Certain teachers were real people and worthy of trust. They were Boot the art master, the one-legged ex-Coldstream Guards colonel, Ken Wilson the PT master and an ex-Royal Marines sergeant, and Basil Bey, who for all his rugged appearance and rugby nature was a perceptive teacher of literature and English thought. And then there was Case Rijsdijk, the science teacher, who had been in forensics in the Rhodesian War. An empty AK-47 cartridge placed strategically on a desk never failed to cue him to waffle war stories until the bell rang.

Two schoolgirls walked behind me, on my way from Rondebosch Station to school, in the mornings. If I was behind them, they dawdled very slowly so I would have to catch up and pass them. They would then change pace, to remain 10 yards behind me no matter how fast I walked, tittering and making me self-conscious about my arse, and the way I walked, and my ridiculous boater hat, and everything else. This went on for several years. They enjoyed it a great deal, and gave me an emotional disorder. I am sure they are very nice middle-aged ladies today.

The Net Blankes carriages were empty in the afternoons and interest was provided when a coloured or black person, perhaps being shouted at by a florid Inspector with a brandy-and-coke hangover, hurried through to the other end of the train, having got on in a hurry as the train was leaving. The Net Nie Blankes carriages had unupholstered wooden seats and were so packed that often the nie blankes hung out of the doors. It was inconceivable that if I were late for the train, I would get on at the wrong end. I would have been fair game for verbal racial revenge. Getting into one of those carriages would have been like climbing into a mincer. I stared wide-eyed at the world passing my breezy window. At Claremont Station, two coloured boys sat on the platform facing the Net Blankes windows, displaying their erections. When other passengers laughed, I laughed with them. When they became serious again, so did I.

From Wynberg Station I caught a bus to Constantia and the seating was mixed. There was an understanding among the passengers that no one was less or more equal, although whites were supposed to sit at the front. Hell's teeth, I was one pale white boy amongst 30 or 40 blacks, I wasn't complaining! I had to wait more than an hour for a bus at Wynberg Station, playing pinball in the Muslim shop on the corner for a while, and then just standing among the street people daydreaming. Dirty pigeons competed about my feet in the spiced air.

Constantia then was shabby and real, with houses among dilapidated farmland awaiting the phony gentrification of the future, commons overgrown with Port Jackson willow where determined so-called bergies avoided relocation to Mitchell's Plain, and where we kids ran around on gravel roads with bare feet and airguns, and played tok-tokkie. A good place to grow up.

After reaching the silent house sometime around four in the afternoon, I went to the horses. No lift was available so I walked the five kilometres, and the saddle, being cumbersome to carry, I usually left behind taking only the bridle, and rode bareback. At this I was as good as a Cossack. Taking Shari off the tracks in Tokai Forest I felt an upwelling of freedom and sprinted through the thickest parts of the trees, dodging them from left to right, jumping unexpected tree trunks, and we excelled in our coordination and timing. She was a strong and intelligent horse, very agile on difficult ground, not big but deep-chested, hard and slender. She had the slow measured gait of a big horse that at my word, would snap into the violent gallop I know she loved as much as I did.

On the weekends I rode with some or all of the eight or so other Silverhurst stable tenants, a mixed age group laughing in the forests of European trees, oaks, planes and pines. It was a whole day's activity, sunny and healthy, with jokes enjoyed easily at the trot and races in the long green gallops near the streams. And at nights, too, when the Christmas beetles hummed beneath the balmy summer stars, as grey shapes we rode in silver moonlight singing sad songs about kings and ships, and other things we'd never see.

My riding friends were interesting and despite our varied ages, treated each other as equals. This was good for me. Of all of them Mary was the closest, believing in my dreams and encouraging my vision, uncompromised. In return I fell in love with her. She was bloody naughty (for which I am grateful) – twice my age with fortune beaming broadly upon her womanhood. Early one morning on the way to the horses in the Land Rover with the back full of noisy children, she looked at me and whispered quietly, "I want to fuck you." She held up her finger. "Just once." We spent some nights together over about six weeks, a time of pride and mystery. She picked me up at school and was my golden queen. When it ended in my anger and tears that December after I left school, she was less surprised than I was.

So that's what I came from. Little did I know where I was going.

2
1 SAI: Basics

Back when we were 16, the Department of Defence sent the school forms we had to fill in. It was general information and had no immediate effect besides an ominous foreboding. I was assigned a number I was not to learn or even be aware of, for several years, but they had us all by the balls, China! – 78385275.

I left school and drifted mindlessly round my usual haunts in a golden Cape summer, riding, or lying reading, and then a second letter ordered that I report for two years' Military Service at the Castle, at 2pm on 14 January 1981. It included a long checklist of essentials like locks, personal effects and money, which I conscientiously assembled. I suppressed all thoughts about the impending time, and I knew so little about it, except what I had absorbed from the positive media and school leavers. I and my friends had the impression it would be a camp. A crew-cut and a rof suntan. Marching, becoming fit, eating bad food and swearing disgustingly. Although I was very afraid, I did not show it. I also did not trek overseas as others I knew had done, because I was young and afraid of leaving home, and foreign exile seemed by far the greater unknown. As by a secret fear my last summer school holiday was made cold.

On the day, my mother and I had cold Eugenia-fishcakes with Mrs Ball's chutney for lunch without much said, because I had butterflies in my stomach like no swimming gala or athletics meet had produced before. We kissed goodbye in the car, in the street next to the Grand Parade, and without looking back I walked over the moat bridge into the big hot courtyard of the Castle, through a ragged hubbub of parents and boys, then across a divide of empty cobbles between them and already-separated boys seated on the ground against the far wall with their suitcases. I carried mine disembodied across the open space and joined them and sat at the back. From there I stared at others experiencing what I had just done. I watched their faces to see how they handled it. One boy, tallish and gaunt got my attention. He slouched with hunched shoulders and wild blue eyes in unhealthy sockets. His drab brown hair reached past his shoulders. His nose was large and hooked. He looked like he was refusing to acknowledge the world around him. Joining a crowd of complete strangers. Later we met and he told me he had been fall-down-drunk and loaded with pills. We became best friends.

Names were being shouted out by a tall soldier in brown with a green beret, who spoke only Afrikaans. This took over an hour, then the onlookers were herded out amid pathetic calls of farewell, and another tall soldier spoke to us, telling us about the trip ahead and threatening punishments for misbehaviour. I was a little surprised – I had no intention of misbehaving. Then the shouting started and did not ease off for six months. We were brutalised by noise every waking minute, all of it violent, threatening, ugly. We walked in a mob across Strand Street to Cape Town Station and boarded a Bloemfontein-bound train, which stopped at every station or barren siding on the endless dry plains, where one or more terrified boys stood with stern family groups awaiting the train. The journey of two days was mayhem and very nearly murder.

"Is there any room in here?"

"Fuck off you cunt!" A chorus.

"Is there any room in here?"

"Y-Yes. Come in. My name's André G-G-G-G-Glazewski. And yours?" He was blond and slight with a thin face. Very Nordic. His eyes were sky blue and they stared levelly through glasses.

"I'm Evan Davies."

"What?"

"Evan Davies."

"P-P-Pleased to meet you."

We shook hands. His hand felt thin and cold yet strong. His movements were neat and considered, almost practised.

"Which s-s-school did you go to?"

Aside from groups of frightened subdued boys who tried to separate themselves from the chaos, there were hundreds of drunks, scarred bullies, tattooed gang members and eccentric youths of every description with the lone mugger and stabber thrown in. The train reverberated with the released anger of a thousand convicts fighting, shouting, breaking – and some quietly crying – with ghetto blasters five to a carriage blasting hard music at the limit of their range. Suitcases, possessions, bedding, bottles, seats, toilets, even windows, were thrown out of windows. When the train turned a bend, we all leaned out the windows and threw things at each other and screamed. People were injured and I shrank inwards. Glazewski and I talked away most of the time. In such a situation you are desperate to make and keep connections. The second youngest of an unlikely 14 children, he had developed his stutter in the noise and competition of a paternalistic Polish Catholic family. Unlike me he had taken school sports very seriously, with long-distance running being his strength, and source of confidence.

We watched first the Karoo, and then, on the second day, the golden plains of the Orange Free State with their willow-grown rivers. Because of the natural beauty, I managed to hold on to a romantic vision of the adventure ahead. But by midnight, every creative hope and clear perception I had, and each beautiful dream, would be smashed and completely obliterated in a flood of muck. We shunted into a less public siding at Bloemfontein Station and were herded by packs of abusive psychopaths into trucks. They kicked and shook us and hit and screamed. We ran and tripped and cried and swore. We were hurled from the trucks onto a floodlit dust-patch, where many more monsters waited, baying for our blood. "Kontkop! Soutpiel! Jou ma se poes, rower! Varkpoes! Ek gaan jou verkrag!" (*Cunthead! Salt-prick! Your mother's cunt! Pig-cunt! I'll rape you!*) I heard in the bedlam. They chased us and we ran, and rolled in the gravel as they told us to. By dawn we all quivered in a state of shock and I didn't even know where I was, for I had been in a nightmare cloud of dust all night.

"Julle fokken rowers is fokken slegter as fokken slangkak! Daai fokken halt het geklink soos 'n fokken koei wat in die fokken pad kak! Voorste fokken posisie af! EEN! twee! drie! drie! drie! drie! drie! kom Hanekom jou fokken maatjies wag vir jou, vier!" (*You fucking recruits are fucking worse than fucking snake shit! That fucking halt sounded like a fucking cow shitting in the fucking road! Missionary [push-up] position! One! two! three! three! three! three! three! Come Hanekom your fucking little friends are waiting for you, four!*) And we sweated at four o'clock in the fucking morning. We'd again failed the inspection we'd been woken up at three to prepare, after a clattering of dustbins beaten by their lids all over the seven-thousand-full camp, and now fucking Hanekom can't do a proper push-up after all the practise he's had. "Neen-en-fokken-neentig! ... " screamed the korporaal, and "Hanekom jou poes! Ek gaan jou opfok!" (*Ninety-fucking-nine! ... Hanekom you cunt! I'm going to fuck you up!*) hissed several quivering, sweating, stinking and groaning rowers in the dark at ground level with the corporal's torch flickering over them. He still had an hour to fuck us up before breakfast and he was going to put as much into it as he could. The gravel in the wet clay bit into our hands. We took our trommels and ran with them. It was sit-ups in the mud. Glazewski and I carried each other – we were the same weight. He had endurance, more than the others. Under our breath, we cursed the korporaals with death and hatred. We held our R1 rifles above our heads, running, always running.

Finally at dawn in the queue for breakfast, which was miles long, we were running on the spot being abused by other korporaals who strode up and down victimising people. "Fuck them," said Glazewski resolutely and without stuttering. "Stare them straight in the eye and smile." But a rower near the front of the queue was being shaken like a rat by a bull of a man, with black hair and solid red eyes and menace graven into his face (he had literally burst the blood vessels in his eyes from shouting). The rower's steel helmet was flying backwards and forwards over his face and hitting his nose. When he dropped his rifle with a clatter, the man yelled straight into his ear, holding him off the ground by his collar. "Varkpoes! Dink jy jy kan my teepraat jou kont! Gaan agter in die ry!" (*Pig-cunt! You think you can answer me back you cunt! Go to the back of the queue!*) And he released him, throwing him viciously to the ground.

This one terrified us. He was motivated by hatred. In the mess he strode along the table tops kicking off helmets as we stuffed food in our mouths, shrieking, "Vreet nou kou later! Dink julle dis ñ vakansieplaas? Ek sê vir julle dis 'n POESPLAAS hierdie! Vreet, julle varke vreet, en kry die FOK hieruit!" (*Feed now, chew later! You all think this is a holiday farm? I tell you, this is a cunt-farm! Feed, you pigs, feed, and get the fuck out of here!*) and he picked on one rower and stood squarely in his food, and then wiped his boots in his hair. Then, with his boot against his forehead, he pushed the boy and his chair backwards until he crashed to the ground and lay on his back staring up. "Wat kyk jy, Liefie? Ek's nie jou fokken ma nie, is ek? Of dink jy ek's jou fokken tjerrie? Wil jy my naai? WIL – JY – MY – NAAI? Voorste posisie af, ALMAL! EEN! TWEE! DRIE!" (*What you looking at, Lovey? I'm not your fucking mother, am I? Or d'you think I'm your fucking sweetheart? You want to fuck me? You want to fuck me? Missionary position, everyone! One! two! three!*) and so the whole room was filled with heaving racked rowers with food in their mouths, imagining his brutal death by their own hands, hating.

We had been in the army for 12 days, and it was hell. After a week of being given numbers, injections, medical classifications, haircuts, lectures, brown clothes, steel helmets and rifles, Basics had started. This had been rumoured on the train to be terrible, and it was. Its aim was to select its survivors and to alter them forever into beings that kill. We were cowed, bullied, exhausted, made miserable and literally kept awake for three months. It led to spontaneous hatred. We did not know what it was all for.

It had become abundantly clear that there were no channels of recourse to any benign authority, and we were completely dominated. There seemed to be no end to the misery our minders could heap on us, and they were bigger, stronger, more aggressive and louder than anything we had ever seen before. Later, we became equal to the situation, but by then we were acting within the system, not against it.

The day began with despair at three in the morning, when you remembered where you were, shocked from the beautiful sanctuary of sleep in a cacophony of screaming that ended at 11 o'clock at night, though one seldom slept before midnight. Each and every day kicked off with a kit inspection at four. The bed had to be 'square'. Down on my knees I chewed the edges with my teeth, sprayed shaving cream along the sharp edge and ironed it with two hot irons, so that it looked like a wooden box with bedclothes pulled tightly over. It was compulsory to sleep in the bed. Your clothes all had to be washed and ironed, and your boots shined to an unlikely lacquer gleam. All would deliberately be muddied each day. The rifle's parts were to be shiny and displayed along with every item of your possessions, so that your entire being was on display. You had to be clean and shaved. The test for this was a wisp of cotton wool dragged across your face. If any fibres got left behind, the whole bungalow of 95 people failed the inspection. We engaged the limits of our endurance to meet these requirements, but had we been less fucking stupid or at least rational we would have seen them to be impossible. Floors were tested by rolling a squash ball on them. Any dust stuck to the ball meant, you guessed it, failure. This is how we lost our self-respect – we drowned in a sea of disappointment.

Inspection was therefore followed by an hour or two of imaginative punishments. The korporaals were at liberty to deny you breakfast, lunch or supper. If you did make it to eat, no time was wasted in the long queue: various strenuous activities could be forced upon you as you waited, and a favourite trick was to pull a whole platoon or company out of the line and exhaust them utterly, and then send them to the back. Keep them going while others went past them and ate. Or until the food ran out. The actual eating took about three or four minutes, because of the eat-now-chew-later principle, and the murderous bullies who wandered bellowing around the mess. The volume of noise in that big metal shed was indescribable. Then you prepared for Inspection Parade on the main parade ground.

Today, as we stood in dumb immobility under the hawk-like gaze of Samajoor Stone, seven-thousand, in large training companies of roughly three-hundred souls each, we were prayed at by a sieltiffie or chaplain. I watched Glazewski falling asleep on his feet in front of me, and a korporaal saw it too. He sidled quietly up to him, then with his knuckles punched him in the solar plexus. "Jy moet wakker bly soutpiel. Miskien sal dit jou help." (*You must stay awake, salt-prick. Maybe this will help you.*) And he drew back Glazewski's rifle barrel and slammed the front sight into his shoulder joint. I could see from the corner of my eye that tears of pain and frustration were very close. Such a lamer lasts a week. Overcome with mute rage, I imagined taking a loaded rifle and shooting bullets into the korporaal's head until it became unrecognisable. This type of bloody imagining became an everyday fantasy, and it was a good thing there was no ammunition available in the camp at that time.

Among us were quite a few guys with criminal and aggressive tendencies and low stress levels. Fights broke out continuously and sub-classes emerged, based on fighting ability and domination. We were the cattle pen wherein we were pitted against each other, and emotions were explosive and people got hurt. There was no protection from the barbarian besides your own talents. I watched several pikstel-knife fights, in a spatter of dark red blood between snarling boys with flared nostrils, who slept not four feet from each other. The most dangerous were the midgets. I learned to be polite to small people, for they were strong and bristled with anger. They were animals. I made friends who slept near me in those months, circumstantial friends. For though today I hardly remember their names or faces, I spent many hours in their company, both in free time cleaning kit, and en masse training or being punished following shouted commands, with us responding as one man. In our discourse we were always victims, and as such, found common ground in shabby complaining.

After parade, we invariably went through hours of drill marching, liberally interspersed with PT punishments involving a lot of groaning. In every direction brown hordes could be seen running, marching, suffering, to demonic cries. The days were all the same and very long and time was a torture. Of some interest though, was opleiding, in the middle part of the day. It consisted of basic infantry knowledge, but the courses were aimed at the lowest intellect present, which was indeed very low.

The korporaal was asking Hanekom, "Hanekom, dit is 'n geweer. Oraait, Hanekom, wat is dit?" (*Hanekom, this is a rifle. All right, Hanekom, what is this?*) Hanekom, believing this to be a trick question, stood silently with his mouth hanging open, too afraid to reply. "Die antwoord, Hanekom, is 'dit is 'n geweer'. Verstaan jy?" (*The answer, Hanekom, is 'this is a rifle'. Understand?*) Hanekom had a black eye from being persuaded to pull his weight a few days previously, surrounded while he was naked and squinting in the showers. "Ja Korporaal!" yelled Hanekom unconvincingly. "Hanekom jou dom poes, jy verstaan fokkol!" (sycophantic laughter from the rest of us) (*Hanekom you dumb cunt, you understand fuck-all*). Though I was emotionally more shattered than I even understood myself, I wrote the first of many brave letters home.

Dear Mom,

I have just phoned you and you are leaving for Clanwilliam. I wrote a letter to Granny this morning, but I'll send the two off together. Today is intercompany sport, which I greatly wished to watch, but somebody had to keep watch (although I have not yet come across open stealing except on the train, where 2kg of biltong were tragically stolen). Some of the people are unacceptable totally. Most of them are rock spiders and have incredibly bad manners and many have only got standard 6. In my bungalow is one gangster from Woodstock, and next to me sleeps a murderer. (TRUE) But he's a very nice person, shy, with a passion for walking around the quiet bungalow for a couple of hours after midnight. It's now Sunday but tomorrow's Monday, and the Corporals say that we are going to start kakking off because our training starts tomorrow. Some of the Corps are sadists. They stand there and laugh as we suffer doing press-ups for 2 hours. Today we went to church; it was very pleasant but for the fact that we had doubled there (2km). We got our pay on Wednesday; the pay system is crooked. It didn't get sent to the bank: I got a straight R58, from which was deducted for exercise books (I'm enclosing some of my rough notes), funds and R1 for a town flooded in the Karoo. We pay for T.V., but our set is broken. Last week my knee started hurting (from the Cedarberg still) and I think I might have a permanent injury. I'll only report sick if it gets bad, because I don't want to be a G3 just yet; also it could lessen my equestrian chances. A boy here by the name of Karl Lynch wants to give his father my name and number. Karl Lynch is a Springbok Gymkhana rider. Karl Lynch's father is the C.O. of the Equestrian Military Academy, a Colonel, and he knows our C.O. well. This is the army, and there's a fine dividing line between serious trouble and a shouting by the Corporal. Every evening I steal bread from the mess and if we are on cleaning duty I get jam in the daytime. We really crave for extra food in the evenings. Do you think you can send a parcel containing sufficient quantities of: Milo (or something), Powdered milk, Sugar (a small packet), Biltong powder (Granny sent me some, I loved it, but it's finished), Biscuits, + a small traveling element. (Don't let it look like food, please, don't have any tins, rather plastic honey bottles). I've made friends from Durban, Calvinia, Durbanville, Cape Town and one millionaire who doesn't live anywhere in particular. I'm worried about my big toes. They've gone completely numb and have been like this for a week now. Anyway they haven't gone gangrenous so they should be all right.

We learned through courses that we were in a part of Bloemfontein called Tempe, and the name of the camp was 1 SAI (1 South African Infantry Battalion), though it took me in my brainless ignorance two weeks to realise they were not saying 'One Side'. The camp was several score hectares of grey gravel, with evenly positioned prefab bungalows, each sleeping almost a hundred trainees, with about 60cm between beds, and at present, with the extra numbers of unspecialised conscripts, olive-green tents in symmetrical villages. There was not one particle of living matter in the camp beside unhappy humanity, and the grey gravel at inspection times was expected to bear no footprints anywhere, and was swept and raked. It was a place of dust. The climate seemed to be the harshest imaginable. Scalding days of windless sun would alternate swiftly with violent thunderstorms that would turn the world to sucking mud, and dust storms preceded these: vast dun curtains bearing across the sky, blocking out the sun, and shrouding the camp in a brown fog, and dry lightnings cracked before drops of mud fell from the sky. And the mud was quick to dry – the earth becoming dust again in a few hours.

On one of the clear sunny days between these disorders, we were undergoing opleiding just outside the barbed wire compound and we were learning about camouflage. Sersant Pretorius was prowling between the platoons of Hotel Kompanie sitting dotted around in the long golden grass of late summer. He was seven feet tall and could command complete silence over seven-thousand people and get them to march as one man. "Wie's Engels?" A show of hands. "Wel, hou my goed dop, seuntjies. Ek is 'n Transvaal rock spider, en ek is julle baas," (*Who's English? Well, watch me closely, little boys. I am a Transvaal rock spider, and I am your master*) was how he introduced himself. It was our special gift from fate that he was training company sergeant-major for H Company, and I can't say that he was disliked as he was fair, and he didn't need to be abusive because he was awesome with a granite face bearing steel eyes, and the resonant gravelly voice and strength of will of a tyrant god. He now stalked up to us with a white toilet roll in one hand and eyed each of us until we waited, riveted. "Dit," he stated categorically, "is kakpapier. In die leer is dit bekend as wit goud. Julle troepe moet leer om hierdie gerief spaarsaam te gebruik. Daar is 'n manier om dit spaarsaam te gebruik, wat ek nou vir julle gaan wys." Taking the roll he tore off a single white square. "Dit is al wat 'n mens nodig het," he said authoritatively, "en jy vou hom – so." He folded it twice, quartering it. "En jy skeur die hoek af. Dan steek jy jou middelvinger deur," holding up his finger at us which was very long and looked like a very rude sign, with toilet paper draping his fist. "Dan krap jy jou gat skoon met jou vinger," he said expressionlessly, "en jy maak jou vinger skoon met die kakpapier." And then he demonstrated the action, pulling the paper up his finger with the other hand. "Dít steek jy weg onder 'n klip, maar die afgeskeurde hoekie papier, wat jy níé verloor het nie, gebruik jy om onder jou vingernael skoon te maak." (*This is shitpaper. In the army it's known as white gold. You troops must learn to use this luxury sparingly. There's a way of doing this that I'll show you now. This is all one needs, and you fold it – so. And you tear the corner off. Then you stick your middle finger through. Then you scrape your arse clean with your finger, and you clean your finger with the shitpaper. That, you hide away under a rock, but the torn-off corner, which you don't lose, you use to clean under your fingernail.*) He eyed us without a hint of amusement and swung on his heels, leaving us absorbing the military humour, and we laughed madly in irrational release.

We also learned about the operation of the rifle, about the proper organisation and numbers in a Mechanised Infantry fighting unit, from the smallest part, a section of 12 men, to a brigade of three battalions, and about the Infantry Fighting Vehicle, the Ratel, of which we carefully wrote down:-

Infantry Fighting Vehicle Ratel 20
3 crew and 9 infantry
120km per hour on road 60km per hour off road
6 cylinder in line 12 litre turbocharged water-cooled diesel
Automatic or manual with 6 forward and 2 reverse gears
6x6, 6x4 or 6x2 wheel drive
Solid axles with single coil springs and double acting shock absorbers supported by wishbones and longitudinal arms
Hydraulically assisted steering
Brakes: hydraulic-pneumatic on front wheels, Pneumatic-mechanical on rear four wheels, Pneumatic-mechanical crawl brake, Mechanical hand brake on rear 4 wheels
Armour 10mm armour steel on sides 20mm in front
Armament dual feed 20mm cannon with choice of Armour Piercing or High Explosive shells, rate of fire 1000 rpm total 1,200 rounds. AP effective range 1,000m HE effective range 2,000m. Coaxial 7.62mm machine gun rate of fire 600 rpm total 2,000 rounds. 6 gun ports for infantry. 4x81mm smoke grenade launchers
800 litres diesel
500 litres drinking water
14.5 tonnes empty. 18.5 tonnes combat loaded

Every week we were tested until all the new information became common knowledge among us, but its relevance was clouded in insomniac anesthesia.

Opfoks were routine about three times a week and were known as a bosbus, because the corporal or sergeant was the driver and we were the dazed passengers. He would drive us into all sorts of difficult terrain (like bogs) outside the camp at different speeds (but usually as fast as the bus would go) crash (and here we would all crash onto the ground), tell us to help our fellow passengers (carry them) and generally try to get us scratched, bruised and dirty.

After several weeks I caught a bad cold that became tonsillitis and bronchitis. It was made worse by the dust in the camp, and one morning I reported sick, hoarse and coughing, at the medics. "Is this the queue for the medics?" I asked the wan group standing against the prefabricated wall of the medical bungalow. It was a dumb question. There were bandages, coughing and feet in slippers among them. I stood at the back and soon two others tagged on behind me. There were nearly 30 of us and each went inside for a few minutes. A little ahead of me a conversation about motorcycles was in full swing. They were mostly from other companies – I hadn't even seen them before. I wondered why patients looked worse leaving the room than they did entering. This matter was cleared up after almost an hour when I reached the front of the queue. A rower limped out and said, "The fucking poeses ek sê!" He made a vague gesture at me, "Go in." I opened the door and went in. Inside, a very hefty bosomy nurse and a tall pale expressionless young medic awaited me. The nurse was Afrikaans and intimidating and the medic English and homosexual, which might explain their reserve with each other, but both were lance corporals. The medic asked me what the problem was, then told the nurse, "Another one. Double B-Co please Corporal."

"Yes Corporal."

She went into another room and reappeared filling a large syringe with a thick long needle with a white viscous-looking substance. "Take off your pants," said the medic. The nurse pulled down first one side of my grey issue underpants, then the other and quickly gave me a fat injection in each cheek. "You can go," he then said. "Tell the next one to come in." I found out the substance was a mixture of several vitamin Bs, and the injections felt like the kicks of a racehorse so that I could hardly move. I could not understand this practice, the purpose of which was not to cure you but to prevent you from reporting sick! We were designated 'light duty', given orange overalls and marched around the camp all day with arms stretched out before us, flicking our fingers in unison shouting 'bee-baa, bee-baa' because were not a bus now, but an ambulance. It only increased the misery, so because the next time I felt sick, the identical thing happened, it dawned on me to be sick without any help from the military authorities.

3
Separating the Wheat from the Chaff

"Jy moet bykom Davies." (*You must come right Davies.*) A hand was thrust towards my nose as if it would klap me across the ear.

"What?" What the fuck was he talking about?

"Jy moet nét fokken bykom soutpiel." (*You must just come right, salt-prick.*)

As I walked into the bungalow from supper, Mostert was giving me advice. Being the biggest among us, he could do this. Jesus Christ, how could they complain about me? I was a soutpiel and a rooinek, so naturally I was a target, but I thought I was bringing my kant (*side*). I felt hunted and exasperated – there was no letting up and I felt almost ready to cry. But perhaps the korporaal had instructed Mostert to 'sort out' the bungalow. Glazewski came in after me and began to receive the same treatment. "Bykom yourself," he said without stuttering, but I could tell what a near thing it had been.

I opened my trommel and placed the still dripping varkpan where it belonged. Supper had been skrapnelhoender – not as good as fried bully beef but much, (so much) better than skrapnelvis. The varkpanne never really got clean because of the filthy cold soapy water in the wash basins outside the mess, and they always had a fatty rancid smell.

"Posparade!" yelled the rower who slept closest to the door. He always called out warnings or screamed "AANDAG!" when rank entered the bungalow. A bit of a shloop. We launched ourselves to the front and tree'd aan for post. It didn't matter if you arrived late for post parade, which began more or less when supper was over. You just quietly joined the ragged end of the squad.

"Kompanie, nommer!" (*Company, number!*) yelled the korporaal.

"Een!" called the first rower on the right. The numbers were called down the line. "Twee!" "Drie!" "Vier!" "Vyf!" "Ses!" "Sewe!" "A-A-A-A-A-A-A-A ... "

Giggling developed all around me. The korporaals were smiling and shaking their heads. "Glazooski, we know, we know, you are fukken number eight ... Bly stil julle fokken werfetters! Gaan aan, nommer!" (*Be quiet you fucking farmyard pus-heads! Go on, number!*) "Nege!" Then when your name was called out you shouted

"Korporaal!" and ran and threw yourself at his feet and did 20 push-ups. He then counted your letters or parcels and calculated how many more push-ups you owed for them. "Davies!" Pronounced 'dah-feese'. "Mr Evan Davies Esquire," he crowed. Oh God, my grandmother! She had such high hopes for me. An extra 20 push-ups at least! Last week she wrote 'Corporal Evan Davies'. That had got me another 50. The trouble was, she really believed I was already promoted. Her grandson – how not? Quite often she sent pink envelopes. At least she hadn't perfumed any yet. The korporaals smelled all letters very carefully for faint traces of female pheromones. Letters from confirmed girls cost a hundred push-ups, and post parade could last for up to two hours. The korporaals had nothing else planned, and sweating boys could be reduced to tearful dusty creatures.

"Aaa, hier's een van 18 De La Reystraat, Wepener ... laat ek dit neerskryf ... dis van jou tjerrie, nê, kontkop!" (*Ah, here's one from 18 De La Rey Street, Wepener ... let me write that down ... it's from your sweetheart, right, cunthead?*)

"Nee, korporaal," panted the rower as he strained his way through the inquisition. "Jy lieg! Korporaal Visagie en ek gaan met haar hierdie naweek lekker kuier, terwyl jy hier in die kamp bly! Ons gaan op pas! Ons ken Wepener soos die back of our hand! Dis nie 'n groot plek nie. Is sy mooi? Nee sy sal nie mooi wees nie, want jy's 'n lelike dom poes. En as sy lelik is sal sy graag wil naai, nê. Nê rower! Of miskien piel suig, nê? Wat sê jy, rower?"

"Ek weet nie Korporaal."

"Hy weet nie! Hulle hou net hande!" he wailed in a jeering falsetto.

"Wel, Korporaal, hierdie naweek sal ons haar 'n paar lesings moet gee." (*No, Corporal ... You lie! Corporal Visagie and I are going to visit her nicely this weekend, while you stay in camp! We're going on pass! We know Wepener like the back of our hand! It's not a big place. Is she pretty? No, she won't be pretty, because you're a stupid, ugly cunt. And if she's not pretty she'll be eager to fuck, right? Right, recruit? Or maybe suck cock, right? What do you say, recruit? ... I don't know Corporal ... He doesn't know! They only hold hands! Well, Corporal, this weekend we'll have to give her some lessons.*)

We listened with sagging shoulders and dull eyes smouldering as the evening grew cool and late. Another evening fucked up. We'd be up all night preparing for tomorrow's inspection.

Dear Mom,
    On Friday we went shooting. We woke up at 2.30 so as to be able to leave for the range at 5. We left at 6.30 and got a turn to shoot at 2.30 in the afternoon. Having inspected my target and being told that I didn't need to

shoot again (good placing), we were told that our next pass is Thursday! 1. We won the sports. 2. It is the Commandant's birthday. Straight after, the Sergeant got us into his clutches (looking very formidable in battle-clothing – tall, very tall, with a set mouth, startling blue eyes surrounded by black eyelashes and wearing a bush hat. He didn't like the way we drilled, so we ran and sweated and got heat-stroke in a time limit. Then we sat in the skietgat and changed targets. Its loud in there, louder than the rifle-shots themselves; it's something to do with the bullets and the sound barrier. (Oh, yes, in the morning we had a demonstration of Russian rifles). At last the day came to an end, after we had declared individually that "no sharp-point ammunition nor live rounds nor any part thereof" were in our possession, corporal. I think they are frightened we'll shoot them or ourselves. The Bedfords arrived and began to remove other companies, and then the sergeant tells us that our inspection was "kak" among other things, so he began to tell us in modulated tones, what we had to do: "Run to the third pole (400m away), turn right and run to the 500m mark. Turn right and come back to the road; turn left and run to the 600m mark. Turn left and run to the third pole. Turn right and run to the 700m mark. Turn right and run to the road etc ... till you get to the 1,000m mark, and then come back by the road. My knee pained a lot and I ran and walked. Many people walked, and when at last we got back, dear old sarg. says run that again. We arrive back, and run half the distance again. Then the army played us a dirty trick. It was raining, but my shirt under my raincoat was wetter than my pants, and it remained that way until 9.30, still raining, pitch dark, very cold, when I at last boarded a Bedford, my sore knee bent double, for 1 SAI. Supper is usually at 5 o'clock. We slept Saturday and Sunday, apart from church. Now they tell us that National Service is now 3 YEARS!!!!!!!!!

People were removed from among us, for various reasons. If they went AWOL, or were in any way criminal, they were caught and sent to Detention Barracks (DB), which was far worse than 1 SAI. DB was a short distance away from our camp, so that from a hill we could occasionally see the inmates being horrifyingly mistreated. Any Jews who had by some administrative error found their way among us, were taken off to separate Jewish training camps, so that we ended up being uniformly Christian, because our food was definitely not kosher. People with known drug associations were also considered unacceptable, and these, mostly people who had been known to smoke dagga, went to Klipdrif, a rehabilitation camp with a reputation almost as bad as DB's. Conscientious objectors were absolutely the lowest form of life, and were subjected to not two, but three, years of DB. Of them, Jehovah's Witnesses were deemed even lower, *laer as slangkak, uit soos boknaai* (*lower than snake shit, out like goat-fucking*), and we sometimes saw groups of these in blue overalls digging ditches for sewerage piping, and being treated like animals by their supervisors.

Once, when we were left unwatched near a group of these using picks and shovels deep in a muddy trench, we wandered over to them. I stood on the edge looking down. A boy, like me, looked up at my form silhouetted against the blue sky with glazed blue eyes and then quickly averted them back to his deep earthy prison. A sergeant ran from a building, scolding, "Kom weg! Moenie met hulle praat nie, hulle is slegter as kaffers!" (*Come away! Don't talk to them, they're worse than kaffirs!*) The unhealthy (including homosexuals, or 'rugridders') were despised, and also vanished.

"Is jy 'n fokken hommel, Glazooski?" (*Are you a fucking queer, Glazooski?*)

"N-N-N-N-N-N-N-N-No Corporal."

"Then why the fok do you sound so fokken guilty, rower?"

Being unhealthy was also tantamount to a sin, even if you only wore glasses for reading. Droves of the unhealthy were taken to learn to become chefs, orderlies, storemen or medics. The latter were not deemed too bad. Usually they had only minor eyesight problems, and when trained they rejoined us and bore arms. All these alternative forms of national duty were represented as kakker than ours. One thing we could always rely on was undesirables being discovered by their 'buddies' and reported, often not before being beaten up (as they were fair game). I virtually crept around for fear of being singled out for some yet-unrevealed deviancy.

There was a strong verkrampte contingent that was enthusiastically vocal and aggressive amongst the trainees. I forget his name, but one of these (let's call him 'Doos') used to walk up and down the aisles of the darkened bungalow when we were trying to sleep, shouting abuse at the top of his voice. He brown-nosed the instructors by agreeing with everything they said and discovered secrets among us. In return he (and others) were favoured and given more or less free rein to bully and lord it over us in the absence of instructors. One night, he walked past lifting the foot of each bed and dropping it with a crash saying, "Kom rowers julle moet slaap! Julle moet slaap!" (*Come, recruits, you must sleep! You must sleep!*) From across the dividing wall a voice called out, "Gaan slaap jý jou dom Doos!" (*Go to sleep yourself, you stupid idiot!*) A ragged chorus joined the voice. We didn't really know the people on the other side of the wall, they were another platoon.

"Wie sê dit?" (*Who said that?*) boomed Doos apoplectically. He couldn't believe he was being challenged. He stormed around the end of the wall. Except for his confident heavy booted tread there was silence until the sudden sound of steel furniture being hurled around. We leaped to the top of the wall and stared over, an even row of faces. All the other platoon were sitting bolt upright in their beds. Someone flicked on the lights. Doos was fighting like crazy and losing. Two rowers in boxer shorts were laying into him with fists and headbutts. When they released him blood ran from his nose and eyebrows and an ear was torn. He slunk back to his bed sobbing pitifully. Not a peep was ever heard from him again, and trouble from his sort slowly died away.

Before too long we were uniformly Christian and healthy (and white, obviously), and we were much reduced in numbers and in will. This was the fundamental infantry material, whose beliefs were in limbo and could be manipulated, and from which could be formed single-minded combat units. It was easy, now, to train us. Disagreement was limited, and the manipulation of peer pressure a strong element in the control the army had over us. This group could be taught the army propaganda, while the few dissenters were forced to remain silent. It did not pay to raise moral issues. "As julle almal weet," Sersant Pretorius said on one occasion, "die doel van die weermag is om die vyand dood te maak. Dit help nie as hy weghardloop nie, want dan skiet hy jou later in die rug. 'n Kaffer is net sleg, en dis 'n mors van die land se tyd en geld om hom gevange te neem." (*As you all know, the purpose of the army is to kill the enemy. It doesn't help if he runs away, because then he shoots you in the back later. A kaffir is just bad, and it's a waste of the country's time and money to take him prisoner.*)

> Dear Mom,
> The other day we had a propaganda session about Communism. The Afrikaans Corporal (who always gives us such talks) directed his address mainly at English-speakers, i.e. he spoke English. Afterwards we were each given two pamphlets, only the English people. Not one Afrikaner got a pamphlet of any sort. I have read the enclosed pamphlet. I certainly find it very disturbing, and would like to know what the Army would like me to believe. What is the South African Political answer to Russian aggression? Please write your first book and send it to me. Also, the pamphlet indicates a 'Capitalist' victory in Argentina. Tell me about that too. I'll believe anything you say. Remember that.

We filed into the lesingskaserne early one morning red and sweating from the run here, which had deviated from the straightest path (300m) so that it had lasted three quarters of an hour. Our bodies still quivered from the buddy PT, and my joints ached. My knees especially pained and I wore a brace on one. We dragged ourselves to plastic chairs and put our rifles and polished doybies on the ground beneath our

SEPARATING THE WHEAT FROM THE CHAFF

seats. Pencils and notebooks emerged from leg pockets. A korporaal was giving out little pamphlets. I flipped through mine. 'The Total Onslaught'. A demonic black wielding an AK-47 and a hammer and sickle banner graced the cover. There was a map of Africa with red covering most of it. South Africa and South West Africa were among the very few countries left white. An unknown sergeant led us through the material slowly, in both English and Afrikaans. First of all, communism was outlined and then described as a disease creeping down Africa towards us. The South African Communist Party, which I had only vaguely heard of before, was based in Moscow and led by an evil puppet, Joe Slovo, who resided in Moscow licking the feet of his masters. He wanted to enslave us all. I felt I was being let into a secret: never in the media was this stuff ever mentioned.

Next, the African National Congress (or ANC) were painted as ruthless communists in the pay of Moscow. Names were mentioned again, names unfamiliar or only vaguely recalled. Nelson Mandela, evil beyond imagining, frightening, and, thank God, locked up forever in the safety of Robben Island. The South West Africa People's Organisation (SWAPO), likewise. The political criminal in this case was Sam Nujoma, and he was still at large, and was leading children to war against us. The last bastions of civilisation in Africa were under threat. "We know what we are talking about. We have fought with them." It was disquieting. I felt trapped in a dangerous and unheroic time. Black hordes swarmed out there, alien, brutal, inscrutable.

Another sergeant stepped forward and began to talk about the South African answer: military strength. We took notes. Next to me a rower fell asleep. His head just nodded sideways and he was gone in 10 seconds flat. The need for sleep numbed me too and I widened my eyes and wriggled my toes. KLONK! There it came! A doybie hurled across the room by a vigilant korporaal whacked into the sleeper's head. He started bolt upright, bleary eyes searching the room in fear. He saw the korporaal's finger wagging at him. I wrote down the reasons why South Africa would win the war. My handwriting became mushy. Mustn't let go! I gripped the pencil very tightly and ground my teeth … BOOF! Shit! I was asleep. The plastic helmet rolled to the floor with a hollow sound. The lecture was continuing. I looked for my accuser. He was motioning for me to go to the back.

"Wat gebeur met rowers wat slaap?" (*What happens to recruits who sleep?*) he said when we were outside, not loudly so as not to disturb the lecture.

"Ek weet nie Korporaal." (*I don't know Corporal.*) I never knew the answers to these questions.

"Hulle swem. Sien jy daardie dam?" (*They swim. See that dam?*)

I looked where he was pointing. It was a puddle, an inch deep and big enough to park a car in. It had rained hard throughout the night (and Sergeant Pretorius had elected to practise fire drill at midnight). "Ja Korporaal."

"Swem!"

I belly-flopped into the muddy water without hesitation. Back inside, sleep attacked me again within a few minutes. My wet clothes made no difference at all. The korporaals had their hands full just keeping people awake. The doybies flew at least one a minute, and the number of wet students grew.

Pale Afrikaners with neat haircuts were allowed into the camp in the evenings (the only type of civvies given this privilege), and would wander through the bungalows bandying their global conspiracy theories and pamphlets about. I did try to get involved with them in discussions, but they really weren't interested in recruiting soutpiele.

"Hotel Kompanie, tree aan vir vetkoek!" (*Hotel Company, form up for vetkoek!*) resonated Sergeant Pretorius one Saturday morning. In less than a minute in three long lines we were given our instructions.

"Die tannies van die Suiderkruisfonds wag vir julle seuns. Het almal sy vier rand?" (*The aunties from the Southern Cross Fund are waiting for you boys. Has everyone got his four rand?*)

"JA SERSANT!"

He eyed us suspiciously, head rotating menacingly above huge, looming shoulders. "Julle moet julle ordentlik gedra. Kompanie!" (*You must behave properly. Company!*) We braced. And doubled off to the Suiderkruisfondstannies. These benevolent ladies supported the troepies by organising fêtes and dos, in and around the training camps. Their job was to smile maternally at us and make us feel they were proud of us. On this fine Saturday, they visited 1 SAI with prodigious amounts of mince and vetkoek. Sergeant Pretorius had threatened us with punishment for not supporting the tannies by buying at least two vetkoek for two rand each. They had an assured market in us. Selling more than 5,000 meals in one day is good business.

We stood in long obedient lines in the sun dying for sleep edging towards the leathery tannies under the vetkoek stand. "I wonder how much they charge for blowjobs," mused a rower behind me. The nearest tannie wasn't sure, but thought she might have heard him say 'blowjob', and glared menacingly in our direction. Terrified, we deadpanned, amazed she knew what it meant. You live and learn. This English rower was quite large and so only received angry stares from the goeie seuns behind his back. Then we took our challenging parcels and sat to eat them on the baking barren ground around the so-called 'Feeshuis', a massive corrugated asbestos auditorium with a dusty earth floor where periodically, appalling variety concerts were meted out to us like punishments, when we could have been in bed sleeping.

The first signs of disaster appeared early on Sunday morning, as lights came on in the bathroom, where troops were starting to visit the toilets. The painful urge hit me at a quarter to three. I barely made it to a booth when the most violent brown explosion I have ever experienced in my life filled the bowl, like an RPG exploding. I went five times again before dawn, and everyone was awake, panting, swearing and groaning. Never was the humble vetkoek so liberally cursed.

We tree'd aan for kerkparade at 7.30 and were marched through Tempe past the Armour Battalion and past the Parabats to the military Anglican church, where the 1 SAI contingent maintained a constant movement to the rear door and back to their seats. There were similar goings on in other churches around town. No one denomination was favoured. Toilet paper quickly ran out at the church and the affliction entered its desperate phase. The retreat to the camp resembled a rout. On the way, I started to experience the warning pain, and knowing I had little time to waste, I said, "Ek het gyppoguts Korporaal," (*I've got gyppoguts Corporal*) and sidestepped out of the squad. Immediately my pants filled with brown liquid, and with heavy balloons at my elasticated ankles, I limped with other casualties back to 1 SAI, discussing the Suiderkruisfondstannies in colourful language. Back at base we regrouped around our bathrooms. Only at sunset did the panic ease off, by which time we were all in considerable pain and had given up the use of the toilets. All the toilet paper was used up, and we went directly to the cold showers, which were left running continuously amid a crowd of naked waiting men. This, and other shared indignities, made for a curious bonding among the rabble.

One afternoon during open air lecture opleiding, a mutinous rower was singled out for an opfok and was given the individual attention of a korporaal. In the Feeshuis compound the two of them interacted, the one tall and wearing a green beret, the other short and stocky and weighed down by staaldak, webbing en geweer. We knew the routine. In our peripheral vision we saw push-ups, sit-ups, running with rifle held high, leopard-crawling, running on the spot, staan-sit, quick marching. Distantly we heard an endless babble of abuse. It went on as long as we sat in the heat struggling to concentrate on the read-out lecture. The rower didn't want to be in the army, and had already made two escapes. We knew he was a fool and avoided him because he meant nothing but trouble. He was wholly defiant. Suddenly there was a commotion and lecture groups everywhere came to a stop. The rower had cracked and was swinging at the korporaal with his R1, screaming, "You fukken poes! You fukken poes!" Korporaals from everywhere dashed to the fight and within seconds the rower was whirling through the air like a doll on a string, wrenched by many strong hands at once, and big fists whacked into his now helmetless head. Blood was everywhere, and then he lay face down in the dust. He was dragged past us for he refused to walk, and he was crying at last, loudly and without meaning like a baby. Blood from his broken nose mixed with his tears, for he was alone in all the world, defeated and cringing in a sea of incomprehensible hatred. Without pity we watched him disappear. We knew how to avoid such treatment.

After one month of Basics we were allowed out on pass, except those who had caused trouble. It must be pointed out that that first month felt like a lifetime. Later, we had four or five months between passes. I caught a South African Airways 737 to Cape Town, determined not waste two of the four days on the road. My salary was R60 per month, less about R10 for mess fees (essentially jam) and floor cleaning materials, so I prevailed upon my mother to buy the flight. The Bloemfontein – Cape Town late-night flight Standby cost less than R60 then in a special deal for National Servicemen. That silence could be a luxury I had not known. The cool clean sheets and the musical crickets chirping seemed the best experience of my life. I slept without dreaming, and woke to silence, sunshine and the scent of vegetation. I did not leave the property. I had no need.

> Dear Mom,
>
> 3 People committed suicide over the week-end, and almost 100 people have not returned from pass; they are mostly hitchhikers. This is out of ± 300. (At this stage in Basics 4 people dead, 1 heart attack). The sergeant was very sarcastic about the whole business, saying that we should not waste time and cut lengthwise instead of across the wrist. Apart from this, everything's going well. Commandant Savides has just become Colonel Savides and generally people are very pleased because he is a good commander. We've been drilled extremely hard this morning, probably because we all slept until 5: it was a very tiring hot night, with people arriving back continually all night. Today has been very hot, perhaps not 42°C, but hot enough for working troops. Today after lunch matriculants were taken aside and then divided into university passes. There is some talk about officers' courses and O+O company, but I don't think this will affect me in any way, 1/ because I think the Equestrian section will send around a selection board and 2/ the officers course is 9 months long and not for people who want to specialise. I've written to Lieut Van Wyk about the transfer, but I haven't given it to him yet. I'm not going to supper tonight because I'm so tired and I think we're going to have trommel P.T., "hotdogs and hamburgers"

(a pleasant game involving 4 repetitive whistle blasts. Fully clothed – at 1, you stand on your bed; at 2, you proceed in a clockwise direction, moving from bed to bed; at 3, you climb into the nearest bed and pull the blankets over your head (HOT!); at 4, you alternate going over and under the beds, in a clockwise direction) and an inspection, but they might say or realise that we've had enough today. (Moral: the sooner I get outta here the better!)

Glazewski arrived back soon after I did. I knew something was badly wrong the minute he started to speak. By the quality of his stuttering I could always tell his state of mind. Now he had started off with eyes wide and glazed, signs of an internal trauma I was never to identify. He was asking how my pass had been.

"It was nice," I said guardedly. "How was yours?"

"I-It was good. D-D-D-D-Did y-y-y-y-you s-s-s-s-smoke z-z-z-z-z-z-zol?"

"No I didn't," I said icily, wishing he wouldn't make this clearly predetermined, and increasingly neurotic, effort to assert himself. "Did you?"

"Yes." The affected gutter jargon in a posh private school accent, bereft of all spontaneity by the terrible stuttering, was mortifying, let alone his unlikely claim. Everyone was listening.

He began again as I waited, deadpanning like an actor in a bad play, committed to struggling on. I knew from the first letter of the word he was stuck on that he was asking if I'd had sex while on pass, implying that if I hadn't, I was a complete bolyn. I braced myself for the inevitable. The silent crowd waited. Excruciatingly, he ran out of breath, but at last succeeded. He was red.

"No, did you?" I said loudly. For years his school had provided nurturing space in which his self-esteem and obvious talents could flourish despite his condition. Without empathy, the army's emotional brutality had at least for the moment, but possibly permanently, defeated him.

"Yes," he said. I felt deeply concerned for him but being in a social hell myself I started unwittingly to search for other friends.

4
The Plains of De Brug: Infantry and Mortars

Ten-thousand ambitionless feet lifted and trod the stony earth like a millipede, to the will of drivers tall and mean. Grey dust coated the boots and faces of the boys as they trudged overloaded and unknowing of their destination. A long flat gravel road led out from Bloemfontein across a gold field of rippling grass that became hazy in the humid sky on the edge of sight. Widow birds, long-tailed and black, performed their falling dance at intervals like funereal banners set free and loose on the wind, on each side of the driven migration from 1 SAI to De Brug.

The camp was emptied. We lagged for miles with blistered feet in badly fitting boots, and with sad thoughts bottled in heads aching with the press of straps in the heavy steel helmets, grown hot in the sun. All our belongings hung about our persons, and swung, and bounced, and shifted. As if that weren't enough, tyres and poles were given to the slow or the mutinous. We were vloeked and beaten to De Brug. This large empty wilderness of grass plains and hills and few trees is where soldiers come to learn their trade. They can run or drive unimpeded and they can shoot in any direction. The sun bakes onto this country, the rains turn it alternately to steaming green savannah, and in winter freezing winds blow unceasingly across the dead grass, and dust and dead grass stalks whip low along the frosty surface. In summer a white man's face turns red or brown and in winter it is chapped and pink. It is a land where you think of cancer. Rooi Hoenderhaan was the name of the place H Company set up camp. Other camps were hidden in the immensity of De Brug, but we saw their inhabitants far out on the vlaktes sometimes, making clouds of dust.

Dear Mom,

If this letter reaches you, it was because circumstances were favourable. I can only send a letter off when someone goes back to Tempe. We had a very hard march out here in the heat, with little water, for 25km & with 20kg on my back. At the moment I'm just resting, and I have been all day except for a 4km walk to the showers. Clean for the first time in 5 days. I have not yet taken my first overalls off. We sleep in little waterproof tents for 5 people which are warm

THE PLAINS OF DE BRUG: INFANTRY AND MORTARS

only if you put a blanket under your sleeping bag (which I do). On our first day (Sunday) we were with the H Company staff, but we alternate our camp every day, meaning a long march in the afternoons. After H we went to Golf Company quarters, 9km away. There we did fire control orders (practical) firing off 50 rounds of R1 ball & tracer over the veld, into chosen targets (wrecks, trees, etc). Tracers are wonderful to watch, but they can set fire to the grass. At Golf Company (G) we were rather badly treated, with very little food (you wouldn't believe the amounts we get. I'll show you how much on my next long pass). Then we marched by night to Juliet Company (J) HQ, where I now am still, on Wednesday. We have done map-reading here; yesterday we went on a surprise march ("as far as you can see") with map bearings on a bit of paper. We ate at 6 in the morning (a minimal amount – 1 egg – 2 slices bread, coffee) and again after the march at 6 in the evening. I then stole – the truth – 15 slices of brown bread which I ate last night. I think we are still here because of the state of many of our feet, and mine are among the worst, I have many, large, painful blisters, especially between the toes; these blisters have split, and other blisters formed deeper under the new skin, and these were filled with blood. When we went to the shower this morning we went in 3 groups:-

1/ Normal

2/ F ... d-up feet

3/ Baie F ... d-up feet

I was with the BFUF. We had to say either:-

Ding – dong, ding – dong, dingaling

or   Beep – Barp, Beep – Barp

or   Pille – pleister, pille – pleister

or   Aspirin – disprin, aspirin – disprin

or   Oink, oink, oink, oink

instead of left, right.

When I returned I had my blisters 'cured'. They now feel worse, because they inject a red liquid into them which stings. 2 corporals sat on me to keep me still. So now we're wondering whether we will hike now or tomorrow. It's now 5.30. Half an hour to supper (officially), although if we march we'll only get supper at 10. Life is hard here, you get thirsty and hungry & tired, but: we go to bed at the latest at 9 o'clock & wake at 5. Usually we sleep at 7. So, in some ways it's better than camp. All we have to do is wash our faces, clean R1s, put polish on boots (do not shine) and clean the tent. But wouldn't I now love to clean bathrooms, make beds and wash clothes! When I come down all I want to do is eat, especially fruit and sweets, and drink tea or anything. We put a jiffy-bag over our dixies so we don't need to wash up. We just peel off the bag after eating and throw it away. De Brug is very large and has many wide, grassy plains. There is continual gunfire and practice bombing by the airforce. Ratels shoot the 90s in among the hills, and occasionally mortars may be heard. There is also tons of wildlife. Yesterday I made a replay of the chase across Rohan in the Lord of the Rings. After our mapped march we were 9km away from our camp across a wide grassy plain, about 200 of us. Then they departed, except for me and two friends, left in a nearby washroom cleaning off military blacking. We came out, and they were already 2km away. We started after them at a whacking pace with me leading, but they were running, and we could still see them at 7km, having a smoke break: a cloud of smoke rising above 200 people. Then they disappeared into the far hills, and we sneaked into camp rather late, and had supper. This is a fantastic lot of staff-members that we are with. We sit around a fire at night and tell jokes, and we get more food than at the other camps.

A volunteer for military training wants to pull through and knows the purpose of the training and so has resistance to hardships. Conscripts, on the other hand, are like captives beaten into submission against their will, which was in any event immature, and we saw no other choice to our attitude. We were a defeated army, an army of boys subjected to grinding humiliations we felt we did not deserve and could see no reason for. We hated the slavery with helpless cowardice and fell into deepest sleep whenever the chance arose, anywhere, a hard floor wearing a steel helmet, on a bench in a shaking truck, in a filthy semen-spattered concrete guard tower in the endless hours before dawn. Things one could normally enjoy were transformed to unendurable drudge. And so, route marches through fine landscapes, visits to the shooting range, Sunday visits to town and church, were made utterly despicable.

Next to me on the church truck one icy Sunday dawn, sat the skinny gawky one I had observed slouching across the Castle courtyard, the one with the long hair, significant hooked nose and unnerving blue eyes. He looked at me as if he'd known me all his life and said, "What church you going to?"

"Catholic."

"Are you fucking mad?"

I was a bit taken aback. I had arrived at this choice of worship only after a systematic rotation of denominations. He stared at me demandingly.

"Well ... none of the corporals go there ... and afterwards there are tea and cakes, and you get invited home for lunch with one of the families."

He absorbed all this with a spiritually open mind, while we both shivered. "So d'you think I should come?"

I shrugged my shoulders and made a vacant face at him. The truck was slowing down at the edge of 1 SAI parade ground. Squads were already forming under the vehement control of corporals. "There's that fucking cunt, lets get out of here!" he spat, glaring out at the red-eyed black-haired bull-man. "Follow me!" he ordered and I found myself treeing aan in the Presbyterian squad. Before half the trucks had even arrived we were being hustled aboard another truck leaving immediately for the dawn service at the Presbyterian church. There were only about six of us and the truck was empty. The sun was just rising when we were dumped at the church. We waited until the truck left and then Michael Eriksen, that was his name, said, "OK let's fuck off." We walked round the block and he led me straight into a Wimpy Bar. After bacon and eggs and coffee we walked briskly in step, so as not to attract attention from the hundreds of off-duty Permanent Force officers that infested Bloemfontein, to the Catholic church. People were gathering outside with a festive air. Inside we relaxed because there was none of the PT that goes on in an Anglican church (stand, sing, sit, stand, pray, sit). We had a good day. We got into camp in the late afternoon, sped off to De Brug at dusk, and separated into our different training companies.

At De Brug we experienced enforced nomadism with its rain, sickness, blisters and exhaustion. We didn't know if we were coming or going quite a lot of the time. But we were like-minded in our rejection of the spirit of the enslavement, and through commiseration many cliques and groups of friends grew up and I met some of the best friends I had ever had. I often met Eriksen and several of his offbeat friends. Michael Eriksen was a neo-hippy-pacifist-pragmatist, and musical, and played guitar well. Peter Barry was short like me but stockier. His father had been a mercenary in the Congo, and he knew a guy in my company called Hoare: their fathers knew each other from mercenary days and they came from Richards Bay in northern Natal. The Natalians had a wild streak in them, something in their subculture that gave them independent spirits. Many of them were suited to being soldiers. Yet like me they were still only boys whipped from their homes at the moment in their lives when the future should have seemed most glorious and full of paths to travel. Barry was luminously irreverent. "Jesus fucking Christ I can't stand Dutchmen. You know what they are, they're plain fucking rude, they're uncivilised. They're just like Russians. They're ugly and rude like Russians. They are fucking Russians, they just don't know it." He gave a falsetto giggle. "Call them Russians, it drives them fucking crazy. And you know what? They love it here. They fucking enjoy the army. They love running and fokken luiperdkruiping around this poesplaas all day long." I was giggling too. This line of invective gave me something to cling to. Any enthusiasm is infectious. "This is worse than prison." He was on a roll. "In fact I'd rather be in prison. Two years! It's a fukken lifetime, a total – fukken – waste of time. And just think: you might get killed!" I did think about it. Often. Of all the chilling thoughts I harboured, this was the coldest. We deeply resented being denied our individuality – no, we were anonymous crew-cut stinking savages amongst a sea of others, farting and cursing and hating.

"Mortiere, tree hierso aan!" (*Mortars, form up here!*) yelled a sergeant with the nametag 'Van Niekerk' and who looked like a young Montgomery. Eriksen, Barry and I sprinted across the open gravel of the parade ground and were in. Those falling in after the required number was made up, were sent back to the riflemen. Straight away we gave our names, fetched our kit and went to new bungalows. Training began immediately after our new officers had fucked us up to gain our respect.

After three months of Basics one was expected to specialise or remain in the ordinary riflemen training companies. I was desperate to avoid these, to somehow escape the brutality. Recruiting officers came to 1 SAI from all over the country to find talented individuals. There were units especially for sportsmen, units like the Recces for the militarily insane, units for engineers and architects, for teachers, and for bikers and horse riders. This particularly interested me. I was a strong rider. But on the day the Berede officer came to camp I was in the middle of an attack of debilitating flu, and I had laryngitis. On a morning after rain I stood in line shivering in the windy sunshine, pale and coughing, and the red-bearded recruiting officer just didn't see me as a likely candidate. What a fool the system was! It was my only possible chance and it was gone. I nagged my company commander three times to try and arrange things for me, but he refused and finally lost his temper with me, so I gave up, bitterly disappointed.

Within 1 SAI itself there were different groupings that received separate training. Most would be trained as riflemen. To be in this group you needed standard six, though that didn't mean matrics weren't riflemen. Others would become drivers, of trucks, ambulances, Buffels and Ratels, and become competent mechanics of the vehicles in which they trained. Glazewski joined them. Gunners were another group. They learned the theory and mechanics of shooting turret-mounted 20mm cannons and 7.62mm Browning machine guns. The last group was the mortarists. Eriksen, Barry and I went for it. Drivers, gunners and mortarists had to have matriculated and would be required to use a bit of brain power. Even if we didn't expect cushy treatment, we expected to be treated as humans, which turned out to be almost true, but only when compared to what the riflemen went through. They were treated like

THE PLAINS OF DE BRUG: INFANTRY AND MORTARS

cattle, and there were some among them like Hanekom who had failed standard six or were unusually dim. But after several months even these had been removed to non-combatant duties, because you can't entrust your lives to idiots.

A mortar is an artillery weapon. It fires a bomb in a high parabolic arc. In the tail end of the bomb is a cartridge like a blank shotgun shell. In the shaft of the tail are perforations that release the blast. When the bomb slides snugly backwards down the pipe the cartridge hits a static firing pin that detonates it: the propellant then expands behind the thick part of the bomb shooting it out. A number of other additional charges may be attached to the tail fins of the bomb, causing a bigger bang in the pipe and shooting it further.

We trained with 81mm mortars with a range of 8km, and 60mm mortars with a range of 5km. Initially lectures and practical handling of the equipment lasted about three weeks. Each mortar weapon consisted of a pipe, a traversing and elevating bipod with optical sights, and a base plate. Other equipment included compasses, maps, and flags to be planted on a compass bearing from the positioned weapon. The base plate was a damn heavy lump of steel, and the whole lot accompanied us everywhere we ran, along with our rifles and all our other gear. The 81s had a crew of three and the 60s a crew of two, and were much lighter and easier to handle. We were told that the 81s were to become a separate unit of their own while the 60s would one day be reincorporated with the rifleman units, as auxiliary infantry weapons. This I didn't mind. The miniature 60mm mortar seemed to me a cooler weapon, and in my section there were three teams, that one day would be part of an infantry company, one mortar per platoon. I fell in with Mark Wetherall, who released the bombs into the pipe while I aimed. He had irrepressible schoolboy humour and complaints. We had a perpetually uneasy relationship, shifting often into adversity, but always nearby on another 60 were Barry and Eriksen. With them I shared a tent and listened to music and in the dark, sometimes miserable nights clung to toilet humour and memories.

The training lasted three months. Most of these were spent out at De Brug, in the coldest part of the year. The mortar company walked there under full kit plus mortars. We set up a camp in the remotest part of the training area and proceeded to hurl mortar bombs out onto the frosty Orange Free State grassland, in a never-ending cascade of hellish noise. Training concentrated on quickness in setting up weapons, and faultless use of the trigonometric range charts. Mortars can be fired visually, by adjusting the aim after shooting in with one or more bombs, or by use of maps, coordinates and compass readings. In the latter case a remote observer is required to relay feedback on the fall of the bombs. Sitting looking up the 60mm pipe it was usually possible to see the bomb and follow its trajectory if the propellant charge was not too great, so you generally knew how accurate you were before the bomb hit the ground. Contrary to myth, mortars are loud when firing. The bomb slides metallically down its pipe, and in a violent report the base plate jerks into the soil. A mortar emplacement of say eight pipes sets up over a wide area, and is aimed and fired as one. It is not intended that individual targets are destroyed, but rather that the bombs fall in a controlled group, and they will never fall in the same place twice because of the shifting of the base plate at each shot. The bombs have a flattened explosion that sends steel bits shooting low along the ground. To be standing within 15m of a 60mm HE explosion means death or mutilation, but steel bits might strike you down at much greater distances. The closer you get to the explosion the more likely you are to be vapourised. Thus a rain of mortars is excellent for disrupting an enemy's activities beyond the actual damage it might cause, and is most useful when you are making movements within range of an enemy, or when the enemy is trying to move to you.

The officers and NCOs never spoke in a low voice but always yelled. In spite of mortars being an interesting weapon and a novelty to use, the sense of drudge soon became overwhelming again. We felt like abject slaves, and it is true that we had no free will at all. We feared our officers completely. They could hit us and we could not counter that. They could insult our mothers and girlfriends and we could only stare back. We did not dare to mutter. They could stop us from being fed and we could complain to nobody. Always the best defence was silence and instant obedience, that became so much a habit that all else seemed unthinkable. We were made to shiver motionless in chilling rain all night, run miles and miles before dawn in full kit to earn breakfast, we had spadefuls of wet earth dumped in our faces as we slept exhausted in hard-dug trenches in the small hours, and we were forced to take cold showers under water tanks lined up naked with shrinking dicks in the biting Orange Free State winter winds. Often at night we were shipped off by Land Rover to remote concrete watchtowers on the edge of De Brug. Here the solitude was no relief in the blackest nights, as the sub-zero winds that blew incessantly froze our noses and ears and fingers and feet, and that was real pain.

"Hey Evan, remember to break off the piss when you finished" advised Eriksen from his pile of bedding. Just his nose protruded from his balaclava. I imagined a frozen arc of yellow pee standing by itself by the door of the tent. Failing inspection because of it: "Wie se donderse fokken pis staan hier voor die tent? Almal van julle, voorste posisie af, twee honderd push-ups!" (*Whose damn fucking piss is standing here in front of the tent? All of you, missionary position, two hundred push-ups!*) "Hey Evan, careful you don't snap your dick off by mistake!" added Barry. He giggled and sniffed revoltingly then cleared his throat like a dying bergie and came and spat out the door. We shook with laughter and cold. He was struggling, trying to walk around still in his sleeping bags and blankets, and he was wearing all his spare clothes at once. He tuned a small radio to Radio 5 and lit a candle. Then he lit three cigarettes in his mouth at once and stuck them into motionless balaclavas that began to emit smoke.

"Fuck! Look at this! Jesus!" We looked. The tent was brilliant white. We couldn't believe our eyes – a million crystals of ice glittering on the inside of the domed tent. We slept six to one of these, blankets below us to keep out the earth chill, pressed together for warmth, lying on our arms to keep them warm, telling jokes and stories in the pitch dark before sleep, and in the black morning waking up, we stuck only our penises through a small slit in the tent flap to piss. And in the cold you had to go. The temperature that particular morning was confirmed to be -13°C. It said so on the weather report for Bloemfontein and surrounds.

After some time the 60s and the 81s separated, for training specific to the different weapons. Always in smaller groups we were treated better, as we became more real to the instructors. At nights we might share a fire and springhaas potjie, tell stories, and listen to anecdotes from the border. In all these sorts of tales there was the sense of victory, that we were the winning side and the right one to be on. Disappearing was moral insecurity, for we were becoming parts of the machine. Herds of springbok drifted here and there across the winter-dun landscape and one afternoon, Sergeant Van Niekerk gave a fire control order that landed a group of bombs among a large herd. There were no downed buck though there might have been some injuries, and they were chased round and round the plain in circles, as group after group fell upon them. Eventually they moved far out on the plain beyond range, and night fell.

After three months had dragged by, the mortar course ended with a special opfok which lasted a week. The food was provided in its original raw ingredients, e.g. a section received two onions, half a pumpkin and some raw chicken to share. Fires were not permitted. Sleep was not on the agenda, and the instructors instructed us to perform meaningless and strenuous activities without respite. It was far worse than Basics, but we were simply getting used to abuse and automatic compliance. This, and the previous hardships and deprivations made us sickly and sniveling, and we broke out in sores all over our bodies, sores from the cold and particularly boils, and our feet were covered in compounded blisters and our hands chapped. Dirt was so ingrained in our skin that it only grew out a month after I left the army.

After the opfok we had a spell of standing guard at 2 Mob, a ranch-sized compound containing vehicles and other equipment in storage yards. I climbed into a walled yard one day and counted over a hundred big tanks close parked. Walking across the roofs of these I found an open turret and sat inside the cool blue cave for more than an hour. It was a strange experience like being a ghost myself, and I found a stiffened leather pistol holster which I took and still have. Some of the guard posts were miles from each other in the middle of nowhere, and I spent some of the loneliest four or eight-hour shifts in the blackest freezing predawn hours I have ever known. Wild thoughts and terrors sprang on you, and you wrapped up tight and stared at the faint horizon, shivering in violent uncontrollable spasms for hours.

One troop saw, in the early morning light, a brown Land Rover stop against the outer fence of De Brug, about 700m from where he stood in number eight tower on a hill on the southern extremity of the 2 Mob enclosure. Two PFs got out and fired a shot at some springbok in the intervening grassland. The troop fired a warning shot vertically upward, which shocked him more than it did them, as there was a sheet metal roof over his head. The PFs stopped for a moment but then let off another shot at the springbok. The troop then simply took aim at them and fired, and they fled, and he fired off a full magazine of carefully aimed shots, and was still shooting when the Land Rover was some kilometres away down the road. Later, we all remarked that we would have done the same, except that we would have taken advantage of being an official guard, and killed those PFs, and no one could have incriminated us, as we thought. The only good PF was a dead PF. That is how we felt.

5
Ratels: Mechanised Infantry

"*Word wakker, word wakker, gister was kak maar vandag is nog kakker!*" (*Wake up, wake up, yesterday was shit but today is even shitter!*) shouted Warwick between the tents. My brain slowly turned itself on. I needed more sleep. I opened my eyes and blinked them forcefully and repeatedly to get them to work. On both sides of my head there were deep waking sighs and a mutter of "Oooh fuck. I'm still here. Giggle." Barry. It was pitch dark in the chopper tent, now filled with the rustling of bedclothes. My arms were buzzing from being asleep, for I had slept on them for warmth.

"I've got to have a piss." I lifted my head off my boots and took out the socks, and pulled them on. I put the boots on without doing up the laces, and taking my rifle and toothbrush probed with my feet to step between the bodies. "Sorry!" I reached the door which I unzipped. Colder air flowed into the musty tent. The cold woke me up completely. The stars and a small moon shone. At the piss lily a dark form was busy. After I'd had my turn, careful to avoid the overflow, I went to the water trailer and brushed my teeth and washed my face. Then I sat down and tied my laces. I was ready.

"F Kompanie aantreep!" (*F Company form up!*) Sergeant Van der Westhuizen's voice sang through the darkness.

Mid-winter had come and the specialisation courses were at an end. Again there was a state of upheaval, lives being organised by faceless authorities, so my friends and I stuck together like horrified sheep in an abattoir, because we knew we could be separated into separate units and never see each other again. Poor Glazewski failed the driver's course. Though he clearly had as much determination as any trainee, he got a raw deal from the officers, because he was made for rejection in the army. His stutter had worsened. His legs were too short to reach the pedals in the trucks, and he had to drive with a cushion. He could not transmit radio messages. This, every viable combatant had to be able to do. He was dumped in HQ Company, a spaarpiel. He was put on a shelf. Though he still had 18 months of army left, the army had no further use for him. HQ Company consisted of all those unsuited to combat roles: gyppogatte, sifseuns and rugridders. I could see he was hating himself. He was fucked. The army had destroyed him.

Meanwhile in 1 SAI a Mechanised Infantry Training Battalion was put together. Its makeup was as follows:
1. A logistics unit of stores, maintenance, command and administration (i.e. The Base)
2. Specialised units – 81mm mortars, Assault Pioneers, Intelligence
3. Three Mechanised Infantry companies
   Each company consisted of the following:
   a) Company administration clerks
   b) Company Command crew in a Ratel, with
      - Company commander
      - Intelligence orderly
      - Company signaler
      - Company medic
      - 20mm cannon gunner
      - Ratel driver
   c) Company 2nd in command crew in a Ratel, with
      - Company 2nd in command
      - Intelligence orderly
      - Company Sergeant Major
      - 2 x 60mm mortarists
      - 20mm cannon gunner
      - Ratel driver
   d) Three platoons, each with
      Platoon HQ in a Ratel, with
      - Platoon commander
      - Platoon orderly
      - Platoon sergeant
      - Platoon NCO
      - Platoon signaler
      - Platoon medic
      - Platoon storeman
      - 2 x 60mm mortarists (i.e. me and Wetherall)
      - 20mm cannon gunner
      - Ratel driver
      and three sections each in a Ratel, with
      - Section leader
      - Section 2IC

- Light Machine Gunner No 1
- Light Machine Gunner No 2
- 6 Riflemen
- 20mm cannon gunner
- Ratel driver

So a fighting company consisted of 153 men in fourteen Ratel 20s, not including extra accompanying NCOs, and the clerks. We were to remain together until the end of National Service 18 months later, with only minor changes. Our training company at that time was called F or Foxtrot Company and was made up of the most disparate examples of South African society. We had our fair share of tattooed scarred ruffians and brekers, as well as pacifists, businessmen and intellectuals in the making. There were friendships and hatreds and fights. All of my friends from 60mm mortars were with me in F Company, although in other platoons. Michael Eriksen and Peter Barry were in Platoon 2. I was in Platoon 1 which had some of the most determined militants and hoodlums, and in the end we became really good soldiers. Dominating Platoon 1, and indeed the company, was a group of bellicose young men drawn from industrial society in Cape Town, as well as some from hard Orange Free State farming stock. Of them, a Capie from Vasco, black-haired hard-eyed Warwick, was the most powerful individual, nobody's fool and supremely aggressive, a born fighter with what used to be known in military circles as 'dash'. He was a gunner, and later proved himself a wizard of this trade under operational conditions. No one fucked with Warwick and it came to be the practice that when there were problems between the company and its officers, Warwick was sent for and quiet words exchanged. Nothing could be done without his approval.

While the ordinary riflemen had already completed three months of fundamental infantry training, combined Mechanised Infantry training now lasted a further nine months, and was highly comprehensive and very demanding. All of it was in the veld, so we gave up life in the bungalows altogether. In the first three cold months we stayed once again at Rooi Hoenderhaan.

Our new tormentor was Cpl Van Jaarsveld. He was a short, stocky and immensely strong man, with dwarfish features (large bean-shaped head, short arms etc.) and a rich brei in his voice indicating he came perhaps from somewhere in the Swartland. His favourite phrases were "kom pieletjies ... " "klim in julle fokken Ratels ... " and "kry julle fokken staaldakke ... " (*Come little pricks ... climb in your fucking Ratels ... get your fucking helmets ...*) We tired of him. We called him 'Tap-tap' after Tap-tap Makathini, the black bantamweight boxer. He dwelt on us, he watched us and knew our weaknesses. He had a very loud voice for such a short man and he loved to use it in close proximity to our ears if he could reach up to them. He accompanied us everywhere like a horsefly that keeps a herd of young bulls on the run. Sergeant Van der Westhuizen, with a blond handlebar moustache you could see from behind, organised the lives of the trainees. While corporals were idiots, sergeants seemed to have got over their ego problems. Sergeant Van der Westhuizen's one true talent was imaginative swearing, but it was never malicious. In the circumstances we liked him. Nevertheless this part of training was our bleakest time in the army. We were oppressed by a man with dark inner demons, the hated, sadistic and overweight training company commander. He was never kind and always heaped on extra misery with a grin. Once, when his sister's child of 12 was in his care for a Saturday in the training area, he treated the boy with such frustration becoming physical abuse, that he became catatonic with fear, and lay quivering in the commander's Ratel as we looked on, appalled. This kind of behaviour fell on us too, but then, we were a few years older and scarcely kept the anger from our eyes. In this environment of perpetual emotional tension, we learned the techniques of violent war.

It was still bitterly cold out at De Brug, but the Rooi Hoenderhaan base area was sheltered and elevated off the windswept flats, and had at its rear a line of steep hills. I know they were steep because I ran up them five times a day, the first time usually to 'wake us up' in the dark, and we stood on the summit and compulsorily yelled, "Goeie more, Suid-Afrika!" (*Good morning, South Africa!*) It was also fairly bushy compared to the grass plains. Generally it was a comfortable spot. A little town of tents was plonked here, and although we had an empty bungalow back in 1 SAI, and went out into the remoter wilderness on training exercises for a week or two at a time, we called Rooi Hoenderhaan home for six months.

For the first of these weeks, training concentrated on infantry skills including camouflage, fighting formations and fire-and-movement. These were first practised in sections, and later in platoons. Live ammunition was not used initially for our newly issued R4 rifles, and we were made to shout "bah! bah!" to simulate shooting and make us spirited. Instructors rushed around among us, pushing us forward and throwing us to the ground. Throwing yourself to the ground was very important, and had to be done without hesitation and violently, so that we were permanently covered with bruises and scratches.

The introduction to 'black is beautiful' was unwelcome, as this oily black gunge crept into your pores, dirtied your clothes and was damn uncomfortable to wear, and yet we were expected to appear neat and clean soon after any training ended. Blacking was part of camouflage, which also included sticking bits of grass and tree branches to your helmet and webbing, and this also worked its way into your clothing and gave 'itchy and scratchy' a whole new meaning. But camouflaging became so natural that at an order we blended effectively with surrounding vegetation within minutes. The aim was to hide your human outline, and the blacking reduced the features of your face to a dim shadow which is overlooked among vegetation. The nutria brown of our clothes was very effective too as it is a neutral colour, and blends with most backgrounds in Africa, in both the dry and the green seasons.

"Ek's fokken invisible!" Sitas van Dyk said in the middle of a flat plain. With a lazy Capie slouch he prowled among the platoon. Like Warwick he was a well built black-haired gunner and the two were lifelong friends. Unknown to the officers the two of them smoked zol at night on the koppie. Now he paraded himself in a virtual haystack of long rooigras tufts. From his helmet they stuck up three feet higher than he was, and three feet outwards from his body in all directions. "Hey ouens, kan julle my sien?" (*Hey guys, can you see me?*) We hooted with laughter. He looked like The Incredible Grass Monster. Van Jaarsveld came scampering up on his short legs to put an end to play.

"Sitas! Watse fokken kak vang jy nou aan! Die luitenant is netnou fokken hier! Hier kom die sersant!" he yelped. There wasn't a remote chance of humour on his big face. "Hoe weet jy dis ek, Korporaal?" said Sitas in aggrieved, whining tones. "Ek's gekamofleer." (*Sitas! What fucking shit are you up to! The lieutenant is here soon! Here comes the sergeant! ... How do you know it's me, Corporal? I'm camouflaged.*)

"Jy gaan kak pieletjie. En jou maatjies ook. Kamofleer jou fokken ordentlik. Fokken nou!" (*You're going to shit, little prick. And your friends too. Camouflage fucking properly. Fucking now!*)

"Korporaal!" Van Jaarsveld spun around.

"Ja, Warwick, wat wil jy nou he?" (*Corporal! ... Yes Warwick, what do you want now?*)

"Korporaal, ek net 'n nood. Ek wil gaan kak." Van Jaarsveld looked around. "Daar's geen fokken kakplek hier!"

"Wáár wil jy fokken gaan kak?" he snapped.

"Agter daai bos, Korporaal," he said loudly, pointing to Sitas who had drifted off. (*Corporal, I have a need. I want to have a shit ... There's no place to shit here! Where do you want to shit? ... Behind that bush, Corporal.*)

Dear Mom,
    For the last month I've been very bored, bordering on depression: I feel so caught and imprisoned that I'm thinking of removing myself. I am busily involved in an incredible waste of Time. So when you came to Bloem it was quite

a highlight and I'm very glad you came. I'm getting pushed around such a lot by Authority that my rebellious flame has grown very bright. Yesterday I took the Tolkien book & read it today. It's very interesting, an attempt to explain the importance of the 'Fairy Tale', like the 'Lord of the Rings' completely removed the Fairy Tale from all Childishness. There is also an amazing translation of a Viking – Saxon afterbattle scene, which reminds one of tapes with the voices of men about to die, except very old. What we've been doing here is Section Spanopleiding. Although it doesn't really affect me in H.Q. Platoon, it's teaching me all about the Ratel. The chances are that we will not use Ratels on the border, but voetstap, as so far only one company at a time uses them. When you brought me back last night, the camp was empty. I went to sleep in an empty bungalow because everyone had gone to De Brug to put out a fire which was threatening Ou Magasyn. They all returned at about 2 o'clock, and we went to church this morning as usual. Today was so dusty & windy that the sheets on my bed had a brown coating. Have you ever heard a Durbanite speak? It's getting on me: "I've got a kiff graft, my broe's moving to my old man's posie, ek sê. I'm going to suip myself dik, eks."

Section attacks went as follows: first you advanced in one of many formations, from single file to arrowhead formation. On "kontak!" you all dove for cover. Shooting commenced immediately on the designated front, while the section leader decided what to do next. He then manoeuvred his force to positions while keeping some elements firing at the 'enemy'. Then the firefight began. This was a static direction of concentrated fire at the enemy, intended to cow him by the accuracy and intensity of your shooting. When he was cowed, indicated by a distraction in his opposition or a lessening of his will, you began fire-and-movement. The 'evens' remained down, shooting between the 'odds' who jumped up and ran then dove for cover after 10 paces, and as soon as they began shooting, the 'evens' were up and running, and so it went on. It was a highly choreographed movement and required the utmost energy and awareness. Fire-and-movement was conducted under the covering fire of the section's LMG, which during the firefight used the opportunity to move to a flanking position more lateral to, and preferably higher than the enemy, from where it could deliver crossfire, to divide the enemy's attention and keep their heads down. At first, the strongest-looking troops were allocated LMGs, one per section. The LMG, an old 7.62mm Bren for training purposes, was at least twice the weight of an R4, or between 10-15kg unloaded.

Brian Hoy cut a fine figure with a Bren, walking out one morning to the training area with the platoon. We had also seen from opfoks and runs that he possessed considerable stamina. He was a man who could simply run all day, even when heavily loaded. I also in the short time we had been together got the impression he was quite bright, but he kept to himself. Today was his first with a Bren. From my position dogging the platoon commander, I heard all commands for exercises, both direct and by radio, and we in Platoon HQ became backseat critics to the efforts of the infantry going through their paces.

"Kontak!" And the section leaders and then the riflemen all yelled "kontak!" and dived to the earth. Shooting started immediately on the front of the formation, and a cloud of acrid cordite rose around us. "Ses-Een-Alpha jou manne is traag. Mouton se gat steek uit – hy's dood!" (*Six-One-Alpha your men are slow. Mouton's arse is sticking out – he's dead!*) Section leaders ducked about, dealing with problems in the firefight. "Ses-Een-Charlie agteruit links onder dekking. Beweeg!" (*Six-One-Charlie back out left under cover. Move!*)

"Charlie positief." Section 3 in reserve dashed out to the rear in single file keeping low and spread out. To me the platoon commander turned and said, "Davies!"

"Luitenant!" I gave him all my attention.

"Droë bos, twaalfuur, vier honderd meter, vier HEs op jou eie tyd." (*Dry bush, 12 o'clock, 400 metres, four HEs in your own time.*) Wetherall and I prepared the mortar and fired off the bombs. Their crunching made our ears ring. One of them hit the dry bush. The Lieut once more spoke slowly and clearly into his handset.

"Ses-Een Bravo, ek hoor nie jou LMG nie! Hy moet laag skiet. Laag! Laag! LAAG! ... Charlie kom in." (*Six-One-Bravo, I don't hear your LMG! He must shoot low. Low! LOW! ... Charlie come in.*)

"Charlie by."

"Charlie versprei jou manne op die rand twee honderd meter en stuur jou LMG heel links koppie toe." (*Charlie spread your men on the ridge 200 metres and send your LMG far left to the hill.*)

"Charlie positief."

From our position slightly to the rear, Hoy was visible loping along a ridge with the section 2IC and the LMG number two, who carried the ammunition and helped load. Soon above the clatter of the two sections firing to the front, came the strident thunder of the LMG's heavier calibre on the hill. The two front sections prepared for fire and movement. "Maak gereed vir vuur en beweging!" (*Get ready for fire and movement!*)

This order got repeated by all the troops. From the hill covering bullets whipped across the front. How Section 2 was not mown down was a trick of the eye. Hoy with great tenacity fired long bursts, and failed to hear frantic yells of "Hoy! Hoy!" from the lower ground, and failed utterly to see the platoon in swift retreat, except Section 2 who were pinned down in a cloud of dust and flying stalks of grass. Section 3's 2IC jumped onto Hoy and put the machine gun out of action. Sergeant Van der Westhuizen came running up yelling, "Wat die donderse poes is daai fokken kontkop se naam?" (*What the damn cunt is that fucking cunthead's name?*) After this everyone knew Hoy, and many were convinced he had made an attempt on their lives. Hoy became platoon storeman almost immediately afterwards, and LMG men were eventually, after a process of trial and error, appointed on merit, some of them being deceptively small and skinny.

Operation Protea was the buzzword in September and one day we were shipped from De Brug, hot and dirty with blacking, for a big victory parade in Bloemfontein but also to honour the dead of Operation Protea, of whom several had been from 1 SAI. In camp I met Glazewski again, and buoyantly told him about the training, the open air and the live ammunition. I suggested he apply in writing to join one of the infantry companies. God knew he would handle it just fine. He hated the petty discipline and ignominy of HQ.

It felt strange to be in the city in clean clothes with shiny boots again, after months in the comfortless wilderness. The whole of Tempe turned out, and thousands of troops lined and slow-marched the streets of the city. Where I stood half on and half off a pavement in the streetlight dark, I could hear nothing of the speeches and as if it were a dream, we were back in the veld that very night.

We understood through the military grapevine that Operation Protea had been a large successful campaign in Angola. A couple of big battles had been fought in several places, inflicting crushing defeats on SWAPO as well as FAPLA, the Angolan Army, denying them the use of southern Angola, and many of them had lost their lives. Still, the information we heard was just that, information, and there was little that was descriptive of the conditions, or painted any picture for us where we existed on the isolated golden plains of South Africa.

"Fuck. Davies hasn't even fukken heard of Three-Two Battalion!" announced Wetherall rhetorically to the gathered group sitting facing each other between two tents. "Do you even know where you are?"

"Wetherall," said Singleton, "hou op om altyd 'n fokken poes te wees. Davies, kyk hier in die fokken Scope," (*Wetherall, stop being a fucking cunt always. Davies, look here in the fucking Scope*) he offered kindly. In a sensational article I learned about 32 Battalion. They were highly trained bush fighters, an elite and radical unit trained to win against heavy odds. "Fukken check what they are fukken wearing,"

Wetherall pointed out on the pages. Photographs showed a line of men emerging from dry bushveld into a clearing. The resolution was bad. They could have been wearing blacking or they could have been black. We believed they were wearing blacking. They had headbands made from strips of brown army scarf, brown T-shirts and they carried AK-47s. We thought they looked cool. "We'll most fukken likely get to see them, ek sê."

As we progressed nuances and subtleties became familiar and we started getting good, moving fluently and rapidly, like a trained team. We started using the Ratels, learning to initiate these exercises climbing out of them, gradually increasing the size of the formations from a single Ratel with one section, to a full company of 12 Ratels in a row, and 120 men. We were using live ammunition in ever-increasing quantities, and were learning that the Ratels could fight also, as if they were giant soldiers moving among us, big friendly brothers with great roaring weapons over our shoulders. From them, gunners had good visibility of the action and received their fire control orders by radio from the section leaders who disembarked to lead the troops on the ground, so the situational awareness of the vehicles was the same as for the men in the open air. The firing line was kept at the noses of the Ratels.

A Mechanised Infantry unit was highly complex, with many varied human components, methods of conduct, and technological tools that could, with practise, operate in peerless coordination. We were starting to understand what we were involved in – a proficient fighting organisation, and the idea that we would indeed fight, and might do so successfully, was no longer vague. Mechanised Infantry warfare South African style was choreographed chaos, an explosion of destructive energy and power carefully aimed at a specific target. We got used to mind-buggering noise, clouds of dust and acrid smoke, swirling flames and stinging eyes. We got used to singed hair on our arms, grit embedded in grazes on our forearms, blisters from hot barrels on our hands. We felt strong and it felt good to take part in the juggernaut. And we liked our Ratels. They were comfortable to drive in, as they had a smooth heaving motion rather like a boat on a gentle swell, even when driving over rough terrain. This they could do at speeds of around 60km an hour.

An operational mech company drove down from the northern South West African border to Bloemfontein at that time. Known as Delta Company, they were a mid-yearly special intake to bolster the conventional forces in the Operational Area, and they had recently taken part in Operation Protea. The training companies were once again brought in from De Brug to salute their arrival after a successful campaign. Melodramatically we stood across the big parade ground at 1 SAI for an hour until the high-pitched whine of turbocharged Ratel engines was heard and they began to pour into the camp. Troops sat all over them. From where we stood, we could see how faded their clothes were, and torn, how relaxed they were and unhampered by drills or commands. In conversation with their officers, they dismounted and strolled around and finally walked off to the mess with long, stalking strides, stick figures carrying rifles slung about shoulders. Obviously they scorned our straight rows and ironed new browns, and felt little for our welcome as if they needed it not.

To 2 Mob at De Brug the recovering wounded of Operation Protea were sent. There were some with no legs, or with paralysed arms, or with hideously erased faces. Others lay in bed with internal injuries and their friends sat by them speaking quietly to them for hours. We saw these things while we were standing guard in the towers, because the guard bungalow was next to theirs.

"Gee my die HEs." (*Give me the HEs.*) It was early morning at Rooi Hoenderhaan. Van Schalkwyk, the gunner of the platoon commander's Ratel stuck his arm out of the turret hatch. Inside he sweated at the black metal of the open breech of his 20mm cannon, having manually cranked back the powerful spring of the working parts. Behind the turret were two opened boxes of HE shells and two boxes of AP shells. I took the end of an HE belt and dragged them to his hand, holding their weight in the air above him. With short breathless instructions he fed the belt into the belt feed, and then spliced the other one to it. That completed, we did the same on the other side of the cannon with the APs. Then he loaded the first shells of each belt into the loading mechanism and closed the top of the weapon. The safety pins holding back the spring were still in place. "Daarsy!" (*There!*) His broad blond farmer's face popped out, dripping sweat and looking the way it would a year later, when he broke my nose with his fist.

Behind us Piek, the driver, who was determined to swap his Ratel for a BMW as soon as possible, hefted open the engine hatches and went through his checks. In the commander's seat Singleton the signaler (Signalton, of course!) who was forever cheerful, clumsy and spoke in a slow drawl, tested the radios with the three other Ratels of the platoon, and then made sure all the platoon portables were in order. Riflemen assisted the crews or prepared the racks of spare rifle magazines along the cabin walls of the Ratels. There was little need to speak, for we knew what to do. There was just "pass this or that" or "where the fuck's such-and-such." A Mechanised Infantryman's life is busy. Maintenance of vehicles, weapons and other equipment is time-consuming, and kept us all busy with allocated chores when we were not training or sleeping, for the unit is practically autonomous and can operate without outside help.

6

The Captain

"There's a red house over yonder," sang Warwick powerfully to his own rhythm guitar accompaniment. Eriksen's spider fingers followed with some skilful steel string blues. "That's were my baby stays." Firelight shaken by the cold breeze flowed over the encircling faces staring inward, dazzled. Bush TV. There stood Hoy by himself, glasses glinting. After the applause, Warwick began a song he had written. Eriksen watched Warwick's hands for the chords and supplied wistful stretched notes.

"Jou militêre moer!" (*Your military cunt!*) laughed Sergeant Van der Westhuizen loudly, having been made the butt of a knock-knock joke. It had been a gruelling day training but now there was a braai. The instructors stood with us and we drank beers and told jokes and sang together. Things had taken a turn for the better.

> Dear Mom,
>
> Lots of news! A few days ago we were riding along in Ratels in a platoon formation when the H.Q. Ratel got lost from the others, because of a radio breakage. We spotted them and raced to catch up. Going almost 70km/h across the veld, we hit a bomb crater 1½ deep & 4m wide. The front of the Ratel hit the other side and because of the angular shape, 18 tons of men & metal ramped nearly a metre off the ground. I just remember a terrific crash as the hull collided, & then a moment of silence before being bodily thrown forwards, backwards, up, down & sideways. The rubber slats of the seat came loose as I hit them, & my headpiece ricocheted as my head hit a metal projection. Only the Lieut in the tower had his ribs bashed in, the rest were okay. The next day we drew our mortars, and were promised a mortar refresher course in about a week. On Monday, yesterday, ** ** ******* became our 2IC when Cpt Malan arrived and took over the Company. I think he's the best thing that's ever happened to us here at 1 SAI. Before he arrived the rumours were good (he commanded Delta Company), but now I see they were understatements – he is very fair, well mannered & he 'treats us like a white man'. He's installed a new pass system. If we want a weekend pass because of, e.g. someone's 21st or a graduation ceremony, or a mother's birthday, we must just ask him, and we'll go,

provided we've 'gedra'd ourselves'. Also he makes training & lectures brilliantly interesting, & has been the first rank ever to say & point at me, "You, mortar, are vitally important, I'm going to give you lots of practice, don't slacken in your training," or words to that effect. In the past, people just haven't known how to deploy us, saying, "Mortars, climb out, shoot at the target, then catch up with the Ratels" (which means about a 3km sprint). Capt Malan tells us of instances that he himself has seen. He says that SWAPO'S WWII T34 tanks won't bother us, and that he hopes we don't see any T55s. "Anyway, the Ratel 90 can knock them out." So SWAPO'S war is changing from insurgency to conventional. If there are any problems (not small ones), just phone Cpt Malan. He will help & is concerned.

Unexpectedly, after three months of Mech training a saint had appeared among us. One afternoon in the remotest corner of De Brug a captain arrived in a Ratel and stood talking to the training company commander while we went through the final stages of an exercise. Then he asked us to follow his vehicle over a low nek between two hills. The burning sun dried the dusty sweat on the red backs of our necks as the instructors herded us trudging heavily in full battle gear covered with grass camouflage over the rise. The Ratel stood parked down the slope in a natural amphitheatre. Sitting relaxed on its edge he suggested we sit around on the ground.

Captain Jan Malan was perhaps 5'10" tall, with dark brown hair and in a pale clear face were keen eyes perhaps a bit like those seen in photographs of De La Rey, and a military moustache over a strong chin. He seemed very lithe and fit and disciplined in his movements. He looked silently over us for a few minutes, gauging our faces, and then talked softly for an hour, while the sun began to make long shadows of the stones and the yellowing stalks of grass. He spoke in a dignified, straightforward way of peace and war, love and death, God, Africa and ourselves. We hoped he'd never stop speaking. He asked any who felt uneasy to voice their fears, and when several spoke, he answered them directly and truthfully.

He said we might indeed get hurt or killed. He told us we would never be called on to mistreat any person or their property, and that it was our right to refuse to do so, moreover, nor would we be allowed to lose discipline and loot, or take souvenirs. We would not use the word 'kaffer', or indeed any obscene words, or blasphemous ones, in his presence, upon pain of punishment, but we would hit any legitimate enemy carrying arms against us, and hit hard. We were here to fight a war, he said, not to entertain others with our exploits. We could expect no thanks for being clean, he said, but in this business, it made it easier to sleep at night. This way of thinking was the key to decent soldiering. A man must be clear in his mind and bare his sole to the cosmos before taking on the responsibility of killing other men in battle without regret, and he must match his motives for war against the motives of his enemy, and his own motives might appear to agree in their results with popular thinking but not necessarily in conception. It took no time at all for us to be moved by this sincere man. In that warm dusk in a desolate place he then and there gave us the option to step out and stay behind. It was not a trick. He really didn't want unwilling followers. He waited silently for two whole minutes. But for a gently stirring evening breeze and a twinkling star, there was no movement at all.

The training company commander was then given a brief word of thanks and as 2IC, became a vague figure in our lives. Later he was transferred away. Captain Malan was no training instructor, but a professional fighting man, dedicated to his work, and untrammeled by ego. He was polite with the former training company commander. He came down to us from the war and asked us to be his brothers in arms. He asked plainly and we agreed. He took over our training, which entered a final stage. He was true to his word about fair treatment and swearing was banned in his presence, and his presence went with us at all times. Every morning he prayed with us, and his prayers were for us, and we were grateful. He was the most uncompromising individual I have ever met, having no grey areas and no uncertainty. Something either was, or it wasn't. And he had a keen mind also. We were to learn too, that alcohol never passed his lips. He soon learned every first name in his command, and he used patience to teach us, but he was as hard as nails and a perfectionist. He drove us to perfection, repeating exercises regardless of mealtimes or sleep, until he was satisfied. In retrospect, Captain Jan Malan was the most forthright, strong-willed, honest and fair man I have met in my life, and an absolute born leader. I have been positively influenced by him.

At this time there were three Mechanised companies-in-training – Echo, Foxtrot and Golf – and the Captain led ours, Foxtrot. He was determined that we should win the final evaluation that would make us the elite team, the one that would become *the* Alpha Company at 61 Mechanised Battalion, based on the South West African border, and fight from Ratels – the remaining companies would become mainly foot soldiers. Second best is last in war, he told us – it was win or die. Our first victory therefore would be to become the best of the three fighting units. All training now became revision and appraisal prior to the evaluations. The Captain kept us hungering to improve our fighting ability, urging professionalism and pride and driving us with single-minded zeal. We loved him and he loved us and we tried everything to reach his standards. Every day he talked to us and invited questions and he was available to listen to problems after hours.

> Dear Mom,
> I arrived back at Tempe after landing at J B M Hertzog Airport and catching a taxi and driving through Bloemfontein. Then we came straight to De Brug and ended up in our tent. We did another first light attack on Friday morning, and Cpt Malan said it was the worst attack he had ever seen in his life: there was insufficient fire on the right places, & more than sufficient fire onto the open vlaktes (dead ground); the rocket launchers fired onto a bit of open sand in front of them. So we did it again, with success. I really think you should meet our captain. He is so open and honest and is the only army hand who does *not* vloek. He has already told us some of his life history and the only two things we should pray for he says, is for the best job and the best wife. Yesterday, Saturday, we went shooting and I shot better than I have in a long time. From the 300m mark I took almost 5 minutes longer than anyone else, squeezing the trigger slowly & watching the red arrow point to a bull. Yesterday we were plagued by the perfume man again. It lives in Bloemfontein & is allowed to come and sell perfumes to us ("Love is ... " bottles & deodorants & Christmas presents). I hope you don't want any teenager smells. Can you give any ideas as to what Granny, Keith, John, Grandfather & Norah would like for Christmas. Tell me what you think, and I'll ask you to buy & I'll pay for it. I wonder if I could be an illustrator. I'll enclose some scribbles. They're done by ballpoint pen; if I had paints & inks they'd be better.
> P.S. We may be getting quite a long pass over Christmas / N.Y.

Lohatla is a vast unoccupied tract of land near Postmasburg in the Northern Cape. Parts of it are very hot and arid, but there is also a type of grassy savannah going on and on across several horizons. Here heavy weapons were tested and the Battle School convened large-scale training exercises. It took almost a day to drive to Lohatla with stops at several small towns, and it felt good to be on the road in a convoy of fast armoured vehicles, passing through new country. We took over Delta Company's Ratels, and in them found such things as AK-47 bayonets and magazines, and Soviet aluminium water bottles.

"Ag kak Singleton," exclaimed Waite the medic, as a heady stench filled the troop compartment and to a chorus of groans our heads shot out of the roof hatches into the warm flowing air. Singleton the signaler smiled vacuously for the umpteenth time that morning, alone amid a forest of legs. He had started a new and unfamiliar brand of farting, quite strong, and we were not used to it. I expect it was caused by a gut bacteria, for soon we all had it and it became the official company smell. Only Hoy remained below, either because he didn't mind, or he was too well brought up, or he didn't have a hatch of his own, reading an already pulverised paperback and stuffing his face with peanuts. We in Platoon HQ were getting used to Hoy, who was from another planet. We forced him to sit in the service passage in the rear right-hand side of the Ratel. The biggest by far of us, he never tried to assert himself, just collected and collected and collected spare food which, though he ate non-stop, filled increasing numbers of sandbags. The job of storeman was perfect for him. He could read all day and was able to satisfy his obsessive compulsive passion collecting things: a boot, a tin of boiled cabbage – anything.

"Hoy, Hoy, what are you fukken doing, Hoy?" Wetherall sing-songed from the fresh air.

"None of your beeswax," he answered without looking up. He obeyed the Captain's request not to swear dutifully. He held the book 15cm from his monolithic spectacles. Without them he couldn't find them. After we discovered this we hid them, usually somewhere clever in plain sight. Peanuts surrounded him and some lay on his book. We exchanged 'fuck, I don't know' glances and when the air was bound to be clear, went back inside.

Once at Lohatla we began training immediately. The School of Armour was there with Olifant tanks and 90mm Eland armoured cars, as well as artillery, and for two weeks we practised complicated and lengthy integrated exercises that left us in new country every night. We also went on night convoys without lights and by compass, arriving at rendezvous points and times. We showered in mobile bathroom trucks once a week, lining up behind ramps naked, and filing in to shower for one minute each, and we lived fearfully on a store of unmarked tins, which turned out with increasing predictability to be beetroot salad, and less frequently sweetcorn. These the army must have acquired on a special. Hoy collected a pile of them. We told on him out of spite and quivering with agitation he was forced to give them back. "But they're mine ... mine!" he wailed.

The high point was an integrated battalion attack with three Mechanised Infantry companies on a hill supposed to be a well-defended enemy position. We advanced in convoy for some 15km through thick bush and arriving on a low ridge in time to see artillery shells plastering the target, we formed a double line attack formation about 2km wide. The tanks placed themselves across the centre and with their stabilised 105mm guns began a charge at 30km per hour through the bush, firing as they went. They went in a great cloud of dust, like powerboats across a flat lake, the stabilised guns trained and firing on the targets no matter what obstacles the tanks encountered, and firing majestically, and in their dust we followed, a great force of steel and discipline. The tanks swept through the objective and peeled off to the sides, at which point we stopped and climbed out with weapons hammering and thundering around us. After a hellish firefight by the 90mm Eland armoured cars and Ratel 20s, we shot our way through the target in a universe of smoke and noise.

I suddenly saw an antelope, a steenbok, staggering in the bush near our Ratel, and went for it like mad and caught it, just behind the front line of noise and fire. It was pierced through its intestines by a Browning bullet. "Van Schalkwyk! Stop!" I yelled, ducking branches in a stooped run back to the Ratel, holding the animal by its legs. The gunner's hand went to his chest switch as he spoke to the driver. The Ratel stopped and the right-hand door opened. "Fuck, not in here, its going to get kak and hare (*shit and hair*) on everything," objected Marais the orderly the moment he saw it. I ran up the outside and heaved it aboard in the hollow of the spare tyre and at the next stop Van Schalkwyk, the farmer's son, cut its neck with a knife, skinned and gutted it. Within 20 minutes our section was grilling fillets and leg steaks over a small fire at the collection point after the firefight was over, and it was the best meal the army provided in 1981.

In a rainstorm the Ratel leaked like a sieve. Icy water dripped and seeped and the cold steel caused condensation. Beneath me outside on the damp ground slept Piek, Van Schalkwyk, Marais, Hoy, Waite and Singleton. The platoon leadership had a chopper tent. Wetherall and I slept on the two troop seats – it was our turn. The seats got harder and harder all night and it got colder. In the morning I had a stiff neck and couldn't turn to the left. The clouds blew away and all kitted up, the company's Ratels stood in lines having moved to a training area. Their early morning white smoke and steam drifted sideways as we idled awaiting the order. Only the commanders, standing up shivering in their turrets, could see over the rise of a hill. Everyone else sat tense and still with the cold, and in the dark troop compartments there was little talk.

The order came. The front vehicles eased forward until their turret weapons had clear lines of fire, and noise started. We popped out of the hatches, peering down the slopes to where explosions were flashing in well-controlled groups around a field of unoccupied trenches. "Mortiere klim uit!" (*Mortars climb out!*) At the same time the right-hand door was opening and we shot out, collecting all our equipment in one fluid movement. In no time at all, we (and elsewhere, the other 60s) were dropping bombs onto a target which from the ground we couldn't see. I kept alert for the platoon commander's hand signals to modify the shooting. The door opened again, and as soon as we hurled all the steel parts in with a crash, and followed them in a heap, the Ratel moved off as the door started to close. Because of the increased ventilation of the Ratel driving, the hatches were sealed again.

The company made a cautious fire-and-movement advance down the hill. On the flat ground, each vehicle again found cover, and an even advance began towards the trenches, cannons clamouring and cordite filling the cabins and drifting off across the veld in a low mist. Everyone still sat hunched, gripping their weapons, but Wetherall and I were already red and panting. The first platoon disembarked on the right flank, the side the sun was rising, and the puny popping of assault rifles filled the spaces between the heavier 20mm cannons and 7.62mm Brownings. We watched the little human figures through the green strengthened glass of the gun port windows. Suddenly the attack halted. Turret weapons were elevated, smoking, and there was silence.

"Wat gaan nou aan?" (*What's going on now?*) we called, fearing some inadequacy in the exercise, and the ensuing agony of seeing disappointment on the Captain's face.

"Nee, daar's iemand geskiet in Seksie Een," (*No, someone's been shot in Section 1*) came Van Schalkwyk's reply from the turret. The low rays of sun shone on the Section 1 Ratel with open doors, right next to us. Troops were spilling from it and officers and medics sprinted towards it. Preparing to climb out, Mark Rothman had accidentally fired two shots on automatic at the roof of the cabin. At point blank, both had gone through, but shrapnel had hurt five people. Luckily all, as required, had helmets on and there were no head wounds. We watched interestedly from the hatches, not being allowed out, and lit cigarettes. The company's ambulance sped up and the wounded were helped in. Seeing that there were no serious injuries the Captain seamlessly treated it all as a valuable extension of the exercise. While receiving a briefing from the company medic he directed Platoon 1 to pull back and defend the medical team while the other two platoons filled the gap and took defensive positions against the threat of the entrenchment. But shooting was stopped. The ambulance went off to Postmasburg to the military hospital there.

Before leaving Lohatla, the Captain called Platoon 1 to an order group. He called us into an intimate circle around him. He laid a large architectural drawing on the ground amid us. "Ons gaan ons makkers in die hospitaal red," he announced quietly, smiling. "Dis 'n plan van die gebou. Hier op die terreinplan sien ons die inrit. Hier is die voordeur. Hier is die kombuis agter. En hier is die nooddeure … " (*We are going to rescue our comrades in the hospital. This is a plan of the building. Here on the site plan we see the entrance. Here is the front door. And here are the emergency doors …*)

That night, Platoon 1 infiltrated the hospital. The gate guards were held. The platoon commander entered the building unarmed, wearing the Captain's stars, through the main door, and opened the fire escapes. Troops swiftly sealed off part of the building, and giggling nurses and sulking doctors were held in a bathroom at rifle point (they were not loaded). With the rescue team, I entered the ward where the well-rested and fed wounded lay. They were very surprised. While they got ready, I was covering the doors along one wall. I suddenly noticed that behind a screen leaning against the wall there was a cavity. I moved closer and there was a slight sound. I stared into the blackness and a human figure resolved itself into the Captain. He was holding his finger to his lips. He was watching how we performed. My rifle was pointing right through his chest, so I had him well covered. We stood a few seconds like this and then I backed off and kept his secret.

7
Chosen for Action

We were evaluated in November in a week of prodigious effort. Blessedly, the training company commander was replaced by a new 2IC, Lt Van Dalsen, and we never heard about him again. Our old instructors also left us, except for the cross we continued to bear, Cpl Van Jaarsveld, who signed up for another year as platoon sergeant for Platoon 2, and we were joined by new officers and NCOs from our own intake. They had just completed their evaluations on the Officers' Course at the Infantry School at Oudtshoorn, and Foxtrot Company received the winning individuals with Platoon 1 getting the all-out top scorers, 2nd Lt Pierre De Jager as platoon commander, and Cpl Frans Robinson as platoon sergeant. In the company of the Captain almost perpetually, we went through every conceivable drill with determined effort, ignoring pain of exhaustion, mindless of heat or thirst, driven by each other to win.

First we ran a 2.4km race twice, with full kit and without. Incredibly, Lt De Jager gave us the battalion's winning time, and so right from the start his nickname was Speedo. We walked a 30km route march in the shortest time, towing a truck per platoon with a long rope. Then we had a drill competition. After that we laid night ambushes, performed section, platoon and company attacks, and suffered a gruelling inspection of kit and Ratels. We went to the shooting range and aimed to score. Finally, physically exhausted, we were tested on all our theory in a three-hour written exam.

We won the company evaluations in every single test. Then our platoon won the platoon evaluations, meaning out of nine platoons, driven by Warwick within our midst.

"Kom Peloton Een! Wie – is – ons?" (*Come Platoon 1, who – are – we?*) he demanded.

"Peloton Een," we returned in rhythm, stamping our feet in unison at every fourth step, as we double timed around the perimeter of 1 SAI in full kit, mouths closed, breathing through our nostrils, fit.

"En watter kompanie is ons?" (*And what company are we?*)

"F Kompanie!" we thundered.

"A-likja-hys! Alik! Lik! Likja-hys!" put in the platoon sergeant in the pause. Then

Warwick led and we yelled each line of the pathetically stupid song after him:

Ah – dee – ayee, ah – deeyo!
SWAPO boys you better lie low!
Cos when you hear the whistle blow,
Platoon 1 is on the go!

We would become Platoon 1, Alpha Company, and we would in time come to be the Captain's favourite troops and follow him into danger. The company consisted of some 150 men selected from an initial call-up to 1 SAI of 7,000, to become part of South Africa's only permanent mechanized battalion.

Sergeant Van der Westhuizen looked around him. The Captain was nowhere in sight.

"Sitas, daai fokken bokkop van jou lyk soos 'n puis op 'n fokken vark se poes." (*Sitas, that fucking springbuck head of yours looks like a fucking pimple on a fucking pig's cunt.*)

"Ja Sersant!" shrieked Sitas at the top of his voice. Sergeant Van der Westhuizen looked pleased.

"Sitas, nou lyk jy so bly soos 'n hoer wat 'n sak piele opgetel het." (*Sitas, now you look as happy as a whore who's picked up a sack of cocks.*) He became serious. "Kompanie!" We braced. "Kompanie, aandag! U-i-t ... tree!"

"Een! Twee-drie een! Twee-drie een! Twee-drie een! ... twee drie vier vyf ses sewe ag nege ... " We murmured as we continued walking in our dress uniforms out through the main gate of 1 SAI. We were sent out on pass for a whole week with the Captain's blessing.

> Dear Granny,
> I phoned you this morning after sleeping all night on a cold shiny floor in 1 blanket. Yesterday F Company had a day pass, but I stayed in camp. What is there to do without money? What is there to do in Bloemfontein? So I stayed in 1 SAI and watched films last night. The whole of last week was evaluation, which we won except for the shooting (where the other companies both cheated blatantly, getting platoon average of 241 – marksman). Our platoon attack was a great success, and I dropped 23 bombs right onto the target. The Major, who was watching, said he'd like us as Battalion mortarists (go in his Ratel, is part of his entourage), but we can't because there aren't enough mortarists. On Friday Capt Malan urged us to run the 2.4 better than we ever have before, and at the

end I just collapsed in a heap. So we won the evaluation; therefore we'll use the Ratels more than the other companies, we are the best fighting company and are looked up to. I hope that me & Wetherall are the best mortarists – then we'll get that long pass (18 – 8). But chances are that such a promise will fall short, or it will be given to another company's mortarists. We won't get pass over Christmas – but instead New Year – December the 27th to the 5th of January. Like as not on the 25th I'll be standing guard at Ou Magasyn – keep me a piece of Turkey & 5 cents (With cake around it). I've already told Mom about the Christmas presents – can you do that, please, because I won't be able to.

For the first time, we were not appalled by the thought of returning to the barren order of 1 SAI, and when we came back rested and spirited, it was to a whole new experience. With our new members and after a year of training, we were now a Mechanised Infantry company in its completed form, with a junior command structure of our own age and intake, and we became an honour-bound family. Our mindset had changed too. We were prepared now to set off to a far-off legendary place of danger with no phones or TV, where letters would be censored, and where we would remain for four-month stretches or longer. We had grown, but were to grow further.

I saw quite a bit of Glazewski back in 1 SAI and he had become part of the human furniture. He ducked around all day and gyppoed. He was unfit, pale and nervous. Part of HQ Company was to go to the border and he was determined to be with it. Anything to get out of the Tempe hell. He did go.

One year after entering the army, Alpha Company stood in lines behind two C-130s parked neatly on the warm red concrete. The great four-engined transport planes whined gently and cast their shadows over the troops, who felt relaxed but charged, and sat or stood around among their things. Ground crews prepared the interiors and checked the aircraft. The empty maws breathed cold air on the front troops who waited five yards from the rear ramps. Eventually all was ready and we shuffled inside. Above the whine of the engines, only Van Jaarsveld's nagging was audible. He was still calling us pieletjes. He had had a long frustrating argument with Cpl Hoy that morning over what could and could not be brought with. Hoy had received a stripe to formalise being made a QM Stores orderly.

The flight was Bloemfontein to Grootfontein direct, over Botswana and lasting approximately three hours. The plane was unheated and condensation formed on the metal sides. We sat side by side in four long rows, facing each other. It grew cold. The

Captain came round, speaking softly and raising grins on each face, and explaining the route, the height, the weather. Most of us weren't able to see out – there were only small windows widely spaced. At Grootfontein the plane pulled Gs and then fell out of the sky. My lunch lunged at my throat and fought to break free. A yellow cloud of vomit emerged from somewhere and hung weightlessly mid-plane, changing shape and deciding which row of troops to dash itself into. Fifty pairs of eyes glared at it in angry disbelief. It rotated before our faces and then swiftly dashed against the side of the cabin. Small bits of skrapnelhoender. Stink. The airfield had a cylinder of air above it, protected by helicopter gunships that flew inspection rounds whenever a plane used the field. Now, we spun from cruising height in a steep helix into this cylinder.

The heat was not excessive when the ramp opened, but was welcome warmth and quite humid. Two massive white Magirus Deutz transport trucks, 'wit olifante', took us crammed and expectant through thick green forest for about a hundred kilometres north. The late afternoon light was clean and clear, and the land rose, affording long views across rolling wilderness as far as our shaded eyes could see. From my spot in the crush on the truck, I avoided the silent scowls all around me and looked at the bush, thinking how innocent it looked, and pondered the possibility of cruel enemy eyes following our passage from the leafy thickets of the tropical savannah. Dusk, laden with flying insects and haze that rose from the ground, was falling fast as we drove through the Ovambo Gate and the final few kilometres to Oshivello. This was a transition camp where new troops were acclimatised and trained in the real conditions of the Operational Area. In falling dark we unloaded and were allocated an area of bush a short way out of Oshivello base, to set up camp. There were no tents and we were lucky it didn't rain that night. Watches were organised and some tins of food were handed out, and under a heavy sky of stars the company slept deeply, and for most of the night there was no moon. Animals called and in the morning light a herd of elephant footprints was seen to have been made right through our lines, whether before or after we arrived we couldn't tell.

We were shown and given new weapons that impressed us: the MAG, a 7.62mm light machine gun with a healthy rate of fire. Its call was urgent and emphatic, it ripped up the earth. The snotneus, or 40mm grenade launcher, was like a fat shotgun that flung a grenade 300m accurately. The patmor, a 60mm patrol mortar, which was to be my own personal weapon, consisted of a hand-held pipe with a light attached base-plate and a curved bubble level on the handle, with ranges inscribed in phosphorescent figures. It could be fired with a spring-loaded trigger instantly from any position, with a range of 2km dictated by using only low charges – higher charges could break your wrists and burst the light pipe. The RPG-7 was captured from the Angolans in such numbers that they were common among us, and this was awesome as an infantry weapon. Simple and light, its psychological effect was as devastating as its tactical effect, for not only did it blast a hole through some 30cm of armour steel but the noise was shocking: the BOOM-SHHH-BOOM! of the firing, the rocket travelling, and impact. Its range was 920m and it flew in a straight line at about 350m per second, in an angry red flash like a jet.

The other companies from 1 SAI joined us over the next week, until we formed a great tent town in the bush. The atmosphere at Oshivello was one of expectancy and danger, and we thrived on it. We all showered in the afternoon under suspended bags of lukewarm water, became brown in the sun and trained continually, using up mounds of live ammunition. Bushcraft was taught, and mine-detecting, specialists appearing and vanishing after their particular knowledge was given. We learned to scan the bush from right to left. Western literate people read, and out of habit look, from left to right using speed reading skills. This can be fatal in a bush war if eyes are trained to move in large increments and focus on obvious objects, whole words or phrases, as opposed to individual letters. Scanning instead from right to left, the eyes move naturally in tiny increments, so that more detail is seen. We were also taught to train our focus beyond bushes, so that no matter how thick they were, we could see objects beyond.

Shooting skills were honed. Daily, and for hours, under the furious instruction of an athletic sergeant-major called Spacecricket with wild staring eyes, we learnt rifle handling, shooting at coke tins thrown in the air, until we could raise a rifle swiftly, fire and hit, all in one movement without looking down the sights. We were tested in simulated contacts, shooting cardboard enemy profiles hidden in the bushes. We laid ambushes of all types and slept out in the wild, listening to the jackals and the occasional lion far off across the road in the Etosha Game Reserve. We learned that the great rainstorms of the rainy season would thunder upon the land in the late afternoons, but usually the clouds vanished before sunset, giving an hour of sun to dry in before dark.

Dear Mom,
  We've been using & watching very sophisticated tricks of the trade. For the last couple of days it's been extremely hot, & I am continually dripping with sweat, and my bush hat and browns have got white stripes from salt. We wake up at 5 and do PT while it's still cool. Today I washed clothes – they've provided zinc basins for us – and hung them up to dry in the tent. There's all that animal

life we saw in Etosha, & the country is similar to that of the latter part of our tour – plenty of trees and picturesque, green views. Walking through the bush I've seen plenty of elephant shit and kudu tracks. The entire region is very sandy – there is no solid ground to walk on, so you walk twice the distance you want to go. There're a lot of hornbills, the only birds that seem to enjoy life to the full, they're like parrots: screaming all the time and doing aerobatics. I've also seen of lot of kites and vultures very high in the sky. This morning I was searching in my balsak for a magazine, and a scorpion stung me on the hand. It stung while I did the beast in, and it's been numb ever since. But we've come across worse things in our kit: Section 3 found a puff adder in their tent. Interjection!: It's just started raining hard, and about 10 black trackers have just pulled into our tent. It's quite difficult to receive them. Funny – they've decided to pull out now – it's still raining. These people are true fighters of the bush. Some of them might be ex-terrs. I've also just had a shower (in the rain). I've got reason to be quite excited right now, hold thumbs for me.

Some three weeks went by in intensive training. We were well fed, but were starting to take on the typical feral border appearance, thin, tanned and quick, with flashing animal eyes. We spent all daylight hours in the sun, always running, usually with heavy loads in the heat. We adapted easily to the operational routine, eating only two meals a day, one at mid-morning and another at sunset. Our officers became more like comrades, joking with us, sharing hopes and disappointments, identifying themselves with us, but maintaining nevertheless strict discipline at all times. We could hold together a platoon formation in the thickest bush, while conducting hot exercises with live ammunition at the run. Now we were sent into the heavily populated northern Ovamboland to walk patrols. My kit was as follows:

1 pair browns
1 pair boots
1 pair sandals
3 pairs underpants
3 pairs socks
1 bush hat
1 ground sheet
1 shelter + 14ft rope (bivvy)
ablution bag
1 tow rope link
1 webbing

1 backpack
1 patrol bag
1 sleeping bag inner
7 ratpacks
3 1 litre water bottles
set of rectangular aluminium cooking pans (dixie), water bucket, spoon
chlorine tablets, malaria pills
3 magazine pouches
7 full magazines
4 60mm mortar bombs HE (and some 20 members of the platoon carried one bomb each; Wetherall carried eight)
1 M26 hand grenade
1 smoke grenade
1 1,000ft signal flare
1 patmor
1 R4 rifle
2nd line R4 ammunition
1 combat knife (supplied by self)
Hoy took a spare sleeping bag.

8
Black Breasts

Leaving at dawn, Alpha Company drove north in Buffels. Somewhere to the west of Ondangwa, each platoon was dropped off separately in thickening mist, and the Captain wished us luck. With each platoon walked two Ovambo translator-guides. Ours were introduced as Simon and Johannes. It was planned that we would reach a particular spot at midnight and camp there.

So we walked in strange country in a dark mist, and later when the moon came out, we could see the silver-grey shapes of huge trees, palms and little palisaded villages, or cucas, which we avoided always by at least 300m. Apart from our breathing and trampling and the cries of small creatures, there were no sounds. We strode through ploughed fields, a heavy chore in the dark, and always had the eerie feeling of being watched. We walked in an extended arrow formation, and I kept my one link to the group, the single grey moving blur that was Marais the orderly, about 15m out ahead of me, in exactly the right relationship to myself. Night hand signals passed down the lines, consisting of simple movements of pale hands, told us all we needed to know. The moon and stars were rich and fragrant, the air cool but sticky. Dawn in a new place holds great promise. Cocks crowed all around and people appeared, naïve and curious to find us in their midst. Dangly-breasted women with brown shoulder-striped donkeys, men and naked boys with sallow dogs, and multi-coloured herds of ranging tree-climbing goats. Children approached us and sat watching, or tried to sell us live chickens. It was natural for patrolling troops to hand out things from ratpacks they didn't want, and everywhere we went, people appeared either to accept handouts or to trade for food. We tried the fabled trick of giving the kids esbits (fuel tablets) to suck instead of sweets, but disappointingly they were wise to us.

The country was barren, the sand white and blinding in the sun. A clean rural poverty was everywhere apparent, as this traditional peasant society had not yet encountered consumerism. Starving black cattle stood or just lay, bony and motionless in the fodderless landscape. "Maklik om te naai" (*easy to fuck*) was someone's comment. Isolated palms grew, tall like aerials and the kraals, evenly distributed a few hundred metres apart, stood in small gardens of maize or sorghum. These kraals, or cucas, had about five round thatched huts each, and a single entrance that was narrow and hard to find among the gnarled grey hardwood stakes that encircled them. They were quite beautiful and we were lucky to witness them, for they were the last of their kind in this part of Africa. We came upon giant trees, so big that the whole platoon could find cool places to lie and sleep up in the branches, and at these we liked to stop and rest. The sun was harsh.

At a particularly large tree we stopped for a day of rest. OPs went out and the rest of us lazed in the cool branches, or threw knives at a mark on the trunk in a competition that lasted all day. We were knife-crazy during that period, keeping them shaving sharp, and many of us became good at throwing them far. Simon and Johannes sat slightly apart. They were modest, very disciplined and tidy, and never looked half as dirty as we got. They were oumanne in their twenties with the clear skin and precise features you find among Ovambos. A few of us got into conversation with them in the still evenings, and they were quite forthcoming. We were surprised at the things they said.

"Sam Nujoma is nie 'n slegte man," said Simon in his Ovambo lisp. "Hy was toe 'n jong man gewerk met spoorweë. Hy was ongelukkig met die mense wat heeltyd 'kaffer' sê. Hy het SWAPO dan begin. Alles wat hy daardie tyd gemaak het was reg. Ek stem saam met hom." (*Sam Nujoma is not a bad man. When he was young he worked on the railway. He was unhappy with people always saying 'kaffir'. He started SWAPO then. Everything he did then was right. I agree with him.*)

"Hy was reg." agreed Johannes in a soft murmur. We were sitting close together and there was no sound but the stars. "Hy was reg." (*He was right.*)

"Maar as hy reg is, hoekom veg julle teen SWAPO?" (*But if he's right, why do you fight SWAPO?*) said Hoy earnestly.

"Nee, jy sien, wat hulle nou doen ... hierdie landmyne ... Hierdie doodmaak ... dis nie reg nie. My familie, hulle het al te veel seergekry van die terroriste. Ons bly daardie kant. Twintig clicks." He pointed west. "Die terroriste maak te veel moeilikheid nou. Van dit moet ek elke dag met SWAPO geveg." (*No, you see, what they are doing now ... these landmines ... this killing ... this isn't right. My family have been too often hurt by the terrorists. We live that side. Twenty clicks. The terrorists are causing too much difficulty now. Because of this I must fight SWAPO every day.*)

We nodded sagely in the dark. It all made tragic sense.

"Was jy al in 'n kontak, Simon?" (*Were you ever in a contact, Simon?*) I tentatively asked, voicing our real interest.

"Ja," he said quietly. "En Johannes ook. Al sewe keer. Mmm ... Ek soek forretjes." (*Yes, and Johannes too. Seven times ... I'm looking for matches.*)

"Hier ... " offered Wetherall, rattling a ratpack matchbox. "En was jy al gewond?" (*Here ... And have you ever been wounded?*)

"Johannes is nog nie gewond nie maar ek is twee keer gewond." (*Johannes is not yet wounded but I've been wounded twice.*)

"Met wat?" (*With what?*)

"Met 'n myn en met 'n AK." (*With a mine and an AK.*)

"Ja, maar dis 'n fokken kak geweer!" *(Yes, but that's a fucking shit rifle!)* exclaimed Wetherall.

Simon bent to the ground to light a cigarette, and held the glow inside his hand. "Dit is nie kak nie," he said more quietly. "Dit is gevaarlik. Dit maak jou dood." (*It's not shit. It's dangerous. It kills you.*)

The next day he showed us his wounds. Shrapnel all over his legs from an anti-personnel mine and bullet wounds in his side. The entry and exit scars were plainly visible.

We got used to the idea that our weapons were always loaded. A flick of a switch and they fired. After a while we no longer noticed if a barrel was pointing straight at us. They were continuously heavy too, with the extra kilogram of bullets in the magazines. Often I carried a bomb in the mortar pipe, so that I could set the weapon down and fire without a second's hesitation. The platoon bristled with arms and we walked in a heavy plodding glide because of the weight. There were plenty of grenades, and in the breaks we pulled out the pins and passed the grenades around, and put the pins back in again, just to keep things interesting.

Sun-warmed water was collected from shonas or flat pans, in which a million tiny creatures moved about among the swollen goat droppings, or occasionally, from deep green seeps, with strange swimming insects like water scorpions, we had to climb down into. Occasional cuca shops, one-room rectangular lean-tos with colourful and untidy hand-painted signage, supplied good bread and tins of peri-peri chicken, that made a fine bunny chow. From their ice boxes or paraffin fridges we bought cool drinks or Windhoek Lager, which was not available then in South Africa but has ever since been my beer of choice. Sometimes, against orders, half-jacks of brandy were also smuggled into backpacks. At the shops we were offered muhangu or homemade sorghum beer that I quite enjoyed, for it was cool and refreshing in the noonday sun.

For 10 cents a litre of supposedly harmless muhangu, it led so some of us getting drunk in the day. With a splitting headache, one afternoon I lagged further and further behind the platoon. My arms and ammunition bore me down and fuzzy sleep tried to crowd me in. Only when I noticed I was alone, with black forms eyeing me from nearby cucas did I take fright. I was struggling to regain sight of the platoon, thinking a situation could arise where I might have to shoot my way to safety, when suddenly two Impala jets screamed towards me right over a particularly threatening cuca. They were painted in green and brown camo, and both helmeted pilots looked down straight at me as they roared past. They were about 100 feet up. The blue castles on them reassured me, and I woke up enough to start running in my heavy gear in the white sand, and within half an hour I had caught up.

Wetherall named our platoon 'Battlekraal Ovambolantia'. At that time the actual threat from SWAPO insurgents seemed very remote indeed, and we became a bit more relaxed and fluid in our movement. Apparently they moved around mainly at night singly or in small groups, or disguised as civilians by day. Their tasks were to approach the locals and impress on them the need to resist the South Africans, and to recruit youngsters. They also intimidated fence-sitters or those involved in any sort of relationship with the administration, for example school teachers. They sustained the myth that they were more numerous and widespread than they were, by laying landmines for vehicles and pedestrians. The most victims came from their own people. Of course mines were a great fear for us, but ambush at night was also a continual threat, so we walked with long careful strides, and wide eyes reflecting stars. Simon and Johannes unashamedly preferred to walk at the back.

One midday, we were in our arrow formation in an endless series of maize and sorghum fields, when from not far off a machine gun thundered a long burst – about three seconds. Our method of firing was a string of short bursts of two or three rounds in quick succession RR – RRR – R – RRRR – RR. This saved ammunition, kept the fire well aimed on meaningful targets, while maintaining a constant cover. Although the guides insisted this was not SWAPO but Koevoet, we headed in the direction of the noise, and in a clearing came upon a Casspir with a mounted MAG. They were a gung ho and undisciplined lot, to us. Sitting up top was a slinky black girl with large shapely breasts in a tight camo uniform and her arm around the neck of a white Koevoet. There were disapproving mutters from the platoon, as well as the guides, but the heat played cruel games with hormones, and good-looking females were as scarce as hens' teeth in Ovamboland.

At an afternoon order group, where we sat fanwise before the platoon commander, Simon ventured to voice a concern.

"Luitenant," he said rising to his feet. "Dit is nie reg dat jy en die Korporaal en die troepe 'kaffer' sê. Sam Nujoma het gesê dis nie reg nie en dit is nie reg nie. Asseblief sê vir die mense hulle moet nie daardie woord gebruik." (*Lieutenant, it's not right that you and the Corporal and the troops say 'kaffir'. Sam Nujoma said it's not right and it isn't right. Please tell your people not to use that word.*)

"Simon," began the Lieutenant. "Dis is nie … " he tried again. "Dit maak nie saak watter woord 'n mens gebruik nie. Jy sien … " he actually went red. "Jy sien … 'n 'Kaffer' is ons woord vir die vyand. As dit SWAPO is is hulle kaffers. As dit ANC is, is hulle kaffers. As ons die woord 'kaffer' gebruik, bedoel ons nie om julle te beledig nie, dis net ons woord vir die vyand." (*Simon, it's not ... It doesn't matter what word one uses. You see ... You see ... 'Kaffir' is our word for enemy. If it's SWAPO they are kaffirs. If it's ANC, they are kaffirs. If we use the word 'kaffir', we don't mean to insult you, it's just our word for the enemy.*)

But although this had been an impressive bit of verbal gymnastics, none of it was working and Simon persisted.

"Luitenant," he said, "as jy en die ander mense die woord aanhou gebruik, ek en Johannes gaan wegloop." (*Lieutenant, if you and the others keep using the word, Johannes and I are going to walk away.*)

"Dan sal julle aangekla word vir AWOL," said the Lieutenant flatly. "Maar julle het gehoor wat sê Simon. Ek wil hê julle moet almal probeer ophou om 'kaffer' te sê." (*Then you will be charged with AWOL. But you've all heard what Simon says. I want all of you to try and stop saying 'kaffir'.*)

"Dankie, Luitenant, ons vra maar net." (*Thank you, Lieutenant, we're only asking.*) Simon sat down.

Later, in the cooler dust, we went a section at a time to a cuca shop for luxuries. It was run by a generously built woman wearing bright red lipstick, and several old men sat around outside drinking muhangu, while other women chatted and laughed. I smiled at their smiles and the owner came over and offered me some local berries from her land. They were red, small and sweet but without any distinctive flavour. Things like that stick with one, because they seem to hold great significance. And that night I had an apocalyptic dream (probably caused by the Lariam malaria pills). I found myself a voyeur to a scene of dreadful evil. A blind Asian woman was daydreaming in a flat in a tall building overlooking a blue bay. She was naked and attractive, but on her lap sat an eerie child. He had a tall narrow head with a ridge of thin hair cresting his bony skull. His ears were large and membranous and his eyes, which were the colour of slate, were small thin horizontal slits without pupils. The colour of the child's skin was Indonesian, and he sweated in a shaking fever. Also on the woman's lap was a tiny nutty-skinned shriveled man with bright round beady eyes, but she was unaware of him. He was petting the child frenetically, protecting him from all earthly harm. A disembodied voice was explaining to me what it all meant. The child was the child of Satan. The little man was an imp, a protector. The woman was merely a slave receptacle, conveniently blind and vacantly unaware of the nature of her child. She had come here as a refugee but had at one stage been a prostitute. Out the window I could see a sweeping view of a city and the bay.

I woke on my back staring straight up at the full moon. To my right lay a pale spotted leopard, staring at me like a sphinx with eyes of night. For a long time I could not properly wake up though my eyes were open and staring at the moon, and I was still gripped in the terror of the dream. When I finally broke into the real world, I breathed the cool clean air like someone nearly drowned, heard the breathing all around me of the platoon, and looked around at a world silver and white with light. The full moonlight was immensely strong, and you could see black palm trees and cucas for miles across the white sand. These cast defined shadows and it was so quiet that the snoring and my hammering heart seemed loud. Around us I imagined armed figures creeping closer, and I listened for hours before falling asleep.

I woke early when a soft voice spoke my name coincidentally on the edge of our wide circle. Nothing intruded into my sub-awareness more than someone saying my name. I always slept very lightly in the open, and would wake to a faint rustle, or the quiet approach of a midnight guard on his way to wake me for my shift. I never had to be touched or shaken awake – no one got near me. We helped reluctant packs onto each others' backs and moved away before dawn, which was a safety drill. The land dipped and for a morning we picked our way around small clear lakes or ponds with white beaches and palmy edges. Big fruit bats flapped around their roosts high in these, and chanked while we stopped for breakfast as the humid heat returned, and sat spread over a wide area, boiling water for coffee over fuel tablets in little grooves scraped in the sand. We never congregated densely, in case of attack or mortars. The privacy afforded by sitting alone by water in a new place of wondrous natural beauty, making breakfast in silence, was relaxing and blissful. We went about our usual job of questioning PBs at cucas along our route, without finding anything out.

"Een-Een dis Een-Een Alpha ... "

"Een-Een by ... "

"Een-Een, ons het in 'n noordelike rigting 'n dier, 'n donkie, bewapen, ek herhaal, dit is bewapen, vyf honderd meter, wat 'n ander dier, klaarblyklik ook 'n donkie, met die wapen aanval. Miskien is dit 'n SWAPO donkie. Dit lyk gereed om skerp ammunisie te gebruik. Dit lyk soos 'n kontak. Ja, dit is definitief 'n kontak. Wag, uit." (*One-One, it's One-One-Alpha ... One-One standing by ... One-One, we have in a northerly direction an animal, a donkey, armed, I repeat, it is armed, 500m, attacking another animal, apparently also a donkey, with the weapon. Maybe it is a SWAPO donkey. It looks ready to use sharp ammunition. It looks like a contact. Yes, it is definitely a contact. Wait, out.*)

In the late morning we had approached a cuca said by Military Intelligence to manifest SWAPO activity, and stopped concealed half a kilometre away and watched it with binoculars. All day two donkeys screwed enthusiastically in the sand track next to the village, an impressive sight, especially seen through binoculars. The changing shifts of observers mentioned this in their regular radio reports. Nothing significant was happening, and it was decided to be more proactive.

9
"Gemeenskap gehou met 'n koei"

So Section 2 went off on a circular patrol and came upon a minor road. The platoon commander ordered a concealed roadblock there by Section 2, to monitor the general curfew that was effective after sunset, at 8pm. It had been told down to us that a terrorist leader, known grandly as 'Nestroy Titus Komati', was operating in the area and drove a white bakkie. As it got dark we were sitting relaxing in a low mopani grove when seven shots were fired in the distance. A moment later, the section leader Cpl Human on the radio reported shooting at a bakkie that was driving after curfew, and refused to stop when confronted. Of the two occupants, the driver was wounded, and needed medical assistance.

Leaving Sections 1 and 3 at the base camp with all kit and mortars, Platoon HQ ran to the scene. It was fully dark when we arrived and had got windy, and the moon had not yet risen. A cloudy sky hid all stars and it was as black as pitch. A white bakkie was parked in the track road and the driver lay chest-down on the white sand, with bullet shrapnel in his kidneys. He was not conscious, or perhaps in shock from loss of blood, and the medic, John Waite, bandaged him and tried to find a suitable vein for the drip needle. There was the vaguest pulse and no pressure. The veins were empty. Finally after many pricks, the needle slid in easily.

Meanwhile, it was decided to drive the two to Ondangwa and Intelligence Headquarters, and the shot flat wheel of the bakkie had to be replaced. This I did, in the dark, in a record time to try to save a life that, belonging to a real person with a real face for once, and having a very anxious companion standing near, evoked our natural sympathy. It is one thing shooting at an abstract enemy target, but another being faced with human emotions and pain. When the wheel was changed, the bakkie wouldn't start and so we called for a casevac airlift. An Alouette helicopter was soon on the scene. We had quickly cleared an open patch in the low mopani growth, and he was guided in with a torch. Near the ground, he turned on a spotlight and landed. The hurt man then vanished in a cloud of noisy dust into the black sky, and we went back to our camp with the other as a prisoner (my first prisoner! I thought). He was a small old man, and I was made his guard and led him in the light of the clearing sky and big rising moon. His hands had been tied and when we reached camp I released him. There was no need to be aggressive or controlling with him. On the contrary, we were polite.

"Davies, jy moet vir Nestroy lekker oppas." (*Davies, you must babysit Nestroy nicely.*) "Wat's die probleem, Van Schalkwyk?" (*What's the problem, Van Schalkwyk?*) The platoon commander had developed a personable relationship with his future gunner and driver. Many in Platoon 1 came from Orange Free State towns not too far from each other. Wetherall, Waite, Marais and I, all from Cape Town, thought their repartee pathetic.

"Luitenant, ek kan nie slaap nie." (*Lieutenant, I can't sleep.*)

"Gaan vra dan vir *Nestroy* of hy nie vir jou 'n storietjie wil lees nie." (*Go and ask Nestroy if he won't read you a story.*)

'Nestroy' was quite docile and when several troops brought him biscuits, and some tins of food, he seemed to relax, but didn't say anything at all. He ate nothing but drank water, and stripped some mopani bark and quickly made a clever basket for all the things we had given him. Johannes talked briefly to him and said, "Hy is net 'n ou man. Hy sê die ander is sy seun." (*He is just an old man. He says the other is his son.*) He was lent a ground sheet for the heavy dew and under this he went to sleep when we did. The next morning he climbed aboard a Buffel that came to fetch him and was gone with his little basket.

It was becoming plain to us how submissive and unwarlike the ordinary people of this region really were. In the main they may not have been on our side but trusted the SADF to be impersonal but reasonable. Still, incidents did occur when skirmishes affected civilians, or individual troops committed crimes, petty or otherwise, against them. The same could not be said of the Police unit Koevoet, which had a reputation even in the army for callousness and cruelty. Our two guides despised them. I don't think they were terribly approving of us either, from now on.

In a letter to my mother I used what I thought was a brilliant code to escape the censor, that I believed she would understand.

Battlekraal Ovambolantia
Destination unknown
Lunar cycle 2
Day 7

Dear Mom,
 … … This was our second week of our tortuous journey through the bewildered survivors of the Turnhalle settlement. Followed all the time by the henchthings of the mindless, unselfthinking Cylon establishment, we try to

Training at Bloemfontein and De Brug, 1981

A Ratel in the Koeikamp with 1 SAI and the Feeshuis in the background.

F Company's Rooi Hoenderhaan training base at De Brug as seen from the hill.

Bombing up for training at Rooi Hoenderhaan – the future crew of 12A. Left to right: Pienaar, unknown, Scheepers, Cruywagen in the gunner's hatch.

Training at Bloemfontein and De Brug, 1981

Me taking a break at Rooi Hoenderhaan with Marie Biscuits.

Me multitasking on the go-kart toilets at Rooi Hoenderhaan. No National Servicemen failed to have this photo taken.

Oshivello Training Base in the Operational Area, January-February 1982

Ready for night patrol at Oshivello. These were real combat patrols.

Keeping an arrowhead formation in thick bush near Oshivello. Left to right: Marais, 2nd Lt De Jager, Hoy.

Platoon 1 resting between platoon attack exercises at Oshivello.

The 61 Mech Base at Omuthiya

The Everite Hotel.

Platoon 1 HQ at a stalparade. Left to right: (standing) Van Schalkwyk, Cpl Mielmann, 2nd Lt De Jager, Cpl Robinson, Piek, Waite, Marais; (kneeling) Weterall, Davies, Singleton. (Pierre De Jager)

Operation Yahoo!, April-May 1982

On the Bravo cutline.

Ratel cleaning inside the earth wall at the Tsintsabis army base.

Klaus Mais-Rische's farmhouse at Onderra.

Operation Yahoo!, April-May 1982

Breakfast at Onderra. Left to right: Marais, Waite, Singleton, 2nd Lt De Jager, Hoy.

The python at Otavi. Left to right: Piek, Cpl Mielmann, Davies, Wetherall.

Rushing to newly found tracks in the Etosha Game Reserve.

Operation Yahoo!, April-May 1982

A Ratel in line abreast chasing insurgents through Etosha.

Koevoet Casspirs arrive minutes before contact to steal our kills in Etosha.

61 Mech Training at the Bloubaan, June 1982

Advancing in convoy at dawn (that's a 140mm artillery gun ahead of the Ratel).

Forming into attack formation; a Ratel 90 tankbuster is seen integrating with the line of Ratel 20s from behind.

Ratel 90s begin the attack at a range of 1km.

61 Mech Training at the Bloubaan, June 1982

Wetherall and I on the 60mm patrol mortar target deep defence positions. We were in trouble for not having camouflaged our helmets.

Troops debussed for a mechanised infantry fire-and-movement advance through the base. The haze is cordite.

The base overrun, with destroyed trucks and trees.

Operation Meebos, July-August 1982

Alpha Company during Operation Meebos near the Cuvelai River. Cpt Malan (with beard) is in front, below the flag aerial. (www.61mech.org.za)

Maintaining weapons and ammunition in a Helicopter Administration Area. (Pierre De Jager)

Operation Meebos, July-August 1982

The Ural truck that died in the killing ground on the Cuvelai Road on August 4 1982; note some remaining 122mm GRAD-P shells at the rear of the flatbed.

The spaghetti-carrying Ural truck having just been hit by an RPG-7.

An Alouette helicopter gunship victim.

We each took an identically damaged note as a souvenir of this day.

Washing in the Cuvelai River. (Pierre De Jager)

Journal Entries

A recording the 15 April 1982 ambush.

A sketch of a SWAPO insurgent killed in April; note the AKM, the rice pattern camo and the knitted jersey.

A sketch of the recovered Ratel 12A destroyed on 15 April 1982, Tsumeb Airport.

Journal Entries

 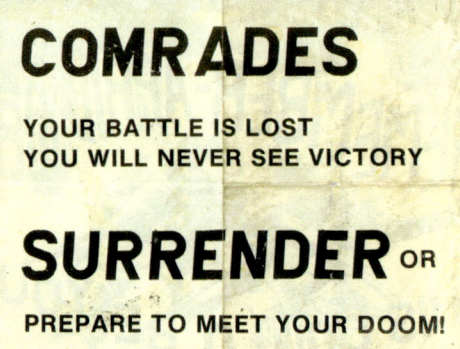

An air leaflet, Operation Yahoo!

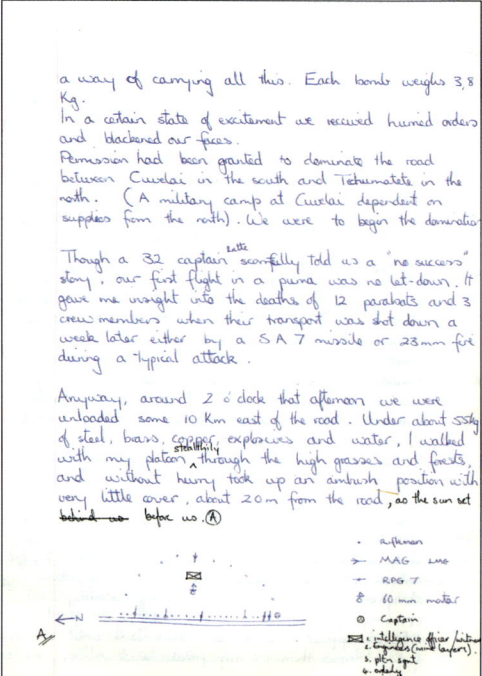

A record of the 4 August 1982 ambush near Cuvelai.

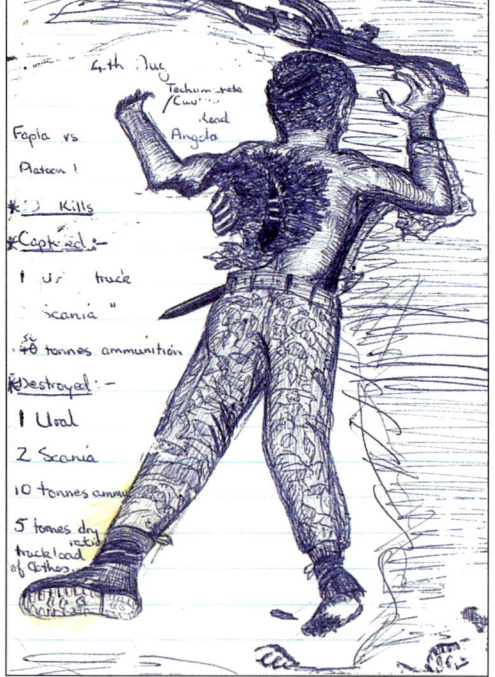

A sketch of a FAPLA soldier hit by 20mm HE shells from an Alouette gunship, Operation Meebos

People

Commandant Roland de Vries, CO 61 Mech. (www.61mech.org.za)

Captain Jan Malan, CO Alpha Company. (www.61mech.org.za)

People

61 Mech Regimental Sergeant Major H.G. Smit (Killer Smit). (www.61mech.org.za)

The author (closest) and 2nd Lt De Jager in a Puma helicopter en route to the 4 August 1982 ambush near Cuvelai. (Pierre De Jager)

bring light & truth to the innocent settlers of far-flung worlds who would long ago have fallen under the tyranny of … the Cylons … I am alive and well & living in Galactica. We have walked quite a way with fairly heavy kit. We see and talk to a lot of the local inhabitants, who are quite wealthy in appliances, though food is scarce. They take advantage of the days when we get our ratpacks & hand out food. I usually give away all my sweets & dog biscuits, so in a day I eat: Pro nutro, 6 coffee packets, 3 of tea, enough sugar, 2 tins of meat & 1 veg, a sausage of cheese spread, a tube of condensed milk, 2 energy chocolate ('tarzan' or 'tazuka') bars, 1 roll of glucose tablets, 1 energy milkshake and a packet of dried fruit. Also you get a container of esbits and a box of matches. We eat better here than in Bloem. We've been having quite a grand time and there's quite a good spirit about us. We get very dirty, sleep in the rain, sit under a bush during the heat of the day, go to winkels and look for water. The other day a local inhabitant found something entering and irritating his stomach suddenly and expectantly, so we called a spiral wing to take him away. It isn't our usual policy to give the local people the gripes. The Ovambos are intelligent and sensible & will protest wildly against words like kaffir & baas. You call everyone meneer in these parts. They are a more slender and well formed people than the Xhosa, who by comparison are rather slow and lumpy. The worst thing you can call a person around here is ngonga, as our translators have proved to us. They like to kill ******, but so far there haven't been any unpleasant incidents. Last night the coy came together & we had a very peaceful braai. I think we'll move out again this evening, and I'll try & write again next weekend. I haven't got any post yet, but they say it only arrives after about a month, and in a bundle. I get no newspapers, magazines, nothing – even a month-old newspaper is quite valuable. They tell me post came in today, but it hasn't been given out yet.

P.S. Lucky number for this month is 27.

Sometimes it rained heavily and after one night of sudden winds and unexpected driving rain, we learned to turn a bivvy into a warm watertight shelter. My bivvy had been tied to sticks and bushes, and was flattened by the gusting wind of a violent thunderstorm. Then the bomb bay of the storm-cloud opened and sleety rain came thrashing down, splashing up from the puddles, so that by morning I was soaked and shivering. I tried to sleep holding my bivvy on my hands and knees, with my head on my arms in half-inch-deep water that lay everywhere on the flat ground. I did manage to have a couple of disturbing dreams, about trying to find my way home in a city changed by war and time.

"Fuck I'm cold! That was a poeslike kak night." In the morning we sat waiting for the sun as everything was wet.

"Hou op om altyd 'n fokken moffie te wees, Wetherall jou etterkop. Hoekom maak jy nie fokken koffie nie?" (*Stop always being a fucking queer, Wetherall you pushead. Why don't you make fucking coffee?*) suggested Piek sympathetically.

"Omdat ek shiver te veel. I'm waiting for the fukken sun to come up. I didn't have fukken Nestroy to cuddle up to, ek sê." Wetherall hunched himself into a pathetic bundle in a wet sleeping bag.

"Ky' daar! Waar kyk die Luitenant so erns in die shona?" (*Look there! What is the Lieutenant looking so seriously at in the shona?*) Singleton pointed out. The platoon commander was gazing introspectively across the wet shona which was reflecting a growing dawn that could drive landscape painters to suicide.

"Wie wiet, bra?" said Marais, "maybe het hy alweer heelnag van Ossewania gedroom, ek sê. Ek, ek wil net meide en koeie naai, en there's it." (*Who knows, brother? Maybe he was dreaming all night about Ossewania again. Me, I just want to fuck cows and maids, and there's it.*) We were freezing, but the sun when it came, dried us quickly, like a herd of wild brown beasts steaming in the dawn. After this, following the two Ovambos' directions, we dug a shallow trench to sleep in and threw the dug sand on all sides in low dykes. On the outside of the dykes a furrow was dug all round except on the head end, and the edges of the bivvy were buried in this. A length of nylon cord tied to the centre of the head end, was stretched and tied slightly upwards to a bush. When you crawled into this strong structure you stayed completely dry, even in the wettest and most violent storm.

Wildlife shared these habitations. Scorpions were common and snakes not unknown. One morning packing my bedding, I was stung on the finger by a small scorpion. Usually of course the wildlife was neutral, little spiders and beetles. I was fascinated by the dung beetles. These were often huge, almost 10cm long. The little ones were called gunships and the larger ones pumas. They would fly in buzzing at the slightest whiff of a crap, and usually so quickly they were with you before you were finished. Overhead they shut their wings and dropped like stones, a danger to immobile distracted humans. Once on the ground, they rushed the hole and fell in, immediately digging and cutting off a generous portion with the sharp edge of their carapace. Competition was fierce and they had to be quick, for soon the hole would be writhing with beetles. Some would make it out the hole in time, rolling their prize along at speed, but the others got a spadeful of sand dumped on them from which they would soon emerge, for they were good burrowers. They were a constant source of amusement to us because they were crazy about shit.

After the 'Nestroy Titus Komati Affair' we heard that Platoon 3 had shot and killed an armed insurgent. He had been shot with a MAG at a range of a kilometre after being chased and then observed with binoculars. He was young and carried a light Chinese-made AK-47. We were also informed that the man we had shot had survived – and was a confirmed SWAPO terrorist.

We met up with Platoon 2 near a small village. When we were released from duties, I immediately went to look for Peter Barry and Michael Eriksen. Barry's face cracked with a massive smile and the first thing he said was, "Have you heard two ous in Bravo Company fucked a cow?" He giggled uncontrollably. I threw back my head and laughed and laughed at the good news.

"All the PF Dutchmen have gone mad!" he said.

"Ja and they fucked … " blurted Eriksen, too amused to talk.

"It was one of those sif sick cows with its arse covered in shit and ticks!" howled Barry.

"And they fucked a whole lot of Ovambo maids as well!" screamed Eriksen. Platoon 1 troops ran up to hear and everyone jabbered at once.

"And – and then! And then they shot the fucking shit out of a cuca shop and set it alight with white phos!"

"Spacecricket's gone apeshit!"

"The PFs are praying for forgiveness."

"Fok hulle gaan hulle gatte kry!" (*Fuck, they're going to see their arses!*)

"Dissie infanterie se naam wat gat gemaak is, hee hee!" (*It's the infantry's name they've made arse, ha ha!*)

"Ja they've made the infantry's name gat! Christ the PFs are going to go befuck!" We were overjoyed at the scandal and lived on it for weeks. But nevertheless, it was a serious matter and we were dosed with dominees and prayed over and given a braai on Sunday. At the same time we were treated with sterner discipline but we laughed at them for we thought nothing they could do could ever bother us again. The two troops involved had been arrested in a drunken stupor by their own platoon commander and were now in a military jail in Ondangwa.

One afternoon the three platoons came together at a large dry shona for a demonstration to the PBs of our military power. These magsvertonings were deemed a necessary adjunct to the policy of winning the PBs' hearts and minds. A crowd of them, mainly women and children, sat on a low rise behind Alpha Company, as directed by the Captain who had arrived in a Buffel, we demonstrated all our weapons, singly and then in unison. I would have been impressed, but I wondered how often they were required to sit through these performances, and what thoughts passed through their minds. Cowfuckers. We waited for a promised napalm drop by impalas, which was cancelled and never came.

We loaded ourselves into Buffels after a month. For four weeks we had been outside, replenished weekly at drop-off points with food. It had been a healthy time, walking in the hot sun in the real Africa, eating sparsely but sufficiently. We were brown-faced with darting eyes and our hair was blonding from exposure to the sun. Not one of us was remotely sick, though a short while later back at Oshivello the company had two cases of malaria. Our shirts were black with an oily substance made of sweat and dust, and we called them our leather jackets. Our boots produced a white layer of salt crystals, that came through the leather from our sweat, and white salt crystals formed in rings on our shirts under our arms. This dirt was only on the outside. Within, we were cleaned out by the constant passing of impurities outwards through our skins.

At the movement of the Buffels we felt moving air and came back to the modern age. A few kilometres down the track we passed Bravo Company getting ready to convoy. "Koeinaaiers!" (*Cow fuckers!*) roared Warwick and they glared back balefully, so we all joined in, yelling like monkeys and throwing dog biscuits at them. Koeinaaiers fokken meidenaaiers koeienaaiers koeienaaiers julle boggers meidenaaiers fokken koeinaaiers.

At Oshivello we now settled into tents inside the camp, systematically – half a section per tent, so that we had a physical address that made finding any unit of the company easy. The tents had electrical cable running through the vent-holes in the apex, and onto this one could clamp a socket with penetrating pin terminals for a light bulb, that was powered by a generator. Soon we had eaten at the mess, and tired out, prepared to sleep. Bravo Company arrived in the dark and unloaded in the furthest corner of the camp. We were up at six for PT which was tough and compulsory every morning. Oshivello was a little to the east of the north-south road, and we crossed this almost every morning and ran along the grassy airstrip that was parallel to the great elephant fence of the Etosha Game Reserve.

Convening bidparade, bug-eyed Spacecricket the RSM marched two troops ahead of him and halted them where all could get a clear view. In strident sermonic tones and with fire and brimstone, he told his tale. "Hierdie twee siele," he began, "het die infanterie naam gat gemaak. Hulle is julle mense, hulle is my mense. En hulle het sonde gedoen." He said the word 'sonde' (*sin*) with powerful emphasis. "Ek praat nie van gewone alledaagse sonde nie, ek praat onbeleefd – siek en godeloos." We braced ourselves in the way squads of infantry do on parade, when they want to laugh but have to look serious. "In Ovambo noord, waar julle almal nou pas patrollie geloop het," he continued, "het hierdie twee van hulle patrollie weggeslenter en AWOL gegaan. Eers het hulle by 'n cuca bier en brandewyn gekoop. Hulle het in die bos hulle eie kamp opgerig en … hulle het dagga gerook," more emphasis, "waarna hulle 'n onspreekbare daad gepleeg het. Julle sal dink dis onmoontlik. Maar dit ís die waarheid." He paused for suspense and rotated his gaze. "Hulle. Het. Gemeenskap. Gehou. Met. 'n. Koei. Ja perde, 'n koei. Julle het almal die Ovambo koei gesien. Dit lê rond, swart, siek en lam. Dit was een van hierdie skraal, sieklike diere wat hierdie twee … vieslike, kalante gevind het in die bos, en in sig van mekaar, daarmee gemeenskap gehou het. Maar manne, dit word erger. Hulle kon dit nie regkry nie, want die gat was te klein. Dis grillerig om te sê, maar hulle het met 'n panga die – vagina – groter – gesny. En nou terwyl hulle hiermee besig is kom die eienaars van die koei, twee Ovambo vroue aan, 'n ma en haar dogter, en – hierdie-onkruid-wat-langs-my-staan-het-hulle-vasgemaak-aan-'n-boom-en-verkrag." We were riveted. "Fluit fluit my storie is uit, dink julle, maar nee! Dronk, gerook, is hulle terug cuca toe en met hulle gewere en hulle handgranate het hulle die winkel vernietig en aan die brand gesteek. Hulle is slegter as slangkak! Hulle het die naam van die infanterie laag gebring, en hulle is deel van julle bataljon! Hulle is hier Oshivello toe gebring en in ons kas toegesluit. Het julle ons kas gesien? Wraggies mooi. Maar gistraand het hulle, met die hulp van hulle maatjies in Bravo Kompanie, uit die kas ontsnap … 'n ambulans gesteel … maar is weer toe in Grootfontein gevang terwyl hulle probeer aan boord 'n C130 na Suid-Afrika klim. Hoe blerrie dom kan jy wees! Hulle gaan nou aangekla word in 'n siviele hof. As hulle hier met ons aanhou bly, sal hulle lewens kort wees, van dit is ek seker. Laat ons vir die Here vergifnis vra. Laat ons bid!" (*These two souls have made the infantry's name arse. They are your people, they are my people. And they have committed sin. I'm not talking about ordinary everyday sin, I'm talking unacceptable, sick and godless. In North Ovamboland where you have all just walked patrol, these two sneaked away from their patrol and went AWOL. First they bought beer and brandy at a cuca. They set up their own camp in the bush and they smoked dagga, after which they committed an unspeakable deed. You will think it's impossible. But it's the truth. They held communion with a cow. Yes, men, a cow. You have all seen the Ovambo cow. It lies around, black, sick and lame. It was one of these scrawny, sick animals that these two … revolting characters found in the bush and held communion with in sight of each other. But men, it gets worse. They couldn't get it right, because the hole was too small. It gives me the shivers to say it, but they made the vagina bigger with a machete. And now, while they were busy, the owners of the cow, two Ovambo women, arrived, a mother and her daughter and – these filth standing next to me tied them to a tree and raped them. You think I'm finished now, but no! Drunk, smoked up, they went back to the cuca with their rifles and their hand grenades, and they destroyed the shop and set it alight. They are worse than snake shit! They have brought the infantry name low, and they are part of your battalion! They were brought here to Oshivello and locked up in our holding cell. Have you seen our cell? It's beautiful! But yesterday evening, with help from their friends in Bravo Company, they escaped and stole an ambulance, and were caught again in Grootfontein while trying to board a C130 for South Africa. How bloody stupid can you be! They will now be charged in a civilian court. If they stay with us their lives will be short, of this I am sure. Let us ask for God's forgiveness. Let us pray!)* And after a venomous prayer he marched his charges purposefully away, never to be seen by the honest infantry again.

For three weeks thereafter we worked hard, non-stop. Platoon attacks dominated the training program, while for variety night patrols, day patrols and shooting practice were thrown in. Under the immediate direction of the Captain again, we practiced 'ground sweep' techniques that seemed simple, but were in fact difficult to do well. There were hints that the next phase of our service would be both dangerous and ugly, for ground sweep was described as a no-nonsense form of attack, that could be used both against sparse resistance in the bush, as well as against a dense firing line of enemy infantry. It was a brutal, pragmatic forward movement. You walked in a long line abreast, in a platoon or company, as slowly as the rate at which resistance was giving in. You could retreat or take cover, or you could move forward, without breaking formation. Each troop fired to the ground ahead of him, picking targets where enemies were likely to be taking cover. The range and rate of fire were decided by the commander, and was determined by how thick the vegetation was, and how close the line could get to the enemy in reasonable safety. Thus as the line moved there was a zone, between 10m and 100m ahead of it, that was parallel to the line of troops, which was a killing ground. Of course, the closer the killing zone was, the more dense and accurate the fire and therefore the more lethal. It was very effective, because enemy fire was likewise less dense and accurate when they were further away, so their options were either to retreat from the killing zone that was moving towards them, or risk being in it. If they risked being in it, then the range would decrease as the line advanced towards them, becoming more dangerous, until the two forces were evenly engaged. But with training, our fire on the front got to be so dense and accurate, that the killing ground, a strip of ground about 20m wide, was a very inhospitable place. And then abruptly, we were transported to our final destination – 61 Mech.

10

Omuthiya

61 Mechanised Battalion was the first permanently integrated mechanised combat group in the world and, as a force dedicated to mobile warfare, was highly advanced. It was constantly being upgraded with new equipment and was governed by avant-garde doctrine. It was the envy of the world's armies. Then, it was South Africa's conventional fighting fist readily available to the commanders in the Angolan war, and was about one sixth of the mechanised forces that could be mustered in a short time if the need ever arose. Although Six-One-Mech's basic skeleton strength was approximately 800 men, of which the Veggroep (*Combat Group*) was some 300, the rest being support, it could be augmented by a number of dispersed units. Residing permanently at Six-One were:

One Mechanised Infantry company (Alpha Company – of which I was a member). It consisted of two Command Ratels and three platoons of four Ratels each. Thus there were 14 Ratels armed with 20mm cannons, and furthermore each platoon had a logistics truck.

One armour squadron. Fourteen Ratels armed with 90mm guns. These could operate autonomously or integrated with the infantry. They proved effective against brand new Soviet T55 main battle tanks, knocking out many of them over the years in vicious battles deep in the Angolan wilderness.

One artillery battery. Four 140mm howitzers and four tow-trucks carrying ammunition, as well as a battery of eight heavy 120mm mortars.

One company of 81mm mortars. Eight pipes as light artillery used in flexible support of the infantry.

Mobile stores. A family of four-wheel drive mine-resistant logistics trucks, or Kwêvoëls, that followed the battalion wherever it went, ferrying fuel, ammunition and rations.

One platoon of field engineers, capable of tasks from laying or lifting mines to building bridges.

One light works troop (the Tiffies). These important guys could fix anything ingeniously in any circumstances. They operated souped-up tow Ratels equipped with steam cleaners, welding equipment, tools, generators, lights – everything.

HQ Company. Clerks, chefs, medics, intelligence and of course the battalion leadership.

The Infantry, Armour, Artillery and Logistics could be doubled or trebled, as the forces existed nearby, but deployed separately in counterinsurgency applications.

Additional ordinary infantry units could also be added. A squadron of 10 Olifant main battle tanks with 105mm stabilised guns was also available for integration into Six-One-Mech. But in its skeleton form 61 Mech was not a force to be sniffed at. Its Combat Group, i.e. the combined Infantry and Armour, when deployed on open ground, formed a front nearly a kilometre long and hit very hard indeed. It was not a force you would want to stand in the way of without tanks, or even with them.

Six-One was based at a place called Omuthiya, exactly where the road turns slightly west to go around the northwestern corner of the Etosha Game Reserve. It's easy to find on a map. Facing north, the elephant fences were on your left and the sand road to Omuthiya led off for about 1.5km to the right. This did not mean that animals were confined to the west of the road. Elephants roamed in our wild training area between Etosha and Mangetti, and at nights we heard zebra, jackal, hyena and other strange calls. The camp was not fenced or in any way fortified, though watchtowers surrounded it, quite far out into the trees. There was a grouping of sheet-metal buildings – hangar parks, stores, magazines, workshops, admin buildings, lecture theatre, a kitchen and mess, recreation and sleeping quarters for the officers. All these were surrounded by tents that had concrete slab floors. The trees were left growing, except on the big parade ground, and continued from the wilderness right through the camp, so it was shady. We stayed six to a tent in spartan comfort, and shared large open shower sheds that were a pleasure to use in the late evening sun. Beside each tent was a deep slit trench in case of air or mortar attack. Near our shower block on the edge of the camp was a waterhole, where in the evenings kudu would sometimes quietly drink and ignore us.

The camp was like a vast family run by strict but benevolent elders, of whom Captain Malan was one. 61 Mech Battalion's commander was Commandant Roland de Vries, a tall, athletic, black-haired man with a strong presence who took his responsibilities seriously. De Vries had been instrumental in the development of the Ratel, and indeed the art of mobile warfare in the SADF. We were intimidated by him as he was a strict disciplinarian, though time would reveal him to be considerate and generous within the boundaries he set. The other large character was the Regimental Sergeant-Major, WO1 Killer Smit, with a basso profundo voice like B.J. Vorster's over a PA system, and the face of a Viking beserker. Rumour had it that he had taken a troop on a bosbus until he died. We were never sure of the truth of this rumour, which conflicted with our discovering, gradually, that beneath his scary outer shell was a down-to-earth human individual. But the respect he commanded remained absolute. At 50m, his glance across the parade ground was so sharp that we knew he could read minds. The PF's wives were seen in camp for the occasional battalion braai. We met the Captain's wife – she was petite, shy and vulnerable with their tiny baby.

Andre Glazewski arrived as part of the QM Stores workforce. Although it seemed he had not one friend in the whole world – I thought I was a bad one – he seemed happy enough, and we talked sometimes at night under the stars in the warm air. Some nights a film was shown in the open-air cinema where the whole battalion gathered, nursing the two beers permitted per person. Films were sometimes interrupted as flaring base-bleed artillery shells roared high against the stars if our battery was practising. Lights went out at 10pm. The day began with coffee and rusks served at 7am, and a brief inspection of weapons and clothing, then straight away tough training would commence in the vicinity of the camp. At 11am we trickled into camp hot and sweating for a quick brunch. The food at Six-One was quite acceptable, unless supplies were running low and we got the traditional 'Noddy cars' – batter-fried bully beef slices, named after the nickname for the inferior-to-Ratel Eland armoured cars. But it was not uncommon to see roast chicken, or boerewors and chops, or bobotie. Either at Ondangwa or Tsumeb was a bakery that produced superlative bread, for it was delicious and I remember its unique taste well. With the training and the reduced meal times we became lean, and could not have been fitter.

We were excited to take over our new Ratels, which were in excellent condition. Somehow, we felt very comfortable in them as if they were mobile homes. We loved the high-pitched whine of their engines and we loved the warmth of their steel in the sun. Nevertheless they meant training and maintenance, and in them, training lasted until 4pm or 5pm, after which PT for an hour, as if that was necessary. Then to the showers where cool water washed away grime and sweat, and aching feet and joints were soothed.

"Can I lend your fukken toothbrush ek sê?"

"Only if I can use your fukken towel." Eriksen and I had this tradition. If we had no money for things such as soap, it had to be borrowed. We shared anything. Looking back, for all the physical hardship we endured, it was the most carefree time of my life. Towel over shoulder we walked in shorts along the soft sand lane, past the Infantry, past the rows of Armour tents, moving in and out of camelthorn shadows. Other troops moved with us or were coming back, drying in the tropical sun. Forearms, faces and Vs around the neck were suntanned and dark. All else was pale. Peter Barry approached us and we stopped and talked.

"Hey I watched you and Wetherall kakking off with that truck, ek sê!"

"Fuck, ja, we must've shot fukken 60 bombs at it and there's it. My arms are numb!"

"Why?" sneered Eriksen as if I had been mad.

"I d'no, the Captain kept telling the Loot, 'HEs oppie teiken, HEs oppie teiken.' Hey, have you heard the new Thin Lizzy?" (*HEs on the target, HEs on the target*.)

"Uh-uh, I'll listen just now. I'll see you at supper." Barry moved off.

"What happened to your arm?" said Eriksen noticing a run of dried blood on my right forearm.

"Slaan'ed dekking on a bit of a twennymil doppie. It's nothing, just blood, ek sê." (slaan dekking – *hit cover*.) At the shower building Eriksen threw our towel over the metal cladding and waited in the noisy splash for a free spot, which we shared. We talked shit with the people around us and took our time. I watched the blood cakes on my arm dissolve. The showers were pipes wired to the rafters, and salty lukewarm water poured out the ends. We washed and brushed our teeth at the same time.

Later after washing clothes and cleaning weapons, in shorts and T-shirts we lined up for supper and after that the shop opened that, when it was available, sold the two beers per person per day, as well as cooldrinks, chips, sweets, soap, shampoo and toothpaste. The shop was run by Frank Fiser, who afterwards went to the same university as me, along with his two brothers. One, Neil, was in my class. In a separate building was a little lounge with splitting sofas, coffee urn, newspapers and dartboards. Usually we fetched coffee there and took it to our tent, mine or to the Barry/Eriksen tent in the Platoon 2 lines. There we sat sharing music or talking quietly on the beds which were the only furniture, hearing, more often than not, the sound of '*Juke Box Hero*' by Foreigner, or '*I Love Rock 'n Roll*' by Joan Jett, consoling the night in the background.

I got to know some of the members of Platoon 2, which seemed on the whole far less belligerent than my Platoon 1, a warrior band to the core, so I was drawn there more and more often socially. In the tent next to Eriksen's lived the crew and MAG team of One-Two-Alpha (12A). Lenny Hough was the driver, who more than anyone in Alpha Company lived his belief that the army was transitory, that it couldn't be allowed to bother him, and that if he kept a low profile and was quiet and decent, he would continue life as before. He walked into Eriksen's tent while we played music and sat unobtrusively on a bed, chatting pleasantly. Corporal Du Toit was the 12A section leader and he and the gunner Johan Cruywagen were friends. Cruywagen was bright-minded and positive and always called an innocent joke or greeting as he went past the tent. Mostert was the MAG man, the same one who had threatened me to 'bykom' in Basics. He had moderated. He was dour but neutral. I sat next to Barry on his bed and looked as he turned an RPG-7 rocket over in his hands. It stands for 'rakat panser granat' (*rocket tank grenade*), if I got the Cyrillic right, for it is Russian, and is written on its supply boxes of Siberian timber. It is, strictly speaking, therefore not a 'rocket-propelled grenade'. It is a simple and brilliant weapon. An illiterate can use it after a minute's instruction and we knew this, and while admiring it, knew that every second SWAPO carried one and longed to bury it in a Ratel.

The tents were filled with live ammunition, as a surprise attack could happen at any moment. HE mortar bombs lay around the floor, and we rolled them idly with our feet. Barry screwed on the RPG's supercharge and passed it to me. I pointed out the aluminium percussion cap on the other side of the shaft.

"The firing pin hits here." Opposite on his bed Eriksen put his eye to the mouth of the launcher and pulled the trigger.

"Ja. You can see it, ek sê."

"Let's check!" I leaned over and took it and stared through it at the light bulb. The pin flicked into the tube with a neat little click. Lenny Hough pulled the rocket off my lap and screwed it apart again. Barry leaned across me and pointed out the rocket jet outlets on the head of the rocket.

"Look, they're slightly skew. They make it rotate, as well as the fins. It rotates ... it rotates anti-clockwise." Lenny shifted and drew in a deep breath.

"Who gives a shit how it rotates?" He got up and left the tent for the living darkness.

But tensions in Platoon 1 ran high always. Warwick ruled there, and the pecking order was hard work and always stressful. Platoon 2 was relaxed and livable. They had no Warwick among them. But maybe that's why we were always the spearhead platoon.

> Dear Mom,
> So we've actually got here, the first place I mentioned in my last letter. Well, it's pretty much like a sauna up here, & it rains at 4.30 in the afternoon & 4.00am almost without fail. We have water restrictions, but we catch a lot in the roofs of our tents, & we can shower at 4.30 in the afternoons. It's now ********* & we've finished brunch a while back. At *** we get coffee & rusks, & at *** brunch. Later on we'll have supper – only two meals a day. We've been working all morning, pulling out bushes and leveling a parade ground. It's very sandy here, & the sun reflects harshly during the day. That's why we will usually

get time off during the day. We've got an order from the captain not to swear at all. However, the only person who swears profusely around here is Tap Tap, or Cpl. Van Jaersveld, everybody's pet hate. At the moment there's a price on his head of R750, provided by his own platoon, unless he changes his ways or goes back to Bloemfontein. I've written this because it's about time someone around here knows about this. See you in approximately the amount of months there are pine trees in the garden, but maybe less. P.S. stamps are kindly provided by the army, & we get paid every two weeks. P.P.S. – another thing, which I forgot to mention, is the inaccuracy of the time ***************. For example, the sun rises at 7 o'clock. Midday is at 3 o'clock about so it's all a bit strange. The sun sets at nearly 8 o'clock.

The training that began at once made us into shock troops. Using Ratels became second nature. Outside Omuthiya was a great simulated trench and bunker fortification that Commandant de Vries had had made the year before for training for Operation Protea. Dotted about it were the wrecks of Soviet vehicles. We attacked this ad nauseam using live ammunition. We would advance upon it in the Ratels from about a kilometre away, in one of the approach formations. Just before it came into view through the trees we formed attack formations, disembarked and lined up between the vehicles. We did fire and movement and the Ratels also did, in quick 50m leaps, keeping pace with the troops. First the 90mm guns picked out visible targets, then as we got closer the 20mm cannons joined them, thoroughly hammering the target with HEs at a range of about 200m, keeping the 'enemies'' heads down. The destructive power of 20mm cannons firing in unison is something to be seen. When the first trenches were reached, the vehicles manoeuvred continuously into positions from where they delivered support fire as requested by the commanders on the ground. Each section leader on the ground directed his own 20mm gunner by radio. It was a symphony of communications. It was a grand, mobile fireworks display. In and between the trenches and bunkers we shot our way using rifles, machine guns, grenade launchers, RPG-7s, hand grenades, phosphorus grenades and patrol mortars, and the noise never stopped.

It cannot be exaggerated the sheer mass of ammunition that was expended in this training. The Ratels had to be completely bombed up each day – that is a ton of ammunition per Ratel. 61 Mech training was costing (then) a million rand a day. Although I caused one close shave, there were never any accidents, even though we were shooting near, between, over and past each other in rapidly moving and changing situations. Shells and bombs were exploding continuously. But one afternoon, we practised a rapid support movement where a platoon darted into a firing position, while the others gave dangerously close support fire. Platoon 1 went in first and when our infantry got out and deployed, I fired mortars off the roof of the Ratel while it was moving.

Bang! I let a bomb slide into the pipe just as we bumped through a trench, and given a sideways knock, it sailed lazily out, spinning like a thrown stick. I watched it in horror and called out to the platoon commander in his turret hatch in front of me. It was already falling towards Section 3. We stared as it fell between the section leader and two troops out in front of him. It didn't explode. The section leader Corporal Koortsen, jumped and spun round to look at us. We stared back helplessly. But shit, he was a nice guy, Koortsen. Later in the mosquito-quiet of the base, he said smiling, "Hoekom wil jy my doodmaak, Davies?" (*Why do you want to kill me, Davies?*) A technical detail other patmor operators will understand, is that we used a static firing pin in our patmors at 61, for a greater rate of fire. After each exercise the Captain called us together, ears ringing from the wall of noise, to talk about and analyse good or bad moments. "Bakgat, manne!" (*Perfect, men!*) he would say, or "Dit was gaggies!" (*That was disgusting!*) For his shear reasonableness we pulled out all the stops and dreaded to disappoint him.

There was always a bit of anger among us, resentments with each other and against PFs, who resorted to more and more drastic forms of punishment to control us. Usually it was most effective to threaten the whole group, then single out perpetrators and punish them individually, to general approval and relief. You could be given a green mamba, an artillery shell, to hold in your arms for say, a day, without letting it touch the ground. A Ratel tow-bar, a hugely heavy piece of steel, was always close at hand and could be carried on shoulders whenever an opportunity presented itself. Oversleeping was dealt with by making the sinners lie in sleeping bags on the parade ground all day, with an ambulance parked nearby in case of heat stroke. I think this happened only once.

I was ordered, after some misdemeanour, to report to the RSM's office for a day of retribution by the expert. I waited with a few other souls, discussing the row of green mambas in deathbed murmurs. Killer Smit ambled out of his office with a clipboard. We snapped to attention and he glared down at us, then rumbled slowly, "Is julle my skurwe seuns?" (*Are you my rough boys?*) He looked at the clipboard. "Mmmmm ... Davies!"

"Ja, Samajoor."

"Davies ... Davies. Nou wat gaan ek met jóú maak, outjie?" (*Now what am I going to do with you, little man?*) He looked at the green mambas and back at me. "Ha Ha

Haaa!" he said, cruelly. "Oraait. Gaan haal jy vir my vier emmers by die KM Stoor." (*All right. Go and get me four buckets at the QM Store.*) And that was it. We hung out with the RSM. All day we were his buddies and went around with him doing odd jobs and chores, except for brunch, when he made sure we were first in the queue. We raked the gravel in front of his office, fetched things, and helped him with some killing. We killed mosquito larvae at the marshy ground next to the showers.

Because life seemed easier at Six-One, we relaxed, which was a mistake. Once the Captain became so furious at the inferior standard of the whole company one training day, that he shipped us all out to the bloubaan, a shooting-in range about 20km from camp. An initial tongue-lashing from him seemed more painful than what followed. From there we manned a long rope and the company pulled a fully bombed-up Ratel back to camp, in full kit with steel helmets and through baking red soft sand that you sank into over your boots. There was no build-up of momentum in the sand, just continual drag. An ambulance followed and picked up two cases of heat exhaustion.

We organised a system of surrogates, people who could take over essential combat duties from killed or wounded comrades. Each Ratel had an assistant driver, gunner, vehicle commander, MAG gunner etc. I trained to be both a hulpgunner and a hulpdrywer, though I became a hulpgunner. The turret took some getting used to, but was then really easy to operate. You held the two winding handles. Each had brake controls that you squeezed to move, and a red firing button (tiet) under your thumbs. The right handle rotated the turret and fired the machine gun. The left handle elevated the weapons and fired the 20mm cannon. At my left shoulder was the body of the cannon, about 70cm long. Beneath it hung the two stainless steel feed belts with their lines of colourful shells extending down into the ammunition bin below my feet. In the left belt were the green and red HEs, and the black and red APs were in the right. Centrally, on top of the cannon, were the safety catch and the selector lever that allowed you to choose HE or AP shells. Before you fired, you had to open the eject aperture in the turret roof, through which the empty cases were flung upward. The spent links cascaded into a canvas bag below the weapon. I leaned my forehead against the soft pad over the optical sight. This was a prismatic periscope that moved with the weapons. When I looked in it I saw the world highly magnified in sharp, wide-angle focus. A vertical black line bisected the view. At night this was luminescent. Short horizontal lines joined the vertical from both sides along its length. Those on the left were ranges for the 20mm, and those on the right were for the Browning. The 20mm ranges went up to 3,500m. As a beginner I had to rotate the turret until the vertical line bisected a target, then elevate the weapons until the correct range also cut it. The vehicle commander used a rangefinder and gave fire control orders. These orders were contained in a formula: 1 – short description of the target, 2 – direction as a clock face numeral relative to the orientation of the vehicle, 3 – range in metres, 4 – firing order. So the voice in the headphones said, "BTR, elfuur, nege honderd, APs vier skote," or "mense in bosse, drie-uur, vyfhonderd, HEs rapid fire." (*BTR, eleven o'clock, 900, APs, four shots ... people in bushes, three o' clock, 500, HEs rapid fire.*)

I lined up on a termite hill 800 metres away and tentatively pressed the tiet. As I was squeezing, the turret exploded and the Ratel rocked. The headphones took most of the shock out of the noise. The sight momentarily pointed at the sky but stabilised quickly enough for me to see the tracer arcing to the anthill. It flew over and exploded beyond it. I lowered the gun slightly and fired again. Wham! This time the fireball appeared in the middle of the anthill and the top half of it vanished. Looking out the window I was surprised at how far the target was. This was fun! But in the main the job meant helping with the maintenance and cleaning of the weapons, which made for plenty of extra work.

Dear Mom,

How is everyone at White Walls? In 61 everyone's fine, except for the boredom & nothingness which occurs with surprising suddenness every day. The rainy season seems to be closing and yesterday clouds of dust poured all over our carefully prepared inspection of our vehicles. As for me I'm fine. Half the week in the evenings are films which are usually quite good. I get a lot of time to read & I'm halfway through my books already. Everyone here wants to get bush babies – they're very small & make 'good pets' but I think they're pretty pathetic – always tied up & always jumping to the end of their string & bouncing back. Spend all day in a box and all night jumping around the tent. We are supposed to have a name for our tent by now – we've thought of several, but they're not suitable: 'The Tent of Immortal Sin', 'The Illuminati', 'The Everite Hotel' – because we're opposite a large Everite water tank. Our tent's very comfortable at the moment – bed, miskit net, electric light, concrete floor, 2 ammo crates for my possessions & a balsak. I think it will be nice to live in a tent when I come out of the army.

11
Into Angola: Operation Meebos 1

No sooner had this last training ended than 61 Mech rolled up the highway north to Angola. Days were spent in the preparation and none were allowed out of camp. Logistics trucks had to be loaded, Ratels and their weapons checked and serviced. Emergency medical training took place. This taught each and every one of us to insert a drip, to give an injection, to apply bomb bandages, to treat different types of wounds. There were also tampons for pushing into gaping wounds. We each received a battalion number to be written or inscribed on all our belongings, as a method of identifying us if our bodies and dog tags became so destroyed we could not be recognised, but also to quickly refer medical records to the medics, for instance blood type. Mine was AO36. Each Ratel carried four spare tyres on the roof, and heaps of extra ammunition cases were carried in them.

When the battalion was ready it streamed from the gate. Arriving at Ondangwa at mid-morning, radio comms told us that the 61 Mech column was still leaving the gate, some 60km to the south. We parked in rows next to the airport and watched aircraft coming and going, including Mirages, and these joined high-flying Canberra heavy bombers which came from the south and headed off into Angola. We followed them the following morning.

The country became very flat, uninhabited and densely green. Huge concrete water towers, 50m high with round platforms supporting tents, dotted these northern regions. Driving to this fabled place, we felt as mariners did approaching the edge of the world. The border at Santa Clara was open. We whined through in clouds of white dust obscuring the small customs and passport control buildings pitted with bullet holes dating from 1975. There was no wear around them and no sign of life. The road became tarred and good and straight, and rose high above the surrounding plain on a causeway, so that we gazed out across the tops of ever-taller trees as we drove straight as an arrow northwestwards. In the afternoon we stopped to practise air raid drill, which required careful driving down the steep causeway to avoid overturning, and parked dispersed under the trees on either side of the road, with all troops disembarked and hidden. Should the attack be real then we and all the 20mm cannons and Brownings would fire simultaneously into the sky, filling it with a dangerous cloud of metal, visible on account of the tracers.

We progressed slowly, and late afternoon we entered Ongiva, a ghost town with wide grass verges to the streets. In the town centre was a modest monument, and a small church. Mortar marks pocked the tarmac, and dents from various projectiles graced the walls of the distinctly Portuguese suburban houses. Some were badly damaged, but most still had glass and even curtains in the windows. People there were none.

The battalion assembled all around the town and one of Platoon 1's Ratels drove into a wet area in a back garden, got stuck, and quickly sank up to its lateral line. Everyone bailed out of the roof hatches. It seemed to pose a difficult problem, for here was 18 tons sunk in a thick black bog. The commander of the Tiffies arrived in his tow Ratel and produced a 30m-long white acrylic rope, about 10cm thick. Digging in front of the stuck vehicle, his men attached this rope to the tow hitch, and the tow Ratel backed up to the bog until it stood close to the other, and was connected, with the rope navy-coiled in between. What happened next was impressive. We were told to move away and take cover and the tow Ratel accelerated at full power, not stopping when the rope sprang taught. Instead, this stretched nearly twice its length and only then did the tow Ratel begin to slow down. With a loud sucking noise, the sunk Ratel leaped right out of the mud and landed on hard ground with a bang.

Mosquito nets were scant protection against night attacks by vicious swarms of the little fuckers. We made believe they could bite you through the soles of your boots. Sleeping was uncomfortable at that time of year – it was hot and very humid, and Tabard mosquito repellant was sticky on top of it. I Lariam-dreamed of white bones in the moonlight, severed heads rotting in helmets and a leopard slinking into camp. We trained in the dense forests to the west of Ongiva, where occasional cucas cropped up in the seemingly endless wilderness.

There was an International Red Cross mission among the local rural population, and when we arrived at another, larger, town called Xangongo, these volunteers lined among the locals up to watch us rumble by. The armour commander told us, "Moenie met hulle praat nie want hulle is kommuniste en neem dwelms." (*Don't talk to them because they are communists and take drugs.*) It was weird after our isolation from the world to see pretty young European women, here, of all places, and we longed to speak with them and exchange words across worlds.

Xangongo had an airfield on a flat scarp above the town overlooking the Cunene River. Here Alpha Company parked, dwarfed by baobab trees. A demolished bridge zig-zagged across the floodplain and water. In it we saw women washing and children swimming, where less than a year before, such a slaughter and frightful tropical battle had taken place during Operation Protea. Signs of recent war in everything.

Hulks of Russian military vehicles, shot-up buildings, cartridges all over, even white bones on the airfield. The Angolans having been driven far away, there was no one to care or clean up.

The sounds of war returned to Xangongo as 61 Mech used part of the deserted town for training – and to give FAPLA pause for thought, in case they wanted to try to reoccupy the area. The buildings were adjoining, and two storeys high. Urban fighting is a specialised aspect of warfare and we trained in large doses. Armour commanders are wise to keep their vehicles out of built-up areas, where a defined front disappears, and they can be ambushed from any direction and from height. Still, their big guns are valuable assets in the streets. Infantry must make the streets safe for them and effectively maintain a defined front, clearing building by building. This is slow, systematic work and can be boring, as not all parts of a firing line are engaged at the same time. The Captain nevertheless thought it necessary for us to know how to operate in towns. "Ondervinding bespaar lewens," (*Experience saves lives*) he said on many occasions. Violent explosions shook the ground and small arms fire popped. The 90mm shells sounded like rushing water as they flew past us, punching holes in walls for troops to enter. At the back of a shop in a courtyard, webbing and helmets and rifles lay about. An RPG-7 launcher stood in the middle of the paving, its Russian leather strap hanging dirtied and limp. We ate from little ratpack tins warmed over fuel tablets.

While we took a break, Platoon 2 on foot was going through its paces, working from house to house with grenades and small arms down both sides of a street, and using reserves to guard their flanks. I imagined Eriksen and Barry hard at work, shirts wet under their webbings. At intersections they covered the side streets with machine guns and laid down smokescreens so that troops could cross the open space invisibly. Then a vehicle, a 90 or a 20, was called up to the corner where it edged its weapon forward to smash open buildings and deliver heavy covering fire. Being used to such noise, it was for us a peaceful scene and a luxury to be between shady walls and indoors.

I won some small local fame during a patrol mortar shooting competition on the airfield, when, as the first contestant up, I dropped my very first bomb into a barrel at 300m with the whole battalion watching from their Ratel roofs. This was virtually unbeatable, and I had the small satisfaction of this being remembered until the end of National Service.

We spent less than a week in the towns and no more than three in Angola. The purpose of the visit seemed mainly to be for training, but we were informed we were also performing a magsvertoning, a projection of power. "Magsvertoning,

magsvertoning!" we complained. "Altyd fokken MAGSvertoning!" We wanted to fight!

Being the end of the wet season, it was sticky and uncomfortable, and the keenest memories are of impoverished rural peasants living discreetly amongst the vagrant armies, ourselves, FAPLA, SWAPO and UNITA. Apparently, according to intelligence briefings which seemed pretty frank, the most popular faction was FAPLA, followed in descending order by the SADF, SWAPO and UNITA, the last two being penniless opportunists and scroungers, and conscienceless abusers. Angolan kwanzas existed but were not considered hard currency and South African rands were much preferred. Towards the end of our time there, for a change in diet I bought a live chicken from a small skinny child for one rand and killed it with the Ratel's hand axe that hung on a clip on the inside of the door. It was hard to find meat in it, but there was some in thin layers. The experience was tarnished by the countless roundworms that writhed like glass Medusa's hair out of the torn intestines and rapidly dried in the sun. But I was determined to go through with the foolish exercise, and cooked with ratpack instant onion soup, I suppose it wasn't too horrible. So Angola was no big deal, we had learned, and drove back to Omuthiya where waiting and training continued.

Dear Mom,

How are things back at WW? I'm fine though I've had a bit of a snotsiekte & the sand fleas and mosquitoes have eaten me to the giblets. I went overseas for a few days last week – that's where the miskits hit me. At the moment things are ********* and *************** at 61 Mech. Bn. Last night Piek and Van Schalkwyk got disgustingly drunk & invited all their friends into the tent. After impassioned speeches and much serious talk about life, and spreading me with fish paste and butter and throwing my kit all over the tent, they passed out at about 9.30. Anyway, Wetherall & I got them back at about 11.30 when, with a great flurry of excitement, we woke them up & said there was an emergency, we had ½ an hour to hand in our kit, and we said it was the next morning 6.30 already. Swearing, cursing & vomiting Piek stumbled out of bed while we burst with laughing. In the north of Ovamboland it's now very lush & green – there is water everywhere & the cattle are fat. Remember I said it was white sand dotted with trees & dying oxen? Well, now there's an increase but the flies have increased also – for every human being perhaps 16 flies & at night they change into evening suits & suck your blood. I'm sorry to know that you're so sick. You'll just have to get better, long before I come home to go mountain climbing.

Just think healthy. At the moment they're thinking of converting the mess into a recreation room. The new canteen is grand – & when the rec room is finished, the canteen will be joined to it. Today and last night I drew some pictures – they're all right. I wonder if, given better pens, I'd ever be able to make extra money by illustrating. I've spent so much time in a Honey Badger for the past weeks that I don't want to hear one anymore. I'd just like to rest in base (not peace) for a month. But I have a very good idea I'll be in one all of tomorrow.

P.S. What is Granny's birthday date?

Halfway into April the Volcano Group came. This big incursion of SWAPO fighters threaded its way through the dense vegetation of Ovamboland and was heading for the area around Tsumeb. They were passing 61 Mech to the east and were somewhere in the vast trackless wilds to the north of the first row of private cattle farms. Tsumeb was to be the HQ for operations, and many units were to be gathered there. We were informed briefly of the state of affairs, the number of terrorists (hundreds), that they were heavily armed and trained in conventional warfare and moving in a single large group.

12

Operation Yahoo!

Alpha Company's Ratels drove south to Tsumeb in the late afternoon. Ratpacks had been issued, the Ratels loaded to capacity with ammunition, tons per vehicle, and we drove through swarms of glittering flying ants in the low gold sunlight. The company stretched out kilometres along the road. I lit my esbit stove on the wheel bulkhead in front of my seat as we drove. I was pleased with my recently acquired ratpacks and heated water for coffee. Ratpacks gave you freedom from routine. Hoy's boots dangled in the service passage to my right, where he sat in the open rear hatch in the streaming air.

Just as my water boiled there were some dull thuds accompanied by a sudden strong whiff of burning rubber. "What the fuck's that?" Wetherall looked at me. We were all puzzled. We looked at Hoy. He sat as before. We climbed out onto the roof and then we noticed wisps of smoke fleeing into the wind from holes in the spare tyre. It was still hard. We looked back at One-One-Alpha driving 150m behind. Everyone was out on the roof staring back at us. Their gunner had accidentally fired his machine gun. Two rounds had missed Hoy by less than 10cm, entering the tread of the tyre against which he had been leaning, behind him. They had followed the curve of the wheel, sliding in an arc under the surface along the steel wire reinforcing for the length of an arm, passing even closer to him, and had exited in front of him, shooting off behind the turret into the bush left of the road. Hoy hadn't noticed, which greatly enhanced his reputation. No harm done, so we didn't report it, but what we didn't realise was that the shit was already starting to hit the fan.

This signalled the beginning of a time of dangerous surprises. We found things out as they happened. At Tsumeb, a pleasant treed town with many jacarandas shedding their blue carpets on the shady streets, we parked in the compound of 61 Mech's admin office. This was where our post was sent to. It was our known address. We were told of a variety concert to be given that evening by entertainers who travelled around the fighting units. It was reasonable. The hall was filled with PF officers and their PF wives. Sitting in their groups were also clerks and some other fighting units. There was a selection of conventional comedy, singing and dance performances. Finally there was an interval, during which we rudely scrambled for cooldrinks and chips. After we were darkened again the stage lights came on, and three costumed lady dancers entered the stage from the wings, followed by the Captain climbing the steps from the front. They looked at him in surprise and he announced to the audience, "'n Groep SWAPOs se posisie is nou net vasgestel. Alpha Kompanie, julle moet onmiddellik aantree buite by julle voertuie. As enigiemand weet van vriende wat nie nou hier in die saal is nie, gaan haal hulle nou, en wees gereed vir orders in tien minute. Loop asseblief nou ordelik uit." (*A group of SWAPOs' position has just been confirmed. Alpha Company, you must form up immediately at your vehicles. If anyone knows of friends who are not here now in the hall, go and get them now, and be ready for orders in 10 minutes.*) We filed past the enquiring faces of women and other troops and out into the darkness. "Let's go to war together," I said melodramatically to Eriksen, and was rewarded by seeing the awe on a nearby woman's face. I was probably wrong. She probably knew more than me and thought, 'maar hy lyk so jonk' (*but he looks so young*). The orders were simple. We were to assemble at the small fortified base at Tsintsabis then drive northward to the Bravo cutline. There we were to deploy along the cutline's south side, concealed over kilometres of its length until morning, in the path of the oncoming insurgents. If contact occurred at any point in the line, reinforcements would quickly arrive from both sides and a fight would follow. It was hoped to contain them north of the cutline and the bush there would be saturated with SADF units.

We organised ourselves outside the camp at Tsintsabis, a small earth-bermed fort. Standing on the earth wall around an infantry major was a group of five Bushmen, the tops of their heads failing to come to his shoulders. In the light of a Ratel's searchlight they took part in an order group with Commandant de Vries and Captain Malan and the platoon commanders, while we watched out of the blackness from the Ratels. From there we drove north, and then turned left and went slowly and quietly along the cutline, Ratels at the back stopping one at a time every 200m, and concealing themselves in thickets. The troops then disembarked and spread thinly between the vehicles and hid. We listened like bat-eared foxes all night. The moon was half, and dew fell. The gunners and drivers stayed in their seats, the gunners scanning the opposing bush through their magnified optical sights.

We lay under bushes in the growing day and heat, waiting. Eventually an order came to group into platoons and move down the cutline to pick up trackers, deploy in separate platoons, and search. But at about 10am, an urgent message from Platoon 3 said they had landmine casualties and needed assistance. Platoon 2 had already found and was following tracks, so we went. With Lt Van Dalsen in the Company 2IC vehicle, we drove west from our position in the centre of the three platoons, until we came upon the distraught group. Our five Ratels parked well-spaced, with turret weapons pointing alternatively left and right of the cutline. Then ours, with Lt Van Dalsen's, drove forward to assess the damage. On seeing tracks on the cutline, troops from Platoon 3 had dismounted. The detonation of a black widow anti-personnel mine had removed Bezuidenhout's leg entirely. Four others had been less seriously wounded by shrapnel. All troops were immediately confined to their vehicles and necessary walking was done on tyre tracks. After we arrived, our medic John Waite went to assist and we dispersed into a circular defence and flattened an area of bush for a casevac.

Lt Van Dalsen, in his turret with his hand on the pressal switch at his chest, was talking while staring east along the cutline and presently the drumming of a helicopter could be heard from that direction. Soon a Puma arrived with noise and wind. We watched the stretcher running through the heavy rotor wash, bushes flapping madly. All of a sudden 2nd Lt Pierre de Jager our platoon commander stiffened, hands pressing headphones. "Peloton Twee is in 'n kontak!" (*Platoon 2 is in a contact!*) he rapped. Simultaneously, limping wounded were being turned away from the Puma. It took off immediately and roared low along the cutline eastward back in the direction we had come. We fixed stares at the Lieut.

"Hinderlaag. Mense is dood." (*Ambush. People are dead.*) He stared into the east with his hands to his earphones. "Eie troepe." (*Own troops.*)

"Wie, Luitenant?" I asked, hit with fear for my friends.

"Ons sal later uitvind." *(We will find out later.)*

Something bad had happened to Platoon 2 several kilometres away. The news bounced around the two platoons in 30 seconds. Everyone was asking questions. Platoon 3 was left to overcome its problems, but we were ordered to make a sweeping patrol with our vehicles in order to find signs or tracks, parallel to the cutline and to the north of it. We forced our way through thick green bush all day on foot among the vehicles and saw nothing, constantly fearing mines and violent ambush, and in dribs and drabs picking up Platoon 2's news.

Earlier that morning, Captain Malan with Platoon 2 had joined up with a contingent of SWATF members and trackers, and the group of five Ratels loaded with extra passengers had come upon a clear trail of debris on the cutline: pamphlets, empty cans, AK-47 rounds, sweet papers, as well as many footprints, in platoon strength. This trail they followed for several hundred metres, until it turned off north on a track at a right angle, into the thick bush. The trackers led, and it became obvious to those following that something was afoot, something not right. The insurgents did everything possible to be found.

The plan was to place stopper groups to the north and flush the insurgents towards them. So the platoon sergeant Cpl Van Jaarsveld was sent ahead in One-Two-Alpha with the Territorial Force tracker team to confirm the direction of the trail so that stopper groups could be placed. A radio message from 12A said that some distance from the cutline the tracks led across a wide black pan or shona. Such a feature was completely sudden and unexpected in this thick bush. The section was told to follow across, enter the bush on the far side for not more than 100m, to make sure there were no changes in the trail's direction or composition, and return. Splitting up the small force near the enemy was a mistake, plus it was standard procedure in thick vegetation to have troops disembarked in screens around their vehicles, although the threat of anti-personnel mines vindicated staying on board.

Across the shona they drove with the extra people making 17 on board, up into the dense growth and then immediately into a small clearing. The two trackers on the ground started running back to the Ratel, and then many things happened. The first RPG-7 hit the Ratel's sight block. The driver, Lenny Hough, caught the raw blast on the back of his head. Miraculously, before he died he operated the pneumatic door-opening levers, to let the others escape the bruising noise. The Territorial Force officer, a local farmer who was standing in the command hatch, and his son-in-law, and a Bushman tracker, sitting by him on the turret, died immediately. The gunner, Cruywagen, was seriously wounded in the head, neck and legs and afterwards lay shrivelling in a coma for many months. Then six other RPGs, or maybe some of them were rifle grenades, exploded into both sides of the Ratel. Petersen, killed outright, had red blotches all over his face and body from the searing copper droplets and screaming steel chips. Wolfvaard's remains were collected only later. It is easier to pick up bits of blackened, shattered bone than the fresh flesh sprayed over the inside of the Ratel. An RPG detonated on his chest as he emerged from the door. Corporal Van Jaarsveld, 'Tap-tap', who trained us, lost his legs, his arms, his lower torso and the top of his head.

After the RPGs, automatic fire intensified. Unaware he was bleeding fast from his back, and crawling through the long grass with bullets for a ceiling, the section 2IC Lance Corporal Scheepers found a remaining tracker, grabbed him and shook him out of his terror, saying, "Kry net die Ratels, die Ratels," (*Just get the Ratels, the Ratels*) and forced him to backtrack. Being shot at from two sides had completely disoriented everyone. The others squirmed through the long pale grass of the clearing and in a loose group, escaped the killing ground and found visual cover. Of them Pietie Pienaar had been sitting outside on the spare wheel when an RPG went into the edge of the engine covers. These blew open, catapulting him unhurt to the ground. Moments later a rifle grenade took a mango-sized chunk from his backside.

Piet Swarts, sleeping as was usual for him on the Ratel floor and protected from serious hurt by the central seating bulkhead, escaped with blast burns, but took two AK-47 or SKS bullets in the left arm once outside. De Villiers escaped miraculously: an RPG was aimed at his middle. It went through the only solid tow bar in the entire battalion (the others being made from pipe), through the Ratel's side and into the diesel tank, whose far side it failed to penetrate into the service passage where sat. But his eardrums burst. Mostert was able to function normally but was bleeding from many small holes. The platoon NCO, Corporal Viljoen, was also wounded by shrapnel. The section leader Corporal Du Toit went back to the Ratel under fire (medals? forget it!) and collected a shirt front full of magazines from the wall racks and brought them to Corporal Viljoen who fired 14 of them empty on automatic on the section's only surviving rifle, at the dense encircling vegetation, until it jammed. Its hand-projector had been blown off in the RPG attack.

At a distance the crews of the other four Ratels heard what sounded like an aggressive firefight between platoons. Deprived of radio comms with 12A, the Captain ordered an advance along the track leading to the noise. Scheepers, white as a sheet from lost blood, and a Bushman, presently appeared running towards them and blurted the worst news.

Drawing up into a line, the vehicles crashed through the dense bush, and emerged on the shona christened by the troops 'Olifantspan' because of the thousands of elephant footprints in the dried mud. Crossing this at top acceleration and reaching the bush on the far side, the troops disembarked, and firing high the line advanced. The ambushers had vanished into the greenery, but with the increase in noise the survivors cowered in an extremity of fear. The first thing Mostert saw was a tracker with an AK-47, an image of impending death.

Medic Piet Spreeuwenberg saved Cruywagen's life, while the company medics and frantic helpers struggled in vain with Lenny's bloody form. But when they turned his head, his brain fell out. The first Puma to arrive contained badly wounded friends from Platoon 3. No one amongst the troops knew clearly what was going on. The first enemy we had ever experienced had hurt us and vanished, and our minds reeled. The fighting seemed global. The trackers counted 42 shallow trenches arranged in L-formation, and confirmed the presence of 42 ambushers from tracks and spent ammunition. The Ratel lay in the exact centre of the L where the track led. The group split up immediately into individuals or groups of two or three. Later in the day one fleeing ambusher was shot by a helicopter gunship from above RPG height. A Bushman, who had gone missing in the ambush, turned up with an infantry unit 40km to the north a few hours later. He had run through the ambush and just kept going. Tannie Pompie, a woman well known for operating a Territorial Force radio relay in the area, relayed the contact report and thus found out that she had lost her son-in-law and husband who had been the Territorial Force members. The event ended in fire when the shot vehicle erupted in flames and explosions and glowed like a furnace for two days.

Platoon 2 was shaken and Platoon 3 never recovered from problems with morale resulting from the good question 'what the fuck are we doing here?' But throughout the company, worry darkened into anger and in the following months we saw ourselves as aggressive gods of punishment. We accepted any hardships and allowed ourselves to be trained to a lethal extreme. There was less resentment from the troops, and we seemed to enter a pact with our officers. We now wanted to be trained into hard men. For the real training had only just begun.

So Operation Yahoo! began with a bang. The insurgents had dealt a blow and broken through. In small groups they were now ranging far and wide in the farmlands, and some were killed as far south as Grootfontein. As far as I know, their strength dispersed for good and they had no further military success, but as terrorists they inflicted many irritations on farmers and Ovambo retainers on farms, and laid landmines all over the region. They were unloved by white and black alike, and were considered in the apoliticised farming lands to be bandits and murderers. After a month they were sufficiently dissipated through being killed and losing heart, and they either blended with the local population or hotfooted it back to the Angolan border. Nearly a hundred were killed, and the operation gradually wound down. Perhaps their victory was in causing such a big deployment by the South Africans, tying them down over such a large area.

After that traumatic day, we spent some time operating out of Tsintsabis. It was a nice small camp with big shade trees. We dreamed tropical dreams around the Ratels which lined the earth wall at night, with turrets and guns just peeping over and we stared out at dense blackness at night when we stood guard. We cleaned out the Ratels every few days. The mess they got into was unbelievable and cleaning was an afternoon's work. Wetherall and I always did the right side and piles and piles of ammunition had to come out and lie in the hot sun and then get packed neatly in again.

"Wie wil veg?" (*Who wants to fight?*) boomed a voice further down the platoon. Sitas, the joker, came swaggering along the vehicles, impossibly clad in weapons and ammunition. He was carrying a MAG and was completely wrapped up in ammunition belts. Furthermore about 20 hand grenades hung on his belt and another six on his bush hat. Mortar bombs hung from his shoulder straps and he had knives strapped to his calves. "Julle klomp moffies, ek sê, wie wil veg!" (*You bunch of queers, I say, who wants to fight?*) a dangerous soft baby voice out of his innocent face. Packets of dog biscuits rained on him from the Ratels, which Hoy picked up. Permanently manning the base at that time was a company of Kavangos, and so we fell under the jurisdiction of their sergeant. We got on with them reasonably well at mealtimes and sharing their facilities, something expected in the army, which was reforming faster than the rest of Apartheid South Africa.

Herr Mais-Rische, a refined old German farmer-gentleman from the northernmost row of cattle farms, now joined Platoon 1 with his team of Kavango trackers. He was an ardent SWAPO hunter, only less obsessive in this role than his four men. They hated insurgents as most men hate snakes, and wanted to kill them methodically. Mais-Rische went everywhere with us with a tracker in each Ratel, and we grew to like and respect all of them. They sure could follow a fugitive, and had strong clean characters.

Platoon 1 was now led by the Company 2IC, Lt Van Dalsen, and so we were a force of five Ratels. This group drove and walked and tracked, from Oshivello to Otavi to Tsintsabis and Tsumeb, on farms and in the cruel unwelcoming tropical savannah, which soon dried out, becoming hard and prickly, the rains having ended. The Otavi hills were hot and uncomfortable, stony and thorny. We patrolled the hills on foot in long hikes under blistering white skies. One day in the hot thorny bush we came across a 3m-long python, which I caught by pressing on its neck with a crowbar, and our section draped it heavily along our shoulders and stood for photographs. It became a strong angry python by the time I released it. At Otavi we were fêted by the local German community and thanked by their DTA representative, standing on the flatbed of a truck. Windhoek Lagers were handed out with ceremonious hospitality, and we wandered through the tiny town and found a sausage shop which produced fantastic Russians, and did good business that day. Beer and deep-fried Russians when you're ravenous … good nostalgia.

We followed tracks in the game country between the cutlines, crossing occasional fences cautiously and alert for booby traps. We sat on the Ratels' roofs staring at the inscrutable bushes, with faces dusty and smarting from too much sun as we drove to new places, hard on the reports of SWAPOs. Into the Etosha Game Reserve itself some tracks led, and we followed them.

Koevoet was always nearby and we saw them often, in the wilderness and in the various bases where we stopped. They seemed to have a first option on contacts, as they were the mobile force dedicated solely to chasing down SWAPO fugitives. They had a high success rate, partly attributable to many army units like us, over a wide area, setting them up to take over at a critical point. We began to resent their arrival. We would track for several hot exhausting days, until we got really close and checked our weapons while adrenaline licked our stomachs. When the gunships whined overhead from behind, we knew shooting was imminent. Koevoet would soon appear, and order us to follow in the rear as a reserve force, or make us drive far out ahead on the flanks of the tracks to concentrate the fugitives. So it was after the long chase through Etosha, which was as much a wildlife tour for us, as a war. Rumours and theories circulated that the Ovambo Casspir crews were offered prize money for kills, and we also heard stories of unconventional methods of gathering intelligence, and that there was no mercy in the dry, thorny, lonely places. Despite their success and reputation, and their vehicles bristling with machine guns, compared to the army they appeared to us to be badly disciplined and poorly controlled.

Once near Otavi we patrolled some farms running next to a range of hills. We went to inspect an old mine that had a long tunnel reaching horizontally into the base of a steep hill. Intelligence suspected that SWAPO was caching ammo there. There were several other smaller tunnels, and leaving the sections covering these entrances the platoon HQ climbed the hill, each of us equipped with a bunch of red and grey teargas grenades. Near the rocky summit, numerous shafts appeared at out feet, either natural or carved in the rock, and the platoon commander decided to drop teargas grenades into these. It was fun doing this until the gas started to stream from cracks and shafts. It was in small amounts but anyone who has experienced teargas will know how we panicked. We ran down the hill but could not get away. The gas came out everywhere. Soon we were bolting headlong down the slope, desperate to escape. At the bottom a situation met us, a classic fokop. The platoon sergeant, Corporal Robinson, with Section 1, had gone into the main tunnel. We couldn't believe our ears. It was impossible to enter, as gas was visibly streaming upwards out from the black mouth in the rock, and no reply came from our radio calls. Soon, echoes were heard and out staggered 11 gasping figures, who collapsed on the grass, red-eyed, with burning lungs and racked with coughs. They slowly recovered. We couldn't help laughing then, but they failed to see any humour. "Luitenant, ek gaan jou fokken aanrand," (*Lieutenant, I'm going to fucking assault you*) wheezed the platoon sergeant.

13

Tracks

Reading a *Scope* one early morning, Hoy questioned some reporting. He sat forward on the edge of the white wooden fold-up chair, his feet centimetres from the hot ashes of the fire. "Ag Korporaal Hoy, wie gee 'n vlieënde fok!" (*Ach Corporal Hoy, who gives a flying fuck?*) Piek called absently from inside the Ratel where he was packing his belongings. Singleton, on top of the Ratel laughed softly and said, "Ag Piek, ou pel, hoe kan jy met Korporaal Hoy so praat?" (*Ach Piek, old pal, how can you talk to Corporal Hoy like that?*) Marais the orderly stopped behind Hoy's shoulder and squinted at the article. "Ne-e-e, fok ek sê … " he murmured and pushed his fire bucket into the coals. Fifty paces away beyond the Ratel was Klaus Mais-Rische's farmhouse on the farm Onderra. The coffee was real and came from his wife's kitchen. I sat at the fire also, with coffee warming up. Smoke drifted into my face. I dipped a dog biscuit and held it there to soak for a minute. I read a Windhoek newspaper that was a week old. I read everything but it all seemed unfamiliar and remote, irrelevant. I didn't want to discuss anything with Hoy, with everyone around ready to kill any real discussion. He looked for too much meaning which tired me out, too.

The platoon commander strode around the vehicle. "Ons moet half nege ry," (*We must drive at 8.30*) he announced, as Piek gave an unseen Hitler salute behind his back. Presently, activity increased around the Mais-Rische werf as all was packed, and the Ratels started and stood idling, their exhausts blowing up dust. Herr Mais-Rische strolled out of his front door putting on his hat while wiping his mouth with a handkerchief, and the trackers materialised from a stand of palm trees where they had had coffee at their own fire.

By mid-morning when we got the call, it had become a particularly hot day, and we had been on the road for some time. We were called to a farm to the north of Tsumeb where a kidnapping had just taken place. It looked a nice farm, the buildings surrounded by tall palms, and other cool trees were dotted about. Our Ratels rumbled into the werf dragging dust behind us. The farm owner was away, and a group of anxious Ovambos stood watching us arrive, and set about explaining that four armed SWAPOs had spent the night at the farm, frightening the women, and helping themselves to food by killing an ox. They had prevented communication with the outside world and in the morning had gone off into the very thick haak-en-steek thorn bush, to the north of the farm house. They had taken an old man, the grandfather, as a hostage, to prevent them calling the army, but after much consideration and debate, they had done so as they didn't believe he was still alive anyway. They were very unhappy and watched us get onto the tracks until we disappeared. We tracked and tore our clothes through the thorns until dusk came. We found him in the dark. The white-haired old black man hung garroted on a fence north of the settled part of the farm. His neck rested on the top wire and a lower wire had been pulled over. His hands were similarly trapped on lower parts of the fence, like a man in stocks. It was a very ugly sight in the Ratels' spotlights, to make your blood boil. His final panicked struggles had mutilated him. We felt no need for speech that night.

Day one. We picked up the tracks again in the burning day. The dust darkened the sweat-run sunburnt faces of the troops and the haak-en-steek scratches on our forearms and legs stung with the salt from evaporating sweat. Our lungs pumped and our feet thudded in the dull dust. There were four sets of tracks moving fast, north and straight, regardless of thorns. They went nowhere near water, sticking to the stony ground, but Mais-Rische's trackers ran like runners on a road. Over open ground, only one ran at a time, kept company by a single section in V-formation behind him. Where the bush thickened, the whole platoon disembarked from the Ratels, and fearful of pom-zeds, or jumping-jack mines, we wove or crept through the stick dry thorns, gingerly tearing them from our clothes. While the situation was constantly being relayed to HQ, the fugitives' path was being mapped out ahead of them and spotter planes were sent to that area. The SWAPOs were aiming for the wild country of east Ovambo, where they might split up, find water, confuse the pursuit and escape to the Angolan border. They had 150km to go, and the first hundred were fraught with a grid of fenced roads, swept and checked daily for tracks. They had no chance but unconditional flight, and in that they put their desperate trust.

We used the wire-cutters on our rifles to loosen fencing wires from the poles to press the wires flat, for the Ratels to cross without destroying them, and ran out of the stony, thorny haak-en-steek country into the long sandy plain that eventually becomes Angola. Part of the platoon went to look for tracks about 10km straight ahead, and soon found them, crossing a sandy cutline into the thick kudu country of game and cattle farms. Thus leapfrogging, the dust changed suddenly from red to white, and the vegetation from dry to murky green. It was more open, with visibility around 50-100m. They ran and the sun went down. The trackers gave up in the failing light, and we returned to Onderra, which was now nearby, for the night.

Mais-Rische's farm Onderra, to the west of Tsintsabis and closer to Ovambo Gate, was where he lived with his wife and some retainers. The children were all grown up and far in the world. Our nights there were always the same – the five Ratels spread around the perimeter of the farmhouse garden, each with a fire, and troops lazing over literature (each other's letters, old magazines or precious incomplete paperbacks and poesboekies), staring at the coals or sleeping, and waking cold and dewy in the silent pre-dawn for German-style meals, bread and homemade blutwurst served hospitably at the kitchen door. But the evening scene was also a setting for arguments, jokes and occasionally, beers. We were terrible drinkers. So fit, so tired out, so sunburnt and unused to it. Drink put us to sleep in a black oblivion. The Mais-Risches were hardened frontier stock. Driving insurgents off the farm was an annual chore which they did vigorously but with evident distaste. A tall masonry watchtower was built onto the house and several of the black retainers were armed with German G3 rifles and could track both game and men. Herr Mais-Rische's own G3 rifle was fitted with an infrared sight that projected a red dot at his target, quite newfangled for then.

Day two. Dawn – and it started again. With the arrival of the sun a quick inversion would take place, raising the ground air temperature by 20 degrees. As morning progressed it became clear that they had never stopped. The trackers pointed out the events of the night's run: a heavy pack had been changed over. A splash of urine. Boots had been removed and the tracks thereafter were made by bare feet. We were shown how to track, to see the mysterious disturbance in the inertia of the environment. See those pebbles? They are unlike the others. And the leaves on that bush? Can't you see the wake on the Earth all the way to the sky? There!

At midday the shimmering tracker out front turned right, signalling the followers to hold. The other three joined him from the Ratels and soon all were following this new route. It lasted a kilometre then turned north again. At times the trace disappeared completely on hard ground or stones. Then the trackers walked circles around the last-known point, and we drew cool water from the taps in the Ratel's sides, until the path was found and the pursuit renewed. They ran and we ran with them. Apparently we were gaining, but they must have believed they would escape, as the sun set as inevitably as before. We separated, we to our cool showers under the Onderra reservoir overflow, they to their possessed insomnia.

Day three. Morning found us once again at a spot marked with toilet paper streamers, the dew drying fast in the undergrowth, and we evolved into creatures of horn, enjoying the potency of our effort, dried out, sweat in white crystalline patches at armpits, shirts becoming black leather jackets with dirt, but we underneath clean like saunaed athletes, fit like racing snakes, drawing power from heat and health from water. There was on this day no more urine, but at midday an empty ampoule was picked up, the contents having most likely been adrenaline. After this they stopped for nothing, running, unbelievably running as if death followed. It did. Again in the afternoon it was close. A spotter plane joined the troops as we entered a square-fenced parcel of land.

Again the platoon split, the trackers sweating and panting and forcing through the whipping undergrowth ahead of three Ratels. The other two, with myself in the leading one, raced along the perimeter track and turned left onto the Charlie cutline, wide, sandy, east-west and bounded on the north side by cabled elephant fences. Overhead flew this incongruous red and white civilian spotter, a Cessna 185, an arm out the window signing wildly to something on the far side. "Stop!" I yelled and Wetherall also yelled "Stop!" The unbelievably real four tracks, hastily raked over by spread fingers but glaringly visible, shot past on the ground next to us. The platoon commander and the gunner spun round in their turret hatches, wide-eyed. They stopped the driver, and then we reversed and they saw the tracks. The vehicles heaved over the verge and snapped through the heavy steel cables of the elephant fence.

Soon the other Ratels arrived, crashing through the trees. Surely they could hear this rampaging. The trackers insisted they were five minutes ahead of us, and the plane could actually see them. As dusk approached red, hot and dusty, a Puma helicopter brought four hounds with handlers to continue the hunt under turret spotlights, but it became a disaster. The dogs, which apparently were young and newly trained, ran terrified from the noisy experience. After recovering all but one of the dogs, we retired to Onderra, the dog handlers confused and worried, the 2IC furious. We now carried three big bloodhound-beagle-cross dogs, and four extra people in the Ratels.

Day four, the last day. They had not stopped and had gained again. The route northwards was, at dawn, still as straight as a laser. By now we were all well into total wilderness, with not a path or pole. The running continued unabated, and became surreal. No fugitive except on the edge of a great horror could do this, a reality so cruel there was no dream but loneliness. Their running awed us and gave me gooseflesh where I leaned against the engine compartment, resting in the hot dead air of my Ratel. The missing dog reappeared unexpectedly, following behind us, and was taken on board our crowded Ratel. It stank of dog, and panted and drooled on us in our hot hole. At mid-morning, we passed a small splash of bloody vomit, but they still did not stop. The trackers began to flag, with seizing leg muscles and others were called in.

They soon arrived in Buffels, a ragged platoon of Angolan Bushmen or Flechas, 31 Battalion, and they sincerely wanted to kill. They ran, all of them together like an angry family, with venom and hate, small figures in floppy browns carrying oversized R1s, leaning into their running like Bushman paintings, sprinting even. They ran the morning away without slowing, until, after several hours of the afternoon, the track bent, turning right and slowly south again in a great arc and bending in small increments, from south to west and from west back to north. Then the Bushmen screamed rejoicing in high-pitched hysteria, as the Ratels crossed their own tyre tracks and bore north again. For on the wheel tracks, clear for all killers to see, trod bare feet, and in absolute mastery of their energy the Bushmen put on speed, panting like lovers. Our part in this war was wrenched from us by its true owners: men with old grudges hard to understand.

And now, true to the character of fate, our vehicle had a flat tyre. The strange procession swept north. Alone and in silence we changed the tyre. Doing this in soft sand is a special operation with an 18-ton Ratel. First, you untie a spare wheel and drop it off the roof. At the same time a big hole is dug underneath the Ratel and the spare is levelled in it. On the armoured hub goes the hydraulic jack and the vehicle is levered off the ground. The second spare tyre comes down also and replaces the flat. There is much loosening and then tightening of heavy bolts. Then the towbar comes off the side and is leaned at 45 degrees against the Ratel. Up the two wheels are pushed, and simultaneously pulled from above with a rope. They are extremely heavy with their armoured hubs. It is a labour-intensive job but with teamwork and swearing it takes less than 10 minutes. We didn't want to miss the action. We raced along the wheel tracks and soon caught up. Due north the humourless horde followed a last mile into an open hectare, where stood, in a field of sorghum, a stake-fenced cuca near a brown waterhole. Between them grew a stand of thick, low, thorny grey bush, and into this led the tracks.

The sky was wide and blue. The Bushmen spread out and walked stiffly into the open, rifles at shoulders already aimed. The vehicles drew up close, surrounding the thorns on three sides, I, standing on a Ratel with an overview that was to be imprinted in memory: a single Bushman ventures into the thorn thicket, a hunter, crouched low, sweat pouring into his eyes and dripping off him, the R1 pushed far ahead of him, his inscrutable friends lined up abreast behind him. He follows the tracks through the sights of his rifle with the concentration of a chameleon. He is unbelievably ready to fire. His eyes are wide, he is unashamed to show his fear to all the world. It is incredible in hindsight: this small patch of bush, surrounded by gigantic throbbing war machines weighted down with weaponry enough to destroy a town, and this man, this hunter, stalks his enemy at great risk to himself, across a tiny space of thorn-shrouded soil. But you cannot beat a Bushman at this game. His stance is low and rigid like a martial artist's, he is holding his rifle like a bow and arrow before him, when from the bush the green tracers wing into the air like a spirit escaping, and the thorn bushes erupt in a cloud of dust as all the Bushmen open up. Leaves and twigs fly out the far side of the thicket. Then there are a few seconds of silence and suddenly cheering, the Bushmen like the barbarians, Huns and Mongols of all time, waving fists and rifles. I am shocked at the brutal bad taste. The small man is dragging it out, dust films on eyeballs, shot in face, arm and stomach, too dry to bleed and skinny, and alone, for the three others have escaped his self-sacrifice and diversion as intended, into the endless haze sunwards.

A bitter melon gets put on his head by Sitas, and thus posed it is photographed. An expressionless face peers over the stakes of the cuca. Soon two Alouette gunships come, and guided by a white smoke grenade one lands, swirling the smoke up into a wild spiral. The dusty body with the unbelievable athlete's foot then gets heaved into it, and it is decided to launch an assault against the most likely direction, at speed. This impatience has some promise of success, but is inspired by a symbolic need for a demonstration of power and climax, like the tantrum of a wayward god. The gunships that have joined us fire down ahead of us, and we shoot with all we have, 20mm cannons, MAGs, assault rifles and Brownings, whipping into the bush at 70km per hour, a charge, a release of tension.

Clumsy Singleton gets the adrenaline jitters, and pulls off a shot inside our Ratel, and the bullet goes through a box of white and red phosphorus grenades stored beneath the turret. Flames drip out, filling the interior with smoke and the fire grows and burns among a stack of mortar bombs. The driver stops and opens doors and we spill out in confusion. We quickly form a circular defence of troops as the attack recedes in the distance, punctuated by the thunder of the gunships' guns resonating in the sky. A fog of white smoke streams from the Ratel. There is panic. The platoon commander, believing his Ratel will be destroyed, is almost in tears. But the dog is still inside. Climbing back on the roof, with my head through a hatch I see the animal, white within white smoke, cowering at the rear. I lean in and by its collar I lift it out, and dropped to the ground, it starts slinking off nowhere in particular. The dog handler is as confused as ever. He is hiding somewhere behind a bush, waiting for the Ratel to explode like in the movies. Meanwhile it is clear to me the fire can be beaten. I and Wetherall start hurling out the flaming mortar bombs (contempt through familiarity). Others throw sand on them, then we spade sand into the vehicle. Phosphorus is virulent stuff. It burns in little patches whenever exposed to air, and seems to run like liquid. The smoke makes you want to spit. The boxes of damaged grenades are buried and phosphorus mixed with sand is dug out again. We thank fuck that none of the detonators had been hit by the bullet. We decide not to carry this stuff permanently in the Ratel again. Finally the smoke is reduced to a thin acrid haze and we continue into dusk. Somewhere out on that wooded plain they are running still.

The platoon came together alone, without the Bushmen, without the gunships. We drifted southwest in the green trees through the slanting yellow rays of sun until the Charlie cutline lay before us. This came out onto the north-south tar road just south of Omuthiya. It grew dark in the Ratel as low beams of light flickered greenly through the thick side windows.

"Singleton jou poes," said Waite.

"Jou poes, Singleton," I said.

"Singleton jy's 'n poes," said Wetherall.

"Poes," affirmed Marais.

"Jaaa, Singleton. Jy is mos 'n poes," chirped Piek from the driver's compartment.

"Ek stem. Singleton jy's 'n poes," came from Van Schalkwyk the gunner.

"Singleton as bevelvoerder, moet ek bevestig jy's 'n poes," (*Singleton as commander I must confirm that you are a cunt*) said 2nd Lt De Jager, the platoon commander, unexpectedly.

A wide dopey grin stretched slowly across Singleton's face. "Ag kommaan ouens, miskien is ek 'n poes, maar julle is ook 'n klomp poeste." (*Ach come on, guys, maybe I am a cunt, but you are also a bunch of cunts.*) We started to smile and talk. Only Hoy stayed silent. And then, coming out of the bush at an angle onto the tar road, 11A drove over the front end of a small red Datsun 1200 bakkie that the driver failed to see in the poor light, astonishing the black occupants. The bonnet was flat on the road. There was a brief altercation, in which we produced a scrappy affidavit of cause of damage, and told them to find assistance nearby at Oshivello, for we had had just about enough that day. We turned right and within 10 minutes were at Omuthiya, which was mostly empty. The infantry and armour tents were silent and slack. We cold-showered and slept in unlighted, eerie solitude haunted with the presences of many battlefields. Like a lullaby the Ratel's engine still thrummed my body and mind, and amongst the leafy comings and goings I dreamed of an RPG drifting slowly towards me. We left first thing in the morning.

I cannot be sure of event sequences for this time. Perhaps this happened before the other thing, or perhaps after. It was the nature of Operation Yahoo! – an endless series of little adventures with one thing leading into the next. Several times we stopped at Tsumeb. Here was the field headquarters for Operation Yahoo! and many battalions passed through here. A few events from the camp at the airport stand out. On our first arrival there as a company our Ratels filed slowly through the gate in the wire fence and into a long sloping field where we always, after that, parked and camped. The last street of the town ended against the fence, so there was a row of suburban houses, like any South African suburb, with lush gardens and many trees. A blonde girl stood at the gate and stared up into the eyes of the troops perched on the roofs of the Ratels. Dirty, sunburnt and horny, 150 troops stared at her as one man as the vehicles came to a stop in their rows. Almost immediately an order came from the 2IC that no troop was to speak to her or pay her any attention, as she was a vuil slet. Like a flower in a desert the vuil slet stared at us while we cleaned and fixed, and when it grew dark she was still there. "Ek naai eerste," (*I fuck first*) announced Warwick generally and that was that. This established, he wandered off into the dark. Sitas followed him without a word and that was settled too. The entire company remained where they were. Only a small clique of scaly Capeys was allowed or wanted it. One couldn't just stop being a dirty, tired, and yet well-brought-up grensvegter all at once, so for most of us it was army as usual. Later I had to walk past the empty house and garden where she was discreetly screwing troops. I wanted to speak to my mother. I knocked on the door of a house opposite the field and asked the woman who came to the door if I could use her phone. I must have looked young and miserable, because with a moment's hesitation she let me in. There were some young German backpackers in the lounge who looked at me surprised. I got through to my mother who sounded not 2,000 kilometres away but in the next room. I explained I was all right, that I hadn't been hurt. It was just after the destruction of the Platoon 2 Ratel, and I was sure all at home would be anxious. But they weren't. They were completely unaware of it, and I got the feeling I was to them a remote entity on the edge of the world. It was a confusing and embarrassing conversation because my jargon seemed empty, and emotion overcame me so that tears ran down my face. The strangers in the room listened in astonishment.

Earlier that same afternoon arriving at the airport, the destroyed Ratel was discovered on a truck under a tarpaulin. Alpha Company could not be held back. We ripped off the cover and carefully inspected it like a swarm of ants, yet respectful and quiet. It was thoroughly destroyed. The insides were shattered and burnt. Parts of rifles and fragments of mortar bombs littered the floor. Also there were chips of bone and scorched meat. In the compartment below the right-hand door there were even large lumps of cooked meat like shapeless burnt steaks. They belonged in one of the body bags. The RPG-7 holes could be counted all around the Ratel, seven, thumb-sized. The wheels were just tangles of wires around the hubs and the barrel of the cannon was bent earthwards in a quarter circle. On the grass beside the hulk lay two body bags, one half full with a very thick lump, and the other containing a meagre collection of remains in a small lump at one end. Labels scrawled in ballpoint on the one read, 'Van Jaarsveld', and on the other 'Wolfvaard'. There was a constant transit of body bags and we saw them at Tsitsabis, Tsumeb and other remoter locations, and they contained the stinking carcasses of blacks in rice-pattern camo clothes, and we were used to them, so they aroused only casual curiosity. These contained people we knew and we didn't touch them. When we asked, we were told that for the funerals the coffins would be made heavier with sand bags. It was the Captain's job to write to the parents. He was visibly depressed and we didn't envy or blame him. We could see he took responsibility on himself, but he took great pains to raise our spirits. He organised a braai soon after, as an event for the company to come together and release their feelings. He ordered all rank insignia to be removed for the occasion.

"Fuck it!! I'm not hungry. The smell of this braai-ing makes me want to puke," said Barry with scary intensity.

"What d'you mean?" I was astounded. He was a voracious eater.

"It's fucking exactly like the burning Ratel. This meat smells exactly like that. It's the most terrible thing I've ever smelt." He rolled the rs in 'terrible'. "I can't even stand this raw meat, ek sê." Later, when I was interviewing witnesses of the ambush, he told me about pulling Lenny, earless and scalped and bloody and briefly alive, from the Ratel, while growing fires sizzled meat in the troop compartment. "I donno how he managed to open the doors to let the other ous out," he said. But of course on that afternoon, when we came out of the dead Ratel's enclosure, the blonde girl was still there, and all the recollection came later.

14
Outpost Life

The 61 maintenance unit, or Tiffies, had set up a workshop at the airport, and here we brought the Ratels every so often for servicing and repairs. The engine steam-cleaners were in great demand by Ratel crews, as they were the quickest and easiest way to make filthy clothes spotless. Just hang them up and spray a jet of steam from top to bottom and watch the dirt run down and out. The Tiffie commander stopped us doing this as soon as he found out about it, instantly creating approximately 400 man-hours of hand-washing. Within the airport grounds a long-drop was dug, one of mammoth proportions. About 15 toilet tops in a row spanned a wide deep trench. Looking in, the level of the crap was 2.5m down (I don't think it was shallow either). It generated a powerful heat that was an idyllic place for flies to live out their dedicated lives, and the air space below your arse was filled with them, sounding like a swarm of bees. Sitting on a hatch, you had to keep waving your hand between your legs to stop them from sitting all over your arse and balls, and they bumped into you furiously. One fine day, true as God (or Glazewski rather, who saw the whole thing), the platform, which was always a bit bouncy, collapsed, and two unfortunates fell into Hell. The rescue team, poor clerks of course from HQ, would rather have left them to their fate and dug another toilet, but happily they came out alive, if emotionally scarred and with a hint of poo.

A less sensational but sadder tale, was that of Hattingh. On the gently sloping lawn at the entrance to Tsumeb Airport, one of the Ratels was well known to leak air from its pneumatic brakes. First light would reveal it 20-30m downslope from where it had been parked the night before. It could be cold and dewy at nights and the natural inclination was to sleep under the vehicles, for the engine warmth and dryness. This Hattingh did, but under the wrong Ratel, and was killed in his sleep. A big wheel rotated slowly onto his face and he held it there like a chock, all 18 tons of it, until it was moved off him. It was assumed that he must have woken up, but the wheel rolled onto his sleeping bag and caught him. He could neither call out nor move. It was entirely his own fault, we decided, a stupid thing that we were well warned about. Later that day we were addressed by an intelligence officer with a big map, who after a lecture on the progress of the operation, changed his tone and told us that the reason we had experienced such adversity over the previous few weeks, was that our faith in God was insufficient.

The days lacked all routine. We could not know when we'd stop and eat. At one stretch I was unable to loosen the laces of my boots for nine days. We had been chasing round the wilderness in an unbroken series of events, when we drove back into Tsumeb. At the airport we parked and were given the order to run across the town to the admin offices to go and shower. This had to be done in the shower bungalow between the office and the officers' residences. From the two long walls projected enough shower heads for a platoon to shower, and we all undressed at the door. Soon every shower was spurting hot water, and steam filled the big space. Flooding soon followed, and running and sliding competitions on the smooth soapy floor, with a great deal of yelling. We got completely carried away and soap fights broke out. In the noise an even more powerful noise cut. Shrill, hurting the eardrums, it went, "Bly still! Ek is die Kolonel se vrou! Julle raas soos kaffirs! Wie is in beheer van julle?" (*Be quiet! I am the Colonel's wife! You're as noisy as kaffirs! Who is in command of you?*) And there she stood hands on hips in a blue denim dress with white belt and enormous white high-heeled shoes, mouth agape and pouring forth noise, in the middle of the floor. Surrounded by 40 naked men frozen in the throes of an energetic cavort, covered in soap suds and with jaws dropped.

"Ek, Mevrou!" called out the platoon sergeant, marching naked energetically, stopping one pace from her and looking her in the eye, stamping his foot impressively to attention in a spray of soap suds and a quivering of buttocks, and saluting neatly (she was an officer's wife). Proving relatively impervious to this tactic, she achieved imperiously, "Ék is die Kolonel se Vrou, en ek gaan julle rapporteer aan die Kolonel! Watter eenheid is julle?" (*I am the Colonel's wife, and I am going to report you to the Colonel! Which unit are you?*)

"Peloton een, Alpha Kompanie, 61 Mech, Mevrou."

"Dankie," (*Thank you*) she replied and lowering her eyes surreptitiously for a split second she spun and marched from the room while the showers sprayed and we began to laugh. We hung onto each other for support. The platoon sergeant smiled wryly and wrapped himself in his towel. Unrestrained guffawing followed her up the hill.

The Air Force transit camp at Grootfontein was a slum. Bungalows gutted and worn by millions of frustrated troops, bursting with sperm, waiting for the plane that would take them home on pass. The beds were mere steel frames and I tossed and turned on mine all night, trying to imagine comfort and oblivion. Mattresses there were none. The wire grid bore into my bones and cut off circulation. I finally groped in the dark past grumbling troops to Eriksen and borrowed a tape for my Walkman. It was '5' by J.J. Cale and I listened to it for the first time there, in the chill pre-dawn hours. In the growing pink light I watched the drive of the Walkman rotating slowly clockwise. Breakfast a la Air Force was cheese and polony sandwiches and sweet lukewarm coffee, and we couldn't see any stewardesses.

We boarded the C130 at 9am. Eriksen and I sat next to the Captain and his wife who kept their baby warm in the iciness of the unheated plane. The Captain asked to listen to Eriksen's music for a while, and heard *'Heavy Horses'* by Jethro Tull. Back at 1 SAI we were a curiosity for the new intake, legendary figures, and who we now called rowers. We noted how pale and young they were and how fresh their clothes.

The seven days' pass fled by like they always did. I visited some old school friends for a dinner, and because I still couldn't drive, I walked, because it was only a few kilometres and I was trained to walk. It rained heavily and the wind blew icy from the northwest and there was a big fire in the lounge and strange girls and I didn't have much to say. After dinner we slumped around the fire and I started talking to a girl for the first time in a year. I started pouring out my soul and wanted to tell so many things, but they were all talking affairs and art and varsity and economics, stuff that meant nothing to me. I was worlds apart from this company and when they finally politely asked me about 'The Border', I broke immediately into sobs and couldn't control myself and I cried with contorted features for Wolfvaardt, who I didn't even know, Wolfvaardt of the light body bag, Wolfvaardt of the crushed cinders. The girl put her arm around my shoulder while the others smiled embarrassed at each other (I saw them through my tears), and so I wrote to her from the war, and she replied, and said she was a lesbian …

After Operation Yahoo! we got a new 2IC, Lt Buys. Some months of intensive Mechanised Infantry training followed much as before, except that the whole battalion trained as one. It moved out into the bush near the base for three- or four-day periods and practised setting up large temporary camps, moving in various types of convoys, and generally familiarising battalion members with the organisation and activities of a large mobile veggroep. We also did some battalion attacks, manoeuvres that lasted all day from initiation to winding down. Directed by the Captain, Commandant de Vries or the Armour Squadron's Major, they began usually at midnight with orders. Artillery moved off and OPs directed their emplacements. Logistics elements formed a camp defended by reserves, while the fighting units crept off in the dark without lights to forming up areas, about 5km from a target (a 'town' or 'military camp' but in reality a collection of Soviet vehicle wrecks towed into position). From there the fighting formations slunk up on the target which was approached at dawn. Hatches closed, we waited as artillery shells finished pounding the target, then the attack began gradually with visible objects being hit by 90mm shells, the 20mm cannons beginning to join in and then the all-out-firefight at about 500m after which fire and movement began, the dynamic stage of the battle. At around midday the target would be overrun. Then it would be cleared up, a slow movement in the reverse direction to assess and make safe – i.e. completely neutralise it. The retreat from the target had to be orderly and lasted until a laer was formed in a safe position at a new location. The sun would be setting or it would be late into the night.

It was by no means always forward, forward, forward. Retreats were also well-practised, with most things, including fire and movement, done in reverse. We learned that retreats could be carried out that would do damage to an enemy. Using the old Boer fighting idea of 'vlugt volmoed', or 'flight with courage', an enemy could be worn out, demoralised, isolated and brought into a vulnerable situation, before being destroyed in a main attack. As with the old Boer kommandos, all depended on being mobile, energetic and independent. As we expected in Angola to come up against numerically superior forces, the mindset of staying power was drummed into us. The manoeuvres involved a lot of wakefulness, hunger and activity, and you slept well afterwards.

> Dear Mom,
> Things are quite peaceful since we've stopped hunting, but the reason we're not coming home in June is something to do with retaliation. We've been working on the problem and I'm not at all disappointed with myself. I've been reading Tai-Pan for a long time now – mainly because of the long interruption – but I'm really enjoying it. I think that King Rat and Shogun are the next books on my list. I've been finding it very difficult to save money – with our first pay at 61 I banked R50, but since then I haven't had the chance. Our new 2IC (who is supposed to do the job) never gets around to taking in our money for banking. I've got R40 on me – would have had 60, but 20 has been stolen, & I want to buy a new pair of headphones, the old ones Hoy broke by crushing them. His clumsiness would bring him fame in the Guinness Book of Records. A plane ticket is now R83 for NSM's, so it's not too much of a worry for me. I am afraid that music has got the upper hand of me: next pass I'll be spending millions again on records & tapes. They are building a new mess & canteen & recreation complex here – it's nearly finished – you see, we're getting ourselves organised up here on the border. It's too cold here in the mornings to roll up your sleeves. I remember that when we went to Etosha we didn't think it was so cold, but I do now. Someone who's just had a month's recovery leave in CT says he shat

himself from the cold. Since we've been here we've had mosquitoes again because of standing water. I was reading about a malaria epidemic in Queens Town, Hong Kong in Tai Pai so I got myself some pills though no one takes them anymore. I hadn't realised that malaria means 'bad air' and the ancients thought it filtered out of the ground at night. Ignorance is not bliss. Anyway, remember that I love & miss you & I'll (I think) be spending 3 sennights at your top restaurant and hotel.

    P.S. I <u>will</u> be coming on pass 3 days after Granny's birthday.

"I c-c-c-c-c-c-can't b-b-b-believe it. They're sending me back t-t-t-to w-w-w-1 SAI." I urged Glazewski to apply to the Captain personally to join Alpha Company, because I knew we needed infantry to fill the empty spaces. He did see him, but to no avail. The Captain who didn't know him from a bar of soap just didn't see him as a worthy or dependable member of his combat unit, and quite justifiably, for he was untrained. Instead, we were sent some rejects from 4 SAI. Whenever troops were requested from another unit, that unit always got rid of its worst, this being one of the unwritten laws of the army. Glazewski with his honesty, endurance and determination would actually have been much better. He was bundled off to Bloemfontein and I never saw him again. Had he not tried and failed to become a driver, he would have felt useful as an infantryman.

    Life in Six-One developed customs and rituals of its own and it felt like home in a dislocated way. Many things took place every single day that were humane and routine. One night beneath the bright stars going to the officers' quarters to take a guard list to the platoon sergeant, I was surprised to see the Captain on his knees in PT shorts praying in his tent at his bed before sleep. I knew in that moment with the profoundest conviction that he was praying about his responsibility for us. This was a man clear in his outlook without inner conflict, and relating this to the troops a short while later, we agreed that we could trust him implicitly to lead us, for he was so far above us in intellect and integrity, that he made us feel unclean, and that if at his command we died, it would be a good death. For what is a death, and how do you choose between a good and a bad one in a time when you constantly expect to die?

    "I'm BORED, I'm BORED!" screamed a troop in the Platoon 2 tents.

    "ME TOO!" and "BLY STIL JOU DOM ENGELSMAN!" *(Be quiet you stupid Englishman!)* rocketed from various parts of Alpha Company's lines.

    "I can't understand why they don't let us do something constructive with our time!" whined Hoy sincerely. "I mean, we could study, or plant vegetables or something."

"Schalkie, Corporal Hoy can't understand why we can't plant vegetables," Piek said to the gunner in strongly Afrikaans-accented English.

"Really! Corporal Hoy! It's very disappointing!" contributed Van Schalkwyk. "I think you should get the whole platoon to ask Commandant de Vries!"

But to isolate himself Hoy had started humming. Word got around and he had to listen to "Hoy, hoe lyk jou ertjies?" and "Pampoen Hoyyyyy!" (*Hoy, what do your peas look like? ... Pumpkin Hoy!*)

A day or two later at a guard parade, we were told to respect Hoy's rank. This in effect drew insults onto him. If he passed by, people would yell, "STAAN OP!" and stand rigidly to attention. No one spoke to him in a normal voice, but instead with melodrama, "Ja, Korporaal Hoy!"

Besides training and being tired it really was desperately boring, all literature having been read or physically demolished, and the *Scope* magazines and *Lag 'n Bietjie Daars* at the guard posts likewise. The dry season came along, with hot red afternoons and distant shimmering dust devils, and the termites cut up and dragged away every last scrap of dry grass, in long twitching spokes radiating from their holes. The air whined with tired cicadas and game came close to the tents at night, for we had water and they could smell it. One night I was guard commander during a period we were expected to maintain a visible alertness at night, by driving a Ratel round the camp with a searchlight on. This provided entertainment. At about 10 o'clock, when I informed the platoon that there was a lot of game standing around the camp on the track I followed, they all came on the next circuit, following the Ratel behind the lights in line abreast. Thirsty buck would stand still until the light passed them by and they were once again in darkness, so the objective was to walk very quietly just behind the advancing line of light and try to catch one. A couple of times someone got very close and the animal would take fright. But on the third circuit, Piet Voges from 11A, evaluated the best rifleman in the company, actually caught a steenbok by the leg, and then let it go again. Later in the night, when I was not driving but operating the turret, we saw the shining eyes of a springhaas sitting far ahead in the left groove of the track. I told the driver to slow down to an idle crawl. Slowly we crept up to the big kangaroo-like rodent and it watched us approach without the slightest movement. The light went past it, over it, and we were surprised to find it flat as a pancake after the big vehicle had passed. We couldn't believe it had not run away in the 10 or so metres the Ratel had to move between it no longer being in the beam of light and the wheel approaching slowly.

Training at the bunkers one afternoon tensions rose in the hot tight space in the Ratel, resulting in a desperate fist-fight for no real reason in the narrow service passage at the back. I had been pushed over backwards and was underneath. We grunted and wheezed and I fought back hard and used my head, for the passage was barely wider than our shoulders and with the webbing on I was going to stay underneath whether I won or lost. Wrenching my temporary opponent's helmet sideways across his face I smashed the side of his head against the steel wall and alternately punched as hard as I could upwards. Blood poured hot and sticky over my face and onto my clothes and when next we leaped out to throw bombs, the turret crew were surprised to see my face and shirt covered in blood, though I was relatively unhurt. You had to strive for equality at 61 Mech, an outpost society with jungle laws, and this was not the only time I was to fight.

After all our training, our next drive into Angola was intentionally more deadly. 61 Mech was expanded through the arrival of many other parts. The camp grew out into the bush, starting 10 days before departure, with the arrival of a second Mechanised Infantry (Bravo) company, two black light infantry companies in Buffels from 102 Battalion, anti-aircraft crews made up from the State President's Guard (20mm anti-aircraft cannons mounted on the backs of Unimog variants, strictly speaking anti-helicopter), field engineers, and a team of intelligence experts and air force liaison officers or MAOTs. It felt to us like a villager feels when his village hosts a festival, such was the activity and the sea of strange faces.

The thrilling general orders for Alpha Company took place in the lecture theatre. A very large map showed northern South West Africa and southern Angola. The Captain, Commandant de Vries and an intelligence officer in turn made presentations with the aid of a blackboard. They told us of the sophisticated and daring reconnaissance of SWAPO and FAPLA dispositions in progress, even as we sat here in comfort, and the constitution and purpose of the force that was getting ready. Involved were the Air Force, with Alouette gunship and Puma troop carrier helicopters, Impala and Mirage F1 jets, and transports, 32 Battalion – the exceptional unconventional infantry fighting unit made up largely of exiled Angolans (this was a professional 'wild' battalion, extremely dangerous and tough) – the Parachute Battalion (Parabats or Bats) of light infantry who would deploy from helicopters, several ordinary infantry units, and 61 Mech.

It was not anticipated that Six-One was to have the lion's share of either fighting or glory in this operation. The targets were elusive SWAPO training bases and launchpads for incursions into South West Africa. These were positioned over a large area of rugged wilderness, but in furtive logistical contact with supply lines from the north. Supplies came to them by unpredictable routes, but often there were links to small towns, FAPLA outposts and roads. No SWAPO base had a road leading directly to it, or it would be easy to find and destroy. On the contrary, the SWAPOs practised strict path discipline to prevent detection by aerial photography. Furthermore, the bases moved incessantly and on suspicion of discovery, would move instantly.

This posed problems for the South Africans. First, the existence of a base had to be confirmed. Reconnaissance Commandos (Recces) in the wilderness followed leads. These could be tracks, the high movement of marabou storks or vultures, vehicles might be heard in the silence of night, dust might be seen during the day or a lone hunter questioned. Secondly, the base needed to be found, observed for its strength and its coordinates established. Other information was gathered if possible: what the commanders' intentions were, were reinforcements or supplies expected. Often a lone Recce or small teams would dog the base within earshot for days or weeks, and even enter it after dark and talk to its members, quite a feat for a white man, though some of the Recces were Angolans. The third problem was to communicate information to HQ. Being perhaps 400km into hostile territory, alone or in tiny groups, Recces depended on a radio relay system. Usually a high-flying plane, or 'Telstar' operating only at night and at certain times, listened for the little scrambled signal from a small radio. The plane, however high and coincidental-sounding, might alert the base being observed and before morning this would be gone. The fourth problem was bringing an attacking force to the position effectively enough to neutralise the base. It must be remembered that in such limitless terrain, the position itself had no value or meaning: success was based on an equipment and body count, full success being the total destruction of the enemy's ability to fight again another day. SWAPOs could make an extremely fast getaway. A five-minute warning would get them scattered over miles of virgin wilderness, and the opportunity would be lost. The Recces in position had to have good communications with whoever advanced on the base, and guide them in. Aircraft were made to overfly a marker set up in line with, and a certain time out from the base. Foot soldiers were met some distance away and led in. The fifth problem was of not giving the attack away until it actually commenced, and the trick lay either in stealth or speed, or a combination of the two. Elements of 32 Battalion could time a walk on foot to arrive silently at the crack of dawn and attack the camp from the east, out of the first blinding glares of the sun, or Puma helicopters, literally brushing the tops of the trees at full speed, could arrive with a force of Parabats and unload them in a position from where battle could be started straight away. Either option could have air support in the form of gunships or attack jets. A combination approach might require 32 Battalion to form up in battle readiness in the dark on one side of the base. At dawn, Pumas would unload Parabat stopper groups who would lie hidden in wait on likely routes of escape on the far side, and Three-Two would simultaneously begin its assault. The stopper groups would kill everyone appearing out of the bush from the direction of the base. It was the role of subtle tactics to get the SWAPOs to stand and fight.

61 Mech's main task was to form instant logistics bases from where helicopters would operate once a battle started. These were known as a HAG (Helikopter Administrasie Gebied). Some 5-25km from a base, depending on the enemy's artillery capability, here helicopters would refuel and receive fresh ammunition for themselves and fighting troops, troops could be held in reserve or be brought for a rest, and a field hospital would be set up. Here also the leadership would monitor events and direct movements, and artillery too could be directed to provide supporting fire. Mechanised Infantry units would also be on standby to rush off to emergencies should events heat up sufficiently.

Our secondary task (or primary, as we saw it) was to attack and destroy large well-defended more permanent bases that might be encountered, as well as conventional FAPLA units that 'mixed in', or on whose close proximity SWAPO bases were reliant for protection. Well-defended bases included those in hilly terrain, as such terrain gave the defenders excellent anti-aircraft opportunities as well as good lines of fire against advancing ground forces. The problem of a vehicle-mounted force was that vehicles were audible for a long distance. A large force of heavy vehicles like Ratels was audible for 50km or more in the complete silence of the flat Angolan landscape: the sound travelled through the ground as a sub-sonic rumble, not obvious to the untrained, but loud and clear to those long in the dense silences. Obviously, if 61 Mech could attack one of these temporary SWAPO bases, it would be akin to overkill, and in this coming Operation Meebos 2 it was not to happen.

15

Into Angola: Operation Meebos 2

After the orders, the next day was spent in a massive stalparade, or inspection of kit and every item of equipment throughout the gathered force. The Ratels were spotless, all weapons were displayed and in perfect order, and the parade ground was filled with proud troops standing motionless before all their things arranged uniformly on ground sheets. It took all afternoon and into the night under spotlights and we were pronounced ready. Standing on a Ratel, the Captain made a speech honest and riveting in its style and content and after that he came down and held his hand in the air. We packed tightly against him, putting our hands on his hand and those at the back putting their hands onto this great pile of hands, and called our battle cry which belonged to us alone and is secret. Then we slept lightly.

The battalion was thundering with engines before dawn. A traffic jam from the intersection on the tar road backed all the way into the camp, and here the parade ground was tightly packed with vehicles in rows waiting their turn, and around the camp and along newly made roads in the bush next to the camp, vehicles waited bumper-to-bumper and side by side. All who reached the tar road turned north and drove 100m apart at 40km an hour. A long line of civilian cars was forming southwards as they tried to slip into the movement of armour. If any had had urgent business in northern Ovamboland, they would have missed it that day. Ratels and Buffels and ambulances, and artillery and fuel tankers and kwêvoëls and trucks, trucks, trucks. When our Ratel finally turned north in the broad day, we could see the resigned frustration on the black faces in a long line of cars waiting for it all to be over. No doubt they would become more resigned and more frustrated as the day wore on. But we were enjoying the drive, the wind in our hair, and things to see away from camp, even if it was mainly everlasting bush. Inside the Ratels troops made coffee over fuel tablets, read poesboekies and talked shit. On the platoon net, conversation was humorous and was played over the intercoms in the troop compartments. I listened to Jim Morrison singing '*Not to Touch the Earth*' and screwed my eyes up at the wind.

Hoy was no longer with us, having taken charge of his own logistics truck. He sat hunched over in the back of this while it drove, eating and reading. He was thus in a position to collect as much as he wished and indeed he took with him to Angola five balsaks instead of one, and they contained among other things, boots of varying sizes, a sand bag filled with dog biscuits, another sand bag filled with instant tea packets, yet another sand bag filled with fuel tablets, spare sand bags, a stack of old *Huisgenoots* and *Scopes*, two spare cleaning kits, and enough socks and underpants to wear a clean pair every day we were away. All was neatly catalogued in his mind, and he would always know when tea, for example, was missing. Whenever we passed near his truck someone would call out, "Korporaal Hoy! Korporaal Hoy!" And he stared back expressionlessly from behind his thick glasses. These had suffered many knocks and were repeatedly repaired with plasters and he had devised a sturdy contraption for keeping them on his head at all times. Often I was taken aback to see the lenses so covered with dust his eyes were all but invisible.

At Ondangwa, the battalion collected for hours, and once again we watched the movement of the Mirage fighters. Gunships patrolled the airfield perimeter and periodically test-fired their cannons downwards in loud reports. We also witnessed Ovambos spilling out of a bus to pee against the fence, the women doing this standing up which we thought most impressive. Then we took the road to the border post at Eenhana this time, northeastwards to enter Angola without attracting too much attention. From there we entered the most uncomfortable bush country and drove off-road, fumbling our way through thorn thicket. You couldn't drive with hatches closed, because of the intense heat in the steel boxes, but open hatches had discomforts of their own. As the vehicles forced their way through the vegetation, leaves and thorny twigs and broken branches showered in, as trees scraped across the roof. With them came spiders and giant stick insects and other bugs and hairy caterpillars and snakes. We sat sweating inside, grimacing against the shower, our laps covered with kindling and picking thorns from where they pricked us. You had to be careful poking your head out as tough thorn trees with fish hooks for thorns swept without warning from front to back, and you could even be killed by heavy branches. The Captain got gashed in the face by a branch and grew a beard, and I was once hooked off the back of the Ratel by a thorny branch, which was very amusing to everyone else. We endured it for months. The endless anticipation in that unventilated steel hot box can't be expressed, sweating, flicking off vegetation and being burned by the tropical sun where it shines through the roof hatch on the same place for hours, because you can't move.

We passed the old Catholic mission station at Evale, where a few forgotten stalwarts still hung around. Here in the middle of nowhere stands a pretty plaster church with Mediterranean roof tiles. Great shady trees surround it. It's a nice place, picturesque. We continued northwards. One afternoon at a stop a fat puffadder crawled out from under the very bush I was nestling in for shade. In fact I heard it rustling near my head. In the Cape they are mostly grey but in Angola, though they have the same chevron pattern, they are greener. I exclaimed and quickly pinned it down with my rifle barrel and picked it up behind the head. We gathered round to inspect its 2cm fangs, and then I cut off its head with my knife, I suppose for a few good reasons. Besides not being allowed to leave my position, it was a long walk to the edge of the laer, and it couldn't be allowed to wander amongst the veggroep by itself. I needed a snakeskin for my hat. And I had never eaten snake. I braaied it on a small smokeless dry stick fire and it was just like fish that needs salt, but had a million small needle-like bones that stuck in my gums. I burned the head in the remaining coals.

As we approached a place called Mupa we came upon small settlements of the most primitive and forgotten backwoods people as can live in Africa. Their huts and cucas were crude with see-through walls of sticks, and they possessed nothing but what few organic things they had made for themselves, and they were small and pitch black and had no stock. I suppose they were hunters, as they had small spears and bows. Unlike other locals, their settlements were in uncleared thickets and there seemed to be no water present. Indeed there was a lot of game in the area, as well as further north where the country opened up and became quite beautiful. There, gentle grasslands swept through tall straight hardwoods and were crossed by numerous anharas and shonas, flat open spaces that in the rainy season collected water. It was total wilderness, there being no signs that people had ever been there. Perhaps it was afflicted by the tsetse fly, but we saw wonderful game including sable antelope that we were expressly ordered by Commandant de Vries not to shoot. They cantered majestically out of the clearings as we entered them, and we all popped out to watch their glossy black forms with proud manes and sweeping horns.

And further north we continued, through the endless trees, until we were far, far north of the border, lurking secretly to the east of where SWAPO was training its men for war.

One afternoon churning through the soft earth, a Ratel from Bravo Company hit an anti-tank mine. Ratels have a screw-in steel drain plug in the floor to help with cleaning. This one's, for some reason, was made of aluminium, probably because it was a replacement made at Omuthiya. The blast blew up through the hole and cut a troop in half. We saw the casevac Puma in its ascent flying low overhead with the body and saw also the dead boy's twin brother sitting on the edge of the floor looking down at us. They had apparently been inseparable.

Quite soon after this happened we began manoeuvring, slowly and quietly and often at night, into potential positions from which attacks could be initiated. Of course we were the last to hear what would happen next, but in a general order group learned that 32 Battalion was deployed somewhere nearby and that Parabats were at the ready, some south at Ongiva Airfield and others also nearby. We started forming big HAGs and helicopters became an everyday sight. Sometimes 32 Battalion companies camped in or close to the HAG, as they rotated duties. There were constant order groups among the higher officers as intelligence came in from Recces. And then came the first attack. 32 Battalion elements advanced on foot, and when they were in position, Parabats were flown in from Ongiva. It was a failure. The base had been hurriedly deserted, leaving bedding still in place and food stores behind. Many attacks were planned over the following weeks, some at a moment's notice, with similar results. SWAPO was aware they were being actively hunted and their reaction time became very short.

We quickly became bored of our repetitive daily routine in Angola of pack up, move, unpack, always at the ready. To relieve this, idiotic behaviour was often necessary. One afternoon I had a brainwave and cut an oval hole in the bottom of a PVC mortar box.

"En wat maak jy, Davies?" (*And what are you making, Davies?*) enquired the platoon sergeant, passing by with his notebook as he took QM requests from the crews at their vehicles parked every hundred metres under the trees.

"Ek maak 'n toilet, Korporaal." (*I'm making a toilet, Corporal.*)

"My donder, slim kind. Kan ek hom leen as jy klaar is?" (*My damn, clever child. Can I borrow it when you're finished?*)

"Ja, Korporaal." When I was finished, I leaned into the Ratel for toilet paper and a spade, and with the roll on my rifle barrel and the new toilet I walked a short way off out of the laer. I dug a hole and positioned the box over it, set the rifle LMG-like down before me as a loo roll holder and faced the wilderness and sat down. We always crapped facing the outside, to keep watch. It was splendid. It was comfortable. There is nothing to compare with the serenity of ablutions in nature. Piek the driver wandered over. He stood a polite three paces away and admired the new furniture. "Werk dit, Davies?" (*Does it work, Davies?*)

"Ja, dis gemaklik." (*Yes, it's comfy.*)

"Kan ek dit na jou gebruik?" (*Can I use it after you?*)

"Korporaal Robinson is eerste." (*Corporal Robinson is first.*) Very quickly every Ratel had one and they civilised the wilderness immensely.

Finally, late one afternoon, a platoon of Parabats in Pumas coming north from

Ongiva by a roundabout route overflew a SWAPO base by chance. Not expecting action, their commander nevertheless ordered the aircraft down as close as possible to the camp and immediately attacked. This resulted in some SWAPO deaths after a short encounter. Engaging and fixing the enemy allowed for the quick arrival of gunships and extra Parabats as stopper groups, but the SWAPOs were already in rapid flight dispersing through uncharted bush, and a hot fast-moving fight over a large area took place. At the HAG we heard what was going on and saw the departure of four Alouettes. We listened to the battle on the gunships' frequency. It gave a vivid picture of violent events miles away, like live radio commentary. You could hear what the troops were doing, how many had been shot by gunships, that there was a lot of smoke rising from a bush fire, that RPGs were being fired into the air out of thick bush and so on. When the tired dirty troops arrived at the HAG later, there was much discussion, for we all now knew as fact and not hearsay that the greater SWAPO family wasn't far away.

Platoon 1 crowded around the back of the logistics truck. Hoy read the names on the balsaks and called then out. Hands reached up for them and troops wandered back to the Ratels with their belongings, for a change of clothes, or to dig out packets of precious cigarettes. Some non-smokers had brought along several cartons and were able, as smokes became scarce, to sell cigarettes for R2 each. I hung around to talk to Hoy. Evening hung dense and quiet in the darkening thickets encircling us. OPs were already out there in the trees, staring and listening where they lay concealed beneath bushes waiting for the three clicks on the radio from the guard commander's pressal switch indicating that the guard change was on its way, or for noises in the dark out front. We talked about how weird it was fighting people we never saw. Of course I can't remember the conversation but it might have been as follows: "You know," Hoy might typically have been saying, "being here is not immoral. Morals are made by societies in their own interest, and our society has declared these people to be enemies. And when you declare a man an enemy, you take away his human rights, in your society, so it's no longer wrong to kill him. The most civilised societies do this. It's a trick they can do. If right now a SWAPO appears over there," and he indicated a deep shadow between two Ratels, "we wouldn't hesitate killing him, without asking any questions, because he is not a person. And we wouldn't feel guilty. But if you went and dropped a bomb on our own troops by mistake ... " I leaped aside, for we were being rapidly approached from the darkness. Whack! and then "Jou Poes!" Hoy whimpered.

"Jou ma se poes, Hoy!" threatened the dark form, "my fokken balsak is leeg gesteel! Waar's my sigarette? Waar's my zol? Huh? Waar's my fokken entjies! Waar's my fokken entjies! Nooit, man." (*Your cunt! Your mother's cunt, Hoy! My fucking duffel bag is robbed empty. Where are my cigarettes? Where is my marijuana? Huh? Where are my fucking smokes? No, man.*) He leaned in and hit Hoy again. I just heard the liquid thumps in the dark. His thick glasses, laboriously mended and padded with elastoplast, flew off into the blackness. The attacker drifted off ranting. Alone we sat down. We held silence in the deeper dark for some while. I could think of nothing to say so I said good night and left him alone with his truck.

We didn't hear the Mirage and Impala bombers while our engines were running. We had driven to a position that was quite open and on higher ground, and formed a HAG at earliest light under the threat of an air raid alert. We saw the surreal sight of formations of Alouette gunships followed by many Pumas like a linear swarm of wasps speeding from the south in the rising sun at low level. As they overflew us in a measured thumping rumble, we saw heavily armed and blackened Bats crowding out of every door. We could see the red and green of the rifle grenades. While our 120mm mortars finished a bombardment they circled the HAG, then peeling off one by one they disappeared across the treetops, to form stopper groups around a large base that 32 Battalion was at that minute approaching, in a long walking line abreast, with many mortars and weighed down with ammunition. Within minutes we heard of a successful contact and the fighting began.

The next thing, 122mm Katyusha rockets began falling on us, hurtling out of the sky with a noise like trains approaching a station, and bursting in impressive grey puffs among the trees over a wide area. Callsign Zero was nearby with Commandant de Vries, and he and Captain Malan were in conversation when this happened, speaking from their turret hatches, and I saw the animated order to move and then the battalion commander's Ratel rushed off to urgent duties. Apparently the rockets were fired by the Angolan Army, FAPLA, from a town called Cuvelai. They knew our position. Without hesitation we quickly performed a relocation of the HAG to a completely different sector, and the rest of the day was busy and dusty, as helicopters came and went loudly with tired troops, rested troops, fresh ammunition, intelligence observers, water, medical teams and wounded. The base was large and well armed and full of SWAPOs and they put up a spirited fight.

For quite a while in the morning the battle seemed a non-event back at the new HAG. From what we could hear it seemed Three-Two were not attacking but merely exchanging fire from cover and lobbing mortars, and the Parabats weren't engaged at all. Even the gunships were only flying reconnaissance at a safe distance. Occasionally we could hear, when no helicopters were near the HAG, the dull echo of a thump far away. Although we were all on immediate standby and the possibility of being called in was not remote, we made coffee and lunch under arms and relaxed, sharing the noon shade with small creatures in a wide perimeter, and called out "Hoy! Hoy!" half-heartedly each time he came past sweating like a pig, on another lap of his daily jog. But Three-Two had done this many times, and fought with patience and caution and skill like a master surgeon, advancing slowly and always under cover. They were fighting accurately but with an expressionless lack of intensity so as not to panic their enemies, gradually taking out the anti-aircraft weapons so that gunships could move overhead the enemy. This was finally achieved shortly after midday, when Mirages delivered a rocket attack on 14.5mm anti-aircraft guns that were well dug in, and in deep defence. The SWAPOs must have realised then for the first time how concerted and unstoppable the assault was, and how frightening it was to have 20mm cannons in the air above you, as well as a competent army coming invisibly at you across the ground. Gradually at first and then increasingly, the stopper groups became busy cutting down fleeing men. In a short space of time, many had already died, and yet there was to be no escape and no mercy in any heart that day. It was not a mass murder, for there was continual fighting, but Three-Two were pacing themselves to avoid casualties and control the slow momentum of their domination.

It was the day of a Currie Cup semi-final, a golden Saturday afternoon in sporting South Africa, but on this nameless African plain another game was being won and lost, and there was no audience, and there was to be no party afterwards. The HAG became busy and noisy mid-afternoon. Choppers landed only briefly and were kept in the air non-stop. The battle was intense during the second half of the match. 32 Battalion attacked with three companies, yet there was as much interest voiced on the assault radio channels for the rugby as there was for the battle. We heard the gunship pilots saying things like, "Zero, this is Dwarf Bravo, we have 12 kills. Er, tell me, what's the rugby score, over." In every Ratel there were two radios tuned: one was blurting the terse sitreps and requests for assistance and the other was blaring the match to nearby troops with attentions divided. I can't remember the score, or even who was playing that late afternoon, but not long after a prolonged cheer in the HAG at the final whistle, I do remember that 32 Battalion stopped attacking and withdrew. The SWAPOs must have thought their defence had prevailed, but soon they, like us, heard the distant whirring of jets growing in the vast empty sky. Then came the napalm drop by Impalas and the swarms of vultures and marabou storks that were drawn across the high parts of the sky, like tiny spots on a transparency, moving towards the dense plumes of black smoke as night began to fall. For as the day waned, it became clear that many SWAPOs would escape when darkness fell, for they were still fiercely resisting, and so an end was put to them in the most pragmatic way a short space of time allowed. Two Three-Twos died earlier in the morning but I don't know if a proper record exists of SWAPO's destruction. I have heard since that the napalm drop was inaccurate and ineffective.

Not a week after that the veggroep advanced to a reported SWAPO base. We arrived shortly after a bombing attack to find it completely deserted, and we drove through it, looking down at small bunkers, trenches, empty cannon emplacements and little grass sun shelters spread thinly over an enormous area, to avoid detection from the air. They were gone, and indeed the SWAPOs were very jittery and few were encountered after this. But they were still there, hidden in the pathless wilderness, and being supplied by furtive means by among others FAPLA, the Angolan Army. FAPLA being part of the problem, our tactics were revised and new things were tried out.

The task force remained at the same HAG as for the big attack for some time. We got to see 32 Battalion daily, as their companies rotated time in and near the HAG, recuperating near the drop-off point for supplies and minor luxuries. They were nothing other than a fucking hard bunch. Although they carried signs with them of being well-paid professionals, like good-quality electrical gizmos and watches, they unnerved us young South Africans because for us they were unusual, hard-eyed blacks, with angry lines worn in their faces that could stare you down, their eyes unfathomably ruthless, and their humour so dour. And they seemed to reject with contempt the notion that we were their brothers in arms. They never joked or smiled and they were taut muscular figures, born to kill. They never chose to speak with us, and did not encourage our visits with them, until we merely lived near each other in uneasy separation.

16

Cuvelai Road

On a baking cicada midday near the now well-worn HAG in the middle of nowhere, my platoon commander told me to prepare 36 HEs, 16 illumination and eight smoke bombs, for a walk. I ran around the platoon looking for bearers. Every troop I approached reluctantly added a bomb to his load. They wanted the bombs to come along. The Patmor is a good weapon, quick, accurate and devastating, and it gives confidence to troops in the front line to have the bombs falling just 100m ahead of them, or closer, if need be. I put two smokes and four HEs in my own load. I put together a heavy webbing that could carry this, and first and second line rifle ammunition, plus an M26 hand grenade. All around me troops festooned themselves gaudily: dazzling gold belts of MAG ammo, the tracers glinting rubies in the sun. Bright green mines, white and yellow illumination mortars, silver snotneus shells and lime-green smoke grenades.

We received hurried orders from the Captain drawn in the dust near the helicopters, blackened our faces and checked ammunition, bedding, sundry equipment, weapons, water and rations. Permission had been granted to dominate the road between Cuvelai to the south and another town, Techamutete, to the north. We were to begin the domination. A FAPLA base at Cuvelai was supplying neighbouring SWAPO bases and these supplies came down the road from Techamutete. Recces, we were told, had seen a convoy being prepared and it was anticipated that night. I have since read that in fact we were monitoring the FAPLA radio communications. Taking prisoners was briefly discussed: we were not to take any, so they couldn't surrender. We were informed of the sensitive political situation. Prisoners would have been very embarrassing to South African peace negotiators. Listening to recent SABC news broadcasts we had heard our presence in Angola 'categorically' denied by Pik Botha.

We were 48. From Platoon 1 we were 34, and with us went a small contingent of strangers from other units, an intelligence officer to observe (this seemed to be a new requirement, sending these guys out for first-hand experience), an engineer to lay mines, an orderly who operated an HF radio for Captain Malan who would lead this infiltration, as well as several MAG and RPG-7 teams drawn from the other platoons. According to the Captain, a Three-Two officer had shrugged the mission off as a waste of time. It is most likely that this officer was the 32 Battalion Recce Cpt. Willem Ratte, though we had not heard of him at that time. But just for the Puma flight at treetop height, it was worth it for all of us. The big helicopters pitched startlingly away from the slow-moving, two-dimensional world of bush we were used to. We used four, 12 troops in each and I had my legs hanging out the door. I was in the lead Puma. I wished I had my Walkman with me to listen to the appropriate music, but that distraction would really have been impossible. The machine vibrated urgently through the warm thin sky, and we loved it. Banking and watching Pumas behind in that same shallow turn above the racing treetops, would give us all insight into the experience of the Puma that would be shot down less than a week later. I might have been in the same helicopter.

Around four o'clock that afternoon we were dropped some 10km east of the road, hopefully in secrecy. Two Alouette gunships had arrived at the drop-off point first, and were circling around the still white column of their smoke marker. We each carried, apart from first and second line ammunition, five litres of water and a day's rations, a light sleeping bag, an M26 hand grenade, a white phosphor smoke grenade, a thousand-foot flare and a bomb bandage. Five MK2 anti-tank mines, 60 mortar bombs, an apparent oversupply of MAG ammunition, Claymores, snotneus (40mm grenade launchers), rifle grenades and RPG-7 rockets were evenly shared amongst the platoon. This was definitely the heaviest combat gear we ever carried, like a cement bag, and we had difficulty disembarking from the Pumas, hovering as they were about 2m above the ground. I can remember thinking my load would collapse me even if I stepped down one foot, and shouting to the pilot (a captain) in the noise, "Go lower!" and he did, as if we were, after all, only reasonable members of a reasonable society, until the footrests were stroking the wind-flattened grass. In these 'real' situations, rank became a job description rather than a social divide. We each did our demanding job, and tried to help each other as best we could.

After being left in a silence complete but for whining cicadas, we took our hats out of our shirts, quickly camouflaged ourselves with grass and leaves, and drifted stealthily though the chest-high grasses and the forests, in a box formation under the physical weight of war, like grass demons with evil equipment jutting out in all directions. Two riflemen armed with rifle grenades stalked 50m out in front as ambush-triggers, and without haste we finally took up an ambush position with very little cover, for the grass was here not even up to our knees, and the trees were tall straight poles with tufts at the top, close to the road. The day cooled while the sun reddened into the trees before us.

The road was nothing more than a grey soft sand track with space for one vehicle only, and deeply moulded by wheels. The Captain personally positioned every one of us with a quiet word on what to do, what to expect, and he left a radio in the care of his orderly with us. We all filled two sand bags and placed them as cover before us. Each rifleman defined his arc of fire with his two mine-probing sticks pushed into the ground in front of him while the engineer dug his five mines into the grooves of the road, and the platoon sergeant set up Claymores against trees facing the road to be detonated electrically. We found a suitable opening in the tree canopy for the mortar to deploy, and then we became silent and lay still for ten hours.

Along the road for 50m the platoon was to stretch when the rear section was brought forward. The ambush was dense in keeping with night operations. Fire on the front would be intense to create the impression that we were a larger force, and everyone was well trained to shoot to the ground, this being so important at night when the natural inclination is to shoot too high. While the riflemen stayed awake a section at a time, we slept. I dreamt of the leopard. She walked up through the trees and watched me in the starlight. Her head whipped and she stared away to the north. I woke up but the world was impenetrably dark and still. After five in the morning on 4 August 1982 Mark Wetherall urged me from a comfortable sleep saying, "The voertuie are coming," and I checked the bombs, packed the smokes away (it was still black night) and prepared my kit for a quick getaway. Of course now all the bombs had been given back to me by the rest of the platoon and lay in neat rows about me so I was keen to shoot off as many of them as I could. I felt well rested and clear-headed.

A sliver of moon hung in the treetops across the road. As I settled down to wait, I listened to the breath-stilling faint drone of engines while the rear section ran to take up positions north of the ambush. The platoon sergeant came round and asked us if all was well. It was, and we could see his dark shape passing along the front line of the platoon until he lay down with his team of RPG men and his Claymore switches. The changing harmonies and discords of revving and slowing motors at first seemed to be only a part of the natural murmur of the night. They were more than half an hour away. The silence around our own position was absolute. You could hear a pin drop in the sand. As they came closer we tried to identify vehicles. Tanks would mean a quick redeployment to deal with the potentially dangerous situation after the detonation of the mines – we expected them to form a line across the road and make a sweep towards us, at least that's what we would have done. The mines in fact failed to explode, confirming everyone's low opinion of other units, especially engineers – "a useless bunch of cunts!" – but the idea was to move away from the road with RPGs deployed in wait among the trees to attack the armour from the side if possible, and the rest of the platoon split into sections and further back, safe in the darkness, mobile and in reserve. The trick would be to put our eggs into several small but effective baskets, to neutralise the armour and trap the convoy between damaged vehicles. Flight was not ruled out as an option, especially if, as we ourselves would have done, they started shooting dense and low before they saw us. The extra RPG men knew they would draw fire and were picked from willing volunteers. We only heard trucks. The ambush was to go ahead in the static layout as planned.

As the noise became loud and immediate we became rigid with tension. Then I saw through the trees big black shapes, without lights, feeling their way in first or second gear. The moon reflected in the shiny black windscreens towering above us as we lay flat. Like a doctor giving a small child an injection, the Captain's soft controlled voice had been talking reassuringly on the radio all through the long approach. Now from his position at the extreme south of the ambush he was saying, "Wees kalm, wag vir my bevel. Mortier! maak gereed om 'n verligting bom te gooi ... wees kalm. OK mortier ... hang die bom ... vuur!" (*Stay calm, wait for my command. Mortar! Get ready to throw an illumination bomb ... stay calm. OK mortar ... hang the bomb ... fire!*) The bomb rang on the metal of its pipe, the bang slammed through my arms, and immediately a thousand-foot flare whooshed into the sky in a pillar of light from the Captain's orderly who was right behind me. CRASH! At this signal I saw our RPGs and a fabric of red tracer flash left and right across the killing ground. My first illumination bomb opens and hangs above the trees. It's a bit high, but it's there and strange shadows in the bright forest tremble and swing as the artificial sun swings from its parachute, and they grow larger as it descends. Everyone fires their first shot as one, the accumulated sound of many RPGs firing and exploding, an arrangement of Claymores, five MAGs, 30 assault rifles, rifle grenades and mortar bombs. I throw them in my predetermined pattern, one HE 300m left at the road, three HEs right 500m, one illumination across the road. I repeat this pattern as fast as I can, four times, the mortar digging a hole in the ground you can put a small biscuit tin into. There is not the least pause in the sound and every shot is a good one. In the wild flickering light, I see the foremost truck lurch out of the ambush on the left. It careers on and off the embankment. I think that the driver must be shitting himself. The second stops dead right in the centre and RPGs slam insolently. Its windscreen is gone. Smoke and dust is thick. It is a killing ground. But the machine guns have already been ordered to turn, firing north up the road in a river of tracers.

Something on the truck right in front of us starts exploding astoundingly with brilliant white flashes. The shockwaves go right through our hearts and the trees shudder. Immediately from the Captain, traffic light red signal flares, cease fire after 30 seconds max. In the sudden silence we hear the last of my bombs exploding to the north: Boom … Boom … Boom … Laughing and chattering softly with the release of tension, we rise from our stations, move back to a big tree identified the evening before by the Captain as the assembly point, and from there file briskly away in our sections while feeble mortars whoosh and bang where we've just been. The light from the burning attracts the enemy bombs. Our backs are lit by the popping truck – incandescent sprays of Angola's pain into the sky, and the tree stems and us flash white like dancers in a strobe.

Behind me walks the intelligence officer. He is muttering, "Fu-uck … Jeesus … " For 2km we walk into the rising sun and then stop to contact our HQ, the Captain breaking radio silence. Sitting 10 paces from him with my back to a cool smooth tree, I can hear the voice of Roland de Vries and excitement on the other side. Intelligence reports suggest we have just held up two companies of FAPLA infantry and a supply echelon, and so we believe that we are outnumbered about four to one. Radio intercepts tell that FAPLA thinks they are outnumbered. Our northern observation post about 400m off reports in a whisper that he can hear vehicles, possibly tanks, moving around, a counterforce possibly being assembled. He is given the benefit of the doubt. Three RPG men, two MAG teams and the platoon sergeant disappear rapidly and silently northwards into the dappled cool forest dawn, with low orange beams of sunlight striking trees. To us at our rest all seems peace. Our packs are much lighter, the HEs are mostly spent. Most people's first line ammunition is low. They reload. The explosions have ceased. The water in our bottles is not yet hot, so some of us mix milkshakes and cooldrinks, eat energy bars and raisins. There is a general feeling of well-being and friendship across the ranks. We obey orders with something like gratitude.

"Ons hoor tenks noord van ons posisie. Ons tenkammunisie is laag en my manne is moeg. Ek versoek lugondersteuning," (*We can hear tanks north of our position. Our tank ammunition is low and my men are tired. I request air support*) which is not true: we are hyped and have energy for a lot yet.

"Ha! Hulle sê hulle stuur twee miracles!" (*They say they're sending two miracles!*) A short while later a conversational English voice speaks on our frequency.

"One-Zero this is Spirit over."

"Spirit, One-Zero, compliments of the morning, go ahead," and the Captain's face bursts into a broad grin. All of us nearby listening grin back at him.

"One-Zero good morning to you we are at 10 fathoms coming up overhead your position and we can see smoke straight ahead over."

"That is a truck burning on the road. The convoy is stopped to the north of it. We have heard tanks. Confirm and knock them out." At that moment a dull whistling grows in the air and rapidly a roaring reverberates through the forest and blocks out the rest of the conversation. The two Mirages dive above us and shoot the shit out of the road for some minutes. They make us feel much better. The diving and the afterburner climbing and the 40mm guns, blast the gentle morning and once again adrenaline is pumping on the forest floor. The noise is immense. For just a second I see the glint of a Mirage through the treetops above us. I expect a delta-wing, but it isn't.

"I can see one burning truck, but that's all. I see no tanks, and no other trucks."

"Spirit, thanks for coming to my party you are welcome any time One-Zero out."

"Only a pleasure changing to home news out." They fade away. From when we first called them until the silence is again complete less than 10 minutes have passed. Our spirits drop at the suggestion that our ambush has yielded nothing.

We want to search our gain, so we kit up in the returned, but pregnant, silence, and after a long circular walk and late morning we approach the spot from the south, following the road. Four Alouette gunships, one apparently containing the battalion commander Roland de Vries, overtake us along the road, and we turn our bush hats inside out, dayglo sticker up. Because of the noise and our walking, I don't hear the Captain's continuous conversation with him but he calls out to us information as he receives it, to appraise us of what is ahead. The gunships start shooting with the die-you-fucker double-tap of 20mm shot and detonation (RRR! RRR!), and telling us of activity around four undamaged trucks parked in the trees and more some distance up the road, parked on the verge. A FAPLA group has been sent to recover their property. Mirages fly too fast for clear observation of ground activity, although the help they bring is quick.

"Daar is infanterie om te clobber! Oppie looppas!" (*There is infantry to clobber! At the double!*) calls the Captain and we run towards the sounds. My feet are by now blistered and the smelly ear-seeking mopani flies are in earnest again. Several lie drowned in the corners of my eyes. External Angola heat meets internal blood heat all around my skin. My pulse throbs painfully and my heart hammers against my ribs. The remaining loose bombs clank heavily in my backpack.

While two gunships search onwards to the north, shooting, the other two whine back over our heads in the direction we have come, towards Cuvelai. In a few minutes they report a convoy of 10 armoured troop carriers, BRDMs, coming our way, still many kilometres off. Forces are moving to surround us. I don't at this stage hear the Captain's request, but a valgroep of Parabats is sent to him. Two sections, heavily armed with mortars and RPGs, are dispatched with their commander to the south to intercept the armour, and the other two, lightly armed, are sent to our own position, to be under the Captain's command.

A kilometre or so further we sweep up to the first truck. He'd not escaped the ambush after all, but had taken bullets and crashed into a tree. A man lies face in the dust where he had minutes before been trying to run from a gunship. He smells like a fish market, before I see him I smell him, his insides. His internal organs are neatly sliced and visible, and still-laced rings of leather encircle his ankles above where his feet are blown away. There is a cordite haze. Some RPGs, us mortars and a section stop and protect the platoon's rear, as led by the Captain it attacks. I have never seen the Captain so cold or heard his commands so clear and lethal as in this moment, when he organises his small force into an attack formation. Each man is completely ruled by these commands like one possessed and outside of himself. The attack moves off into the trees but the presence of the commander remains whispering everywhere.

We sit with the intelligence officer and strain our ears and eyes for tanks and personnel carriers that might break through and come from the south, from Cuvelai. Shooting erupts from up the road, in fits and bursts. This is not a firefight but a cautious sweep. Ammunition is scarce. At one point someone fires 11 shots urgently on rapid without a break. We count the shots, everyone remembers 11. Troops are shooting as individuals, as and when they need to, though there are some mini-firefights. Johan Peach shoots a FAPLA captain, and 12 others die also in a short time. FAPLA once again hits the road.

Half a kilometre north of the exploded truck is the next truck, the tail of one of my bombs lying near shredded rear wheels. The Alouettes search the area but we are alone. They don't miss anything in the flat, evenly treed Angolan landscape. Half an hour later the Captain arrives back from the further trees surrounded by his favourite troops, shorter than many of them but given every unconscious gesture of respect and approval by them. Destined perhaps one day to be known to thousands of troops, surely he must love this command more than any other.

Like an epicentre of everything lies the second truck, the site of a hundred explosions of the burning Katyusha rockets it was carrying to Cuvelai, to be fired at us. We are instructed not to approach it, except the engineer who is forced to dig up his unexploded mines. How he finds them I don't know, the road looks very different now. You can't even see where the road is. We empty our sand bags where we had hurriedly left them, and pack them and our mine probes away. There is much to discuss as talking is allowed only now for the first time. Who was where, who saw what. The FAPLA captain's wallet contains a thick wad of new 2,000-kwanza bills with a shrapnel hole through it. We each take an identically damaged note as a souvenir of this day.

After the arrival of two sections of Parabats in two Pumas, which landed in the road north of the epicentre truck, to support us in our exhausted and ammunition-depleted withdrawal, we destroyed the first truck with a well-placed RPG because it wouldn't start, and drove away across country resting in the remaining two, a Ural and a Scania. I don't know what happened on the road to the south with the other Parabats and the approaching FAPLA armour. Maybe they turned back.

Our Parabats loped along beside us freely in staggered lines like a ranging pack of wild dogs in hunting silence across the leaf-strewn floor, carrying only rifles with 50-round magazines and water bottles. All the trucks were heavily loaded with ammo, including more Katyusha rockets marked 'GRAD P' in Cyrillic, and from the leading truck we also took some spaghetti (it carried several tons of it, made in Spain), Danish tinned tuna and smoked pork, Dutch powdered milk and half a ton of Zambian yellow mealie meal, which the entire veggroep had for breakfast for weeks after, with our ratpack condensed milk.

17

Shot Down!

We almost forgot about home, in the seemingly endless, aimless creeping from place to nameless place. For a while we were in the company of a contingent of Zulu light infantry volunteers, who somehow crossed our path. When in laer, we chatted with them. They were mostly frustrated and annoyed at not getting any opportunities for action. They were well-trained and disciplined (we could tell the difference), and acted all-dressed-up but with nowhere to go. Perhaps they did get some action later. I wondered who they were politically and why they were here. It seemed strange for South African black volunteers to be here in a time of white conscription, even if a great many South West African black volunteers fought fiercely to defend the DTA democratic process against SWAPO's intended one-party state by armed revolution. Some of our Natal farmers' sons spoke Zulu, and as a token of friendship offered some of our captured yellow mealie meal, but it was refused with contempt – only white mealie meal was considered edible for humans, yellow being animal feed. A Puma flew in steak and Castle beer in cans one afternoon, arranged by Commandant de Vries. The steak braai was a treat but the two Castles each were warm and foamy and when we drank them in the hot evening, being tired, fit and sunburnt, we quickly passed out.

> Dear Mom,
> I haven't heard from you since I left Cathedral Peak, but I expect it's the SAW–PO's [Suid Afrikaanese Weermag (Army)–Post Office's] fault – very little post has arrived. The only way post can get here is by ************** & many other channels. We're quite apart from civilisation, but I listen to Radio SA, English or Afrikaans, nearly every day, and little things like the weather in Cape Town seem very interesting. Some rather sad things have happened here. Last week we talked to a ************* who had been just behind the unlucky ****************. Right now I'm tired of everything, we're always on the move & I just want to come home. If I got a dishonourable discharge & came home immediately I think I'd be glad. So, what to tell you? My walkabout's still going strongly, I've got a ruddy tan on my arms, and how are everyone, Rusty and my hi fi? I may come home in Scorpio or slightly earlier. Write double amounts,

give me every bit of news.

Finally we saw the Cuvelai River we had heard about in the order groups, and which seemed to dominate our wanderings. It was little more than a stream and was not flowing, but was instead a series of rocky pools. Though it did have steep banks, it was fordable to Ratels in places. One day the veggroep strung out along it and we washed. We thoroughly altered the ecology in so doing, because fish and every type of water insect lay dead on the surface afterwards. The water hadn't been perfect to wash in to start with, but we felt clean. Moving along the Cuvelai for a few days we tried our hands at catching fish in the pools using grenades (when no one was looking) and as these proved to be more effective than necessary, we threw in just the detonators, and these worked well. The kurper were small and better not eaten.

We heard, about this time, that a platoon of 32 Battalion, 45 men, had attacked a SWAPO battalion much further to the southwest near the border, and had killed 200 armed fighters in a day-long fight, and captured large stores of ammunition. We were beyond impressed. This was Operation Super which had actually happened months before, but we only heard about it now, while in the company of 32 Battalion.

I had another face-to-face with a snake, but this time the tables were nearly turned. It was dusk and we were digging our daily foxholes when there was a panicked cry of, "Slang! Slang!" and "Dis 'n fokken mamba!" and "Kry vir Davies!" (*Snake! Snake! ... It's a fucking mamba! ... Get Davies!*) With a spade in my hand I rushed off to bolster my reputation and saw, in a circle of Platoon 1 troops, a black mamba. When it moved, the circle moved, and fast. So fast that the retreating side was having to run. I went straight into the centre and immediately the black lightning went for me. I thumped the spade on the ground and it reared cobra-like with spread hood, which it quickly folded again and sped off in another direction. I ran after it and put the spade on its back, and it darted back over the spade and lunged at me. I shrieked like a little girl, and fled, and it followed, keeping pace. Now I got its focused attention, and it chased me at an unbelievable speed with its hood half opened and off the ground. I couldn't get more than two paces away from it without taking my eyes off it and just running like hell, which in that moment of showmanship would have been humiliating in front of the audience. Marais ran in from the side and chopped it in half with a spade. The part with the head kept coming and stayed reared and alert, until after it lost strength and began to die. I will never mess with a black mamba again, and I recommend you don't either. They are grumpy.

"Zero, this is Giant One. Giant Three is down." In an airborne assault on a SWAPO base a Puma helicopter had been lost with 15 men. We spoke to some

Parabats the next day who had been in the Puma following behind: while in a shallow turn to starboard, tracers darting up from rising ground had hit the helicopter in the tail and it had fallen like a camouflaged stone, smashing into pieces and bursting into flames. They had seen their friends flung out and falling like insects alongside the spinning wreckage. There was talk of an SA-7 hand-held missile, but from officers the verdict was a 14.5mm or 23mm anti-aircraft gun. This happened on 9 August 1982.

As anticipated only the dog tags identified the dead and only prior knowledge identified the Puma, for all was utterly destroyed. Among the debris only 14 spines were found, but it was very unlikely that the missing person was either alive or a prisoner. The SWAPOs had visited the crash site first, according to tracks found at the scene. Afterwards, 61 Mech sent out some Ratels with a truck and all was loaded and driven south to Ondangwa, and it was kept away from the Parabats lest they see it. Soon after this we gave the affected company a lift on the Ratels to a new laer and they were sullen, but vengeful, towards SWAPO for what happened. That particular attack had however not been entirely unsuccessful, as equipment and documents had been captured and a handful of enemies killed on the hot stony ground. In the attack a Parabat's camera was recovered, with film showing scenes of bloody slaughter. We were severely warned about the dangers of cameras, because these photos would certainly have ended up in a hostile foreign press.

Not long after this, a second road ambush was hurriedly planned. Recces watched an enormous FAPLA convoy coming down the road from the north, loaded with weapons and ammunition. They counted between 60 and 70 vehicles, trucks mainly, but also armoured personnel carriers with heavy machine guns. It seemed that the last ambush, performed by foot soldiers, had convinced them to come in strength, with armour and companies of infantry. But they could not yet have heard the secret that we, 61 Mech, who had done them grievous harm before, were here en masse. We had always lurked in the pathless forests and had taken no part in the assaults on the bases. For all their strength, they were for us still the softest of targets, trapped seals to a ring of clubbers.

As night was falling we could all see it: a vast straight-edged wedge of fine convoy dust, climbing high in the still air on the northern horizon, not easily discerned from the clearer blue. We were near the road west of where it split into a V, with one road leading off towards the southeast. The convoy was not headed that way. At the junction stood one platoon of four Ratel 20s from Bravo Company with a Ratel 90, hidden back in the trees, which were fairly thick in this area. They would drive forward and spring the ambush when the last vehicle had passed their OP sitting up the road. Trained densely on a broad triangle between the two branches of the road were the 120mm mortars and the 81mm mortars. About a minute after the ambush started, they would bomb the triangle, destroying vehicles that escaped there, and keeping the rest on the road the convoy was expected to take. After a while they would begin elevating their weapons, bringing the fire closer until it was on the road itself. Five kilometres down each branch of the road was a platoon from Bravo plus a Ratel 90. These stopper groups would close the trap on the ambush. Alpha Company with the remaining 90s sat in a long line facing east 500m from the road the convoy would be trapped on. As the artillery began drawing their bombardment towards the road, men and vehicles would start to flee toward us. Once engaged, we would advance towards the road destroying everything in our way. It was a trap only the hand of God could lead you out of.

 I felt a complex anticipation of guilt sitting there, thinking of the men and trucks that would soon come fearful from trees in front of me, young men longing for their homes in the distant north, just like those dead ones we had inspected on the Cuvelai road, and like them, with smiling family photos in their pockets, driven from behind to be killed by me and my friends in the grassy open space, by heavy weapons that would punch great holes in the soft trucks and splash flesh to the wind. The feeling was almost sexual like a grinning devil in my lower belly. And yet I felt, as did the others I was with, the anticipation of satisfaction, just like a snoek fisherman eagerly awaits the run and then the wholesale harvest of living things. There was to be no communication with those caught in this terrible trap, only efficiency when this very night, at midnight, we turned our searchlights on the killing ground in righteousness.

 As the night got later it changed from a regular ordinary night to one of depthless fantasy, with the ground no longer the real ground, and trees no longer trees, but the silhouettes of stage props waiting in the dark for a play to begin. Our minds were getting ready to shield reality from an event that needed to be isolated, and not meld. But shortly before midnight we packed everything up and dismantled – the convoy had cut its lights and engines and stopped. Had they seen our dust earlier like we saw theirs, and had they grown afraid? We moved off, and halfway to dawn lay down in a nameless dark. Sleep wouldn't come, it couldn't overpower the images of things nearly real.

 SWAPO became hard to find, so we walked some wonderful patrols in Earth's most beautiful and empty country, silent except for exotic birds. On one such patrol walking behind the Lieut I counted 1,275 steps by hundreds on my fingers. One-thousand-two-hundred-and-seventy-five of my patrol steps was 1km. The Lieut carried a compass. From my neck hung my rifle and on my shoulder I carried the patmor. As usual my various heavy straps conspired to try and strangle me. I listened to the continuous soft rustle of the platoon as in formation it flowed through the gradually undulating grass. It was like a suburban park: open lawns between neat straight trees. We saw no signs of people at all, past or present, and none of the other patrols reported anything. If the wind was right we could smell the veggroep's diesel and oil far out on our return approach. Because of the revealing smells we were forbidden to use deodorant at all times, and toothpaste and soap were forbidden before patrols. Smoking was definitely taboo.

Late in the day on one such patrol we were picked up by Ratels belonging, I believe, to an intelligence unit. The crews were extremely clean, and the turquoise interiors as new, nothing like our own, which were battle-worn and filled with sand, leaves and bugs most of the time. Even the air conditioning worked in these. I'd had no idea any other Ratel units were operating in our area. They felt like spacecraft, their crews like aliens in this place of Pan, and as I lay in my webbing below the turret at the left-hand door, I drifted into a dreamless sleep, the vehicle moving like a boat over the calm sea near my home, thousands of miles to the south.

Every few days while relocating base, the Captain insisted on PT and training to prevent us becoming tourists. Unexpected calls to deploy jerked us out from where we sprawled in the steel compartments, like fevered puppies out of hot dizzy sleep, feet boiling in boots, dry-mouthed and headachy, to don kit and run like hell in the noon sun in the dusty heat and diesel fumes. Because of the constant dust, sweat and travelling we were dirty. Sometimes I got my boots off only once in 10 days, to find my feet a startling white and slimy and stinking.

One night the 120mm mortars, which were deployed close to where I lay on the perimeter, fired 64 bombs at a convoy some way from our laer, controlled by a Recce in a tree. I must have been tired because I alone in the veggroep did not wake up from the colossal noise of the firing. The lights of the convoy had split into smaller groups and gone out but petrol fires were seen to burn for hours.

> Dear Mom,
> Life goes about its dreary way up here, & dirt follows us like flies (as you can probably see by my finger prints. Stress & strain are my worst enemies, & I'm going to pull together my last pleasantries and pack them into this letter. Are you all well? Is the new studio / house going fine? Tell me if Bishops is still all right & which 1st team is Keith in? (huh?) Mom, has that flu bug definitely gone? It's starting to warm up here. It was always hot by day, but now the nights

aren't as cold as they were. Even I can get tired of these endless flat forests (it being forest, not jungle or bush). This place's main products are mealies & fish – we still live on seized yellow mealie meal; I had a chance to try some fish, but it was like "Lucky Pet" & I threw it away. I've also had such products as imported Dutch condensed milk & canned pork. Didn't I tell you that Michael Eriksen and Peter Barry were injured when their machine rolled some weeks ago. So they're most likely having a grand rest back at 61. Wish I was there. Or better still, I wish I was where you are.

After a gruelling few days and nights of bumpy driving, we had set out a laer and lain down to sleep at dusk in a new area. The Ratels were filled with sand and thorns and leaves and there were few chances to stop and clean, and we were starting to get too tired to care. We were travel-tired and dirty, having washed in the non-flowing Cuvelai River more than two weeks before. I drifted into sleep thinking of my watch at 4am the following morning. The vibrations of the engine still hummed in my awareness, as a sailor feels the sea on his first night ashore. The sun still shone on humid green bush. Lenny still steered his Ratel after the trackers who were ducking under low-hanging thorn trees. The Captain and Corporal Du Toit talked in his headphones. The branches swept up across the sharp brown nose. The leaves and caterpillars showered it. He saw the bark being stripped off the branches exposing the moist white living wood beneath. He heard the white thorns squealing across the thick green glass 10 inches from his eyes. He was entering a sunny green clearing. He saw the Bushmen crouching in their tracks and hurling themselves back towards him. The muscles in their light brown necks were bunched into ropes. Their lifting feet left little clouds of dust hovering amongst the grass stalks. Their mouths were open wide and their eyes were pleading at the command crew in the turret above him, but he could not hear what they said. Over the shoulder of the right-hand Bushman was a thin grey smoke and the front end of an RPG rocket, rotating slowly clockwise. It was greeny-brown and the paint was wearing off and the detonation button shone like silver in the sun. He knew then that he was engulfed in the explosion, but he felt only the clear presence of three others with him in the double world. Two rejected him and they went away, but the small third one waited for him like a happy child. Strangely he felt a rustling restlessness from among the infantry behind the turret, so he reached out his hand and when it moved the left door opening lever, he was aware of another rocket stabbing the Ratel on the right side. Two others became dead there but he still felt an anxiety to get out. So his right arm went out to the right lever and pulled it open. The left door was opening now and people were exiting from it, leaving his awareness. Another one became dead right in the doorway. Lenny went up past Cruywagen and through the open hatch in the turret. He hesitated there a bit, because Cruywagen was watching him. Their noses were touching. More rockets were entering and Cruywagen was flinching at them but they didn't bother Lenny. Finally he left him there and sat in the rising smoke above the clearing for some time. He saw the Captain come with his R5 rifle, and Peter Barry moving at his Ratel with great vigour at the place where the smoke was coming from, but he lost interest and turned his attention to the bright empty sky. A torch in my face woke me. First the air felt cool in my throat and then I was surprised it was only 1am. Adrenaline pumped into my chest.

"Pak op en wag in die Ratels," (*Pack up and wait in the Ratels*) was the instruction from my waker, and soon I heard distantly a Ratel starting up, and then nearer, and soon many powerful engines were rumbling in a steady idle. We sat sleepy in our pitch-dark box waiting for the platoon commander to return from the order group, and after a short wait he climbed up and gave the order to start. The engine refused to ignite, and we called for a tow start from the closest vehicle. Several failed attempts later and we called for the Tiffies. A Tiffie Ratel, basically a giant motorised toolkit with a tow crane at the back, quickly pulled up with a staff-sergeant and two assistants, all of them mechanics. They really stank, because Tiffies worked harder and for longer hours than anyone else, and got excessively dirty and greasy, working continuously on hot engines, and not getting a chance to clean up for the duration of an operation. These guys hadn't washed in months. There is no way you could hand-wash the solid black grease out of those overalls, in any case.

Soon we were rolling across the soft Angolan forest floor in pitch darkness in a strangely silent container. The Tiffies clambered across from their moving tow Ratel with tools and work lights. We gave them space at the back and they opened the internal engine hatch in the rear passage. Meanwhile the platoon commander at the base of the turret gave us orders.

Techamutete, a larger FAPLA garrison town, had to be neutralised and we were about to launch a full mechanised surprise attack at dawn. Techamutete base was supplying a network of SWAPO camps throughout the region with arms and the supplies sent by the Soviet Union and Western nations that came down the road from Cassinga to the north and went as far as Cuvelai to the south. But mainly, a FAPLA brigade, some thousand-odd men with armour, was cause for concern because they were backing up the supply effort to SWAPO. Because Techamutete was surrounded by hills, an airborne attack was prohibited because of the excellent anti-aircraft advantage given by high ground. The memory of the wasteful loss of a

Puma and many lives was still strong. This would be a frontal attack and it was set for 7am or just after dawn, and Platoon 1 (us!) was to lead the assault onto the target and be the central axis around which the veggroep would form up. That is, if the FAPLA brigade was still within 50km when we arrived, and of course if our Ratel started. In the meantime, Corporal Human the Section Leader of 11B (Section 2) led the battalion by compass without any lights. All one could occasionally see was a dim gleam of red cabin light from the driver's compartments in the nearest vehicles, though the light was nearly neutralised when seen from the outside because of the green tint of the armoured windows. Hanging upside down through the open roof hatch, one of the Tiffies swung with arms deep in the engine. We made him coffee and stripped our rifles.

"Gee die olie aan Evan. Now where's that fukken deurtrekker … " We used engine oil to lubricate the working parts, and poured it in liberally, because we knew they could get very hot and filled with carbon, and have to keep working for hours. I passed the oil in a fuel tablet tube to Marais.

"Has the water fukken boiled yet?" I asked. "Wetherall! has the water boiled?" On the shelf before us that was the two rear wheels' bulkhead a fire bucket was perched over an esbit stove. He uh-uhed a no. Normally our own dim red cabin light would allow for nocturnal activities, but now the Tiffies' work light burned brightly.

"What direction are we going?" asked Waite, "Daar's geen maan of sterre nie."

"Ek weet nie, vra vir die gunner," suggested Singleton. "Fok! Daar val die poeslike olie! Op my broek." (*I don't know, ask the gunner. Fuck! There falls the cuntish oil! On my pants!*)

"Singleton, jou sif naai! Wetherall, vra vir Van Schalkwyk in watter rigting gaan ons," (*Singleton, you syphilitic fuck! Wetherall, ask Van Schalkwyk which direction we're going*) said Waite. Wetherall ducked forward and tapped the gunner's leg. "Schalkie, what direction we going?" he came back and took off the boiling water. "Northwest," he said, tearing open a coffee packet. Up in the darkness of the turret, the 20mm cannon and machine gun were being prepared by Van Schalkwyk, assisted by the platoon commander, and Wetherall and I got ready all the 60mm mortar bombs, 10 cases. In the infantry-section Ratels, which were more crowded, the troops must have been finished with preparations and were sitting swaying against each other with eyes closed, gripping their rifles between their knees.

After it had begun to grow light, the Tiffie levered himself out of the engine and said, "Probeer start!" The vehicle whined immediately into life. We left our position at the dusty rear of the column and overtook every single vehicle, and there were about a hundred. We were just in time to reach the very front in the centre. The veggroep was starting to form into a broad attack formation. Conversation was stopped. Nerves. Hatches were opening and helmets were emerging. I recognised the person beneath every one. We slowed down to 15km an hour, and the column broadened as Platoons 2 and 3 took positions by our right and left. Bravo Company was in reserve behind, and I have no idea where the black light infantry were positioned. Then we stopped altogether, and the Ratel 90s integrated with our line from behind, so that we alternated 20-90-20-90, in a long line stretching out of sight in the bush.

The landscape and vegetation here were quite different from the open woodland we had lain down to sleep in the night before. Ahead of us we could see arid karoo-like low flat hills, though the bush around us on the low ground was thick with long grass, between soetdorings and haak en steek. The roof hatches were ordered sealed against mortars, and we approached the hills at a crawl in line abreast, and when the sun rose, we got the order, "Klim uit." (*Climb out.*) I got out and placed the mortar in the soft soil before me. I leaned on it and looked around in the brightness, feeling shaky and sleep-deprived. Our Ratel 20 was on my left and a 90 from the Armour Squadron was on my right. Ratels faded into the bush on both sides. Away behind me, in his turret, the Captain looked like he was praying. And then, on the flat low hilltop about a kilometre ahead and slightly to the left, beyond which was Techamutete, two standing human forms were spotted. It was Captain Willem Ratte, the 32 Battalion Recce, and he was busy telling Commandant de Vries that Techamutete was deserted. Niks, nada, fokol. FAPLA had fled north in the night.

I suppose that was an excellent result for our manoeuvre, leaving Cuvelai unsupported, but you can imagine our disappointment. Hurry up and wait. Then we drove south. We slept bouncing against each other through the day and in a black nightlong drive, with only one incident, when Piek our driver fell asleep and hit a thick tree, flinging us towards the turret in a startled heap. After Techamutete, we drove straight out of Angola. We followed the anharas, long beautiful sandy grassland clearings lined with green hardwoods. In one long line the convoy drove along the smooth earth at 40km an hour, the vehicles 300m apart, their dust drifting out sideways in the gentle breeze. Powerful emotions swirled through us on that scenic drive and we looked at the beautiful, stunning country rolling out beneath us, and eyed the young goatherds like wealthy tourists momentarily struck with envy of their carefree African lives.

We stopped near Ongiva for a night. We ate a young goat we had stolen from a multi-coloured flock during the drive south. Not being house trained it parked 'pis en drolle' all over the platoon commander's sleeping bag on the Ratel floor, which, at the price of Marais the orderly getting into trouble, was amusing for the crew and made us happy. It was tough like a rubber stamp and we threw most of it away. We slept under huge trees, littered all beneath by unburied ratpack remains, from the Ovambo light infantry of 102 Battalion recently departed. We were appalled by their lack of discipline.

In the morning the Captain gave what amounted to his farewell speech, for he was to be transferred soon. We sat in silence, drinking his words, and we had goose flesh and disobedient tears. He smiled while he summed up our time together in a conversational way, and he advised us on our future lives. He said the most fatherly things I had yet heard from a living man. He told us to get married one day, and to respect and love our wives, as this would make us happy. He told us that we could find beauty in many things, and to find the things we found most beautiful, and make them part of our lives. He was only 26, but not to us. Late that night we were back in Omuthiya.

18
Marking Time Until Uitklaar

The chefs at Six-One were plump and pale. Like invertebrates they moved slowly between their tents and the mess stores, to which they had unlimited access. They avoided the noon sun and sweated when they worked in a dim steamy hell, their tools ladles and their orders 'cook'. The invasion of their fetid comfort by the rugged battalion out of the cruel northern wilderness meant the end of their dormancy, and the troops despised the 'jam thieves' and where possible made their lives harder. We entered their tents and took whatever food we found, as they lay silent and staring from their beds. We regaled them in threatening violent language and complained to our officers about the cooking. Our greatest joy was to see them rounded up and taken for a bosbus into the trenches.

Sergeant-Major Killer Smit had the meanest eyes ever seen in the history of mankind, and these glinted evilly one morning across the parade ground, as he described to the assembled battalion the misuse of kitchen foods by the two chefs standing at attention in front of him, though with bowed heads, while he thumped them on the shoulders with his pace stick, in time with his words.

"Troepe! Ek het gistraand hierdie twee etters geelhandig gevang ... " (*Troops! Yesterday night I caught these pus-heads yellow-handed ...*) Red-handed and red-faced he had caught them misusing army margarine in a sexual act, while on the small hours shift making coffee for the guards. Sergeant-majors the world over love these exposés, and troops love to hear them. So much for the chefs.

The battalion commander Commandant Roland de Vries presented us each with an elite 61 Mech Combat Bar. On a yellow field a silver dagger points towards your heart, and three red lightning bolts spark off the blade. They were beautiful and meant a great deal, and we wore them at all times on our chests. It was the ultimate sign of belonging, and I still have mine.

The tail end of the dry season was hot, dry and ugly. Not a tree had a leaf and all the grass had long since been carried underground by the termites. All was a dirty grey-tan colour and the sun baked the bare ground beneath the dry trees. The only colours to be seen were on the brightly painted ammunition. Animals were in abundance, surrounding the camp at night and visiting the waterhole. A strong feeling that we were freewheeling down to the end of National Service, and our discharge, gripped

Alpha Company. There was a lull in the activities of the camp. Some platoons went off to man places like Ovambo Gate, Tsintsabis and Etosha, or to other lonely outposts where little was happening either. During this sort of nowhere time, Michael Eriksen asked the Captain permission to hitchhike southwest across South West Africa to Usakos, where his sister lived, to attend a family occasion. I was allowed to go with him and with ratpacks issued at the Captain's instructions, we caught the post truck early one Friday morning to Tsumeb, and from there we hitchhiked a lift to Otavi on the main highway south. However, a phone call from there to Usakos told us that the family was away, a bad mix-up in communications. So, decisively, we then and there booked into the Otavi Hotel and spent three uneventful and relaxing days, drinking only beer and eating only Russian sausages, because we remembered them so fondly. We returned to camp on Tuesday morning.

> Dear Mom,
> Here we sit, broken hearted, in Otavi Hotel. R20 per night. I'm sure the proprietor (German) it doing us in, but, right of admission etc. We've decided to stay another night here because Tsumeb is run by the army. Anyway, we plan to get totally motherless tonight. Bottlestore's just down the road. Last night we tried, but 2 super dumpies of Windhoek Lager were like sleeping pills. Had a wonderful sleep. Well, I phoned you last night & ended up telling you a long tale of terror on the high roads of Angolsh. The whole exercise was known as Operation Meebos. All our weight was thrown at elusive SWAPO, though it may be recorded that rules were broken and FAPLA got a bloody nose as well. When we set up first HAG we were thoroughly impressed, first to be bombed by Stalin Organ mortar-rockets, and secondly …

I needed to produce a portfolio of work for admission to UCT to study Architecture the following year, and I walked into Captain Malan's office.

"Yes Evan, what can I do for you?" he said in English the moment he looked up from his writing. I explained my situation, and he allowed me 10 days. Early the next morning I got a lift in an ambulance to Tsumeb. With me I took my R4 rifle and one ratpack. At Six-One Headquarters I phoned my mother, asking her to book a flight the following day from Windhoek to Cape Town, and then I hitchhiked. I passed south through Otavi, Otjiwarongo, Sukses and Okahandja, with a loaded rifle that was welcomed aboard by the drivers that took me, farmers, an old lady and truck drivers, until I reached Windhoek as the sun was setting on a dry country. I had not been in Windhoek before and I made my way to the main police station and asked for a cell for the night. My rifle was put in a safe until my return and I got locked behind a solid steel door (for my own safety they told me), in a windowless room, with a toilet in the corner. On my release from jail at 6.30am, I took a walk and had a full English breakfast (including kudu liver) at the Kalahari Sands Hotel, and in a newspaper read of a South African jet shot down in Angola. A bus took me to the airport. It was sad not to have my R4 at home but I worked all week, drawing the prescribed exercises in my own bedroom, and the return trip was uneventful.

For some time the Platoon 1 HQ section was left alone, out of the whole of Alpha Company, to man the base. I can't remember where everyone went, but probably to Ondangwa. If I remember correctly, the Armour Squadron and other units were still in base. The seven of us without rank collected all the rubbish, and drove it by Buffel and trailer 5km every day to the dump, which was infested with hundreds of marabou storks, possibly the most repulsive carrion bird to inhabit the earth, with stinking filth-encrusted bald necks and heads. Arriving at the dump, we would open fire with our R4s from the Buffel at the great murmuration of stinky storks, and once hit one in the air, and we posed like Big Game Hunters, stretching wide the 2.5m wingspan. We were left mainly to ourselves, and after unloading the waste, would shower and suntan and read, and I started lifting weights in the deserted gym tent. But we stood guard every single night in three-hour shifts, which was quite frightening in some of the watchtowers far out into the trees, especially as we knew there were no infantry reinforcements in the camp to come out and meet an enemy – on the contrary, apart from the armour guys who would man their vehicles, there were clerks and chefs and medics and Tiffies, who instead would run for their trenches. On my first shift I climbed my rattling tower and came straight down again. After that I never went up, because up there you felt like a magnet for AK-47 bullets, but instead I hid on the ground some way off and listened to the night. We had become natural guerillas ourselves.

When the rest of the platoon returned, I was affronted to hear, that evening, that my name was again on the guard list, but not the others in Platoon HQ. So I kicked up a fuss and was exchanged. Within 10 minutes I was accosted between the tents by Mark Rothman who had been volunteered to take my place. Shouting insults he flung his hand at my throat and gripped it. There was an instant crowd pouring from the tents surrounding us, taking sides and yelling. "There's no need to fight," I said backing off, but when encouraged by his friends he persisted, calling me a fucking poes and poking me in the eyes. I hit his open mouth, and blood flew instantly in a generous spray from a split vein in his lip. He came on and I landed a solid punch on his cheekbone but gripping my arms held me bent with my head under his chest.

Blood was everywhere, again not mine. I was hitting hard up at his solar plexus just before my face, and this had some effect as he leaped backwards and just stood there, surprise on his face. I had been lifting weights religiously for weeks in the gym tent, and my punches were harder than I expected myself. "Don't fight," I said again, shaking, "don't fight," and he went and stood guard like a good chap.

There was still training and PT but not with the same need, as we had proved ourselves, and the commanders knew that we would produce what was expected of us. The threat from SWAPO insurgents was very slight because of the complete lack of water in the wild country and on the infiltration routes, so it was fairly easy to get permission to go to Tsumeb for a day, and further afield and for longer.

Some obvious offenders finally got caught smoking dagga, beyond the shower block. One was immediately expelled from Alpha Company, and joined HQ Company as a co-storeman with Hoy, while the others were merely warned – it depended on their value to the fighting formation. MPs weren't long in arriving at the base and they searched us and our tents and our belongings. Foam mattresses were bent and pressed and wrung for hidden packages. Drug hysteria reigned and we lived in a McCarthyite fear of false accusations. Nothing was found, even by sniffer dogs, for apart from isolated aberrations we were, really, a squeaky-clean battalion.

Then Jeremy Taylor visited 61 Mech. Whether he volunteered, or if the authorities had asked him to entertain the troops, we did not know, but his show was a discomfort rather than a great success because the mood of Alpha Company was dark. We were still standing a lot of guard over that time, and during the evening show, we made that our excuse for slipping away from the cleared-out hangar park. Songs like '*Ag Pleez Daddy*' just didn't go down well at all. We were soldiers for fuck's sake, worldly wise and frustrated, and expected more from life, like no-nonsense sex and violence, not moffie kak. The following day we staged a battalion attack in his benefit, which of course was actually training for us. He was visibly impressed and straight after the noise and smoke subsided, he was asked if he would like to fire a MAG. Of course, he said, and picked up the weapon by the barrel. His hand was so badly burned he couldn't hold a guitar after that and had to cancel his whole tour. Shame, a nice guy really, he was probably relieved.

That night there was a company braai in honour of our unmilitary guests, and we all stood in the dark around smoking fires, getting easily drunk. Some managed to get more than the allotted two beers, and I made my way back to the tents to read a book or write a letter, to escape the aggression that was brewing in the darkness and likely to erupt. Several other troops were in the tents in restful solitude, including Piek our driver who was writing a letter on his bed. He was in a philosophical mood about women and BMW cars.

What I experienced next was sitting on my bed with my head aching dully, and meaninglessly saying, "Hoe lank isit tot pas? Waars ek? Ek weet nie waar ek is nie! Vier fokken hele maande! Is dit hoe lankit is? Is ek oppie grens?" (*How long is it until pass? Where am I? I don't know where I am. Four whole months! Is that how long it is? Am I on the border?*)

"Dit lyk asof hy jou hard gepoes het, ou Davies," (*It looks like he smacked you hard, old Davies*) said Piek, half absorbed in his letter and not looking up.

"Wie het my gepoes?" (*Who smacked me?*) I asked confused.

"Korporaal Erasmus, hy het jou uitgeroep en jy't teen die kabels geval. Jy't miskien vyf minute al daar op jou bed gesit en kak mompel." (*Corporal Erasmus, he called you outside and you fell against the cables. You've been sitting on your bed mumbling shit for maybe five minutes already.*) And in vague recollection I started remembering going outside and talking to a drunken Corporal Erasmus in the dark. I don't remember being hit. Erasmus was Mark Rothman's section leader. As a group Section 1 now felt avenged for the fight earlier. There were other fights. Notable was one between Warwick and a troop from his section. Platoon 1 was standing at guard parade late in the afternoon as roll was called, when suddenly the two of them hurtled out of the squad, Warwick on top, whipping his knuckles across the loser's face and head, thus keeping his eyes shut, and his hands in protective warding. Warwick fought economically, never to seriously hurt his opponents, but only to win. He always won.

"Klim terug in die squad," (*Get back in the squad*) said the CSM Staff-Sergeant Koen quietly when it was over. "Warwick, kom sien my hierna." (*Warwick, see me after.*) Dust devils started. If one came for you, you held your hands over your face and waited.

We had special guests in late November. The Ratel design team from Armscor visited 61 Mech, with some directors. The design team were a mixed lot, but notable among them were four Germans who had been tank commanders in the Second World War, or so we were told. They took great pleasure occupying the commanders' positions in the turrets as we took them on manoeuvres and live fire exercises between Omuthiya and the Bloubaan. They brought a new prototype with them. Starting its operational career, and unveiled then at Six-One, was the Logistics Ratel, the eight-wheeled Ratel Log. We all thought it a wonderful development and were very sorry we had not benefited from it in Angola. It was not fast, but had powerful gears and eight-wheel drive, so that when fully loaded, it could tow two other Ratels through soft sand. It was armed not with a turret but had a mounted .50 Browning heavy machine gun. It carried tons of diesel, tons of water and it was equipped with showers. It had a large deep freeze for meat, a fridge for cold drinks, fresh vegetables and other luxuries, a baggage compartment for personal belongings, and a store of ratpacks, medical supplies and ammunition. Although a large vehicle it was efficiently designed and could allow a platoon to be autonomous and operational for a month. Its crew was a driver and a storeman (Hoy!), who would be trained to use the big machine gun (sweet Jesus!), and it was to replace the SAMIL and Kwêvoël trucks by being more mobile and defensible, and offering more in the way of conveniences.

Suddenly the realisation hit us that we had a month left to freedom. Warwick forgot us. The bonding we had created to survive, was shown to be fragile as it disintegrated. What we had imagined were friendships, disappeared, and politeness within groups started evaporating. The self-sustained myth of the ultimate team, of blood brotherhood, was dissolving. Oh yes, we were that team, but now we each saw an individual future. We yearned for change and in that moment hated the place, the army, each other. All that was left was unendurable waiting for the first day of our new lives, and blank frustration at each wasted day in between.

A troop from another sub-unit went bossies one night and held some of the officers of the battalion hostage. He kept them flat on the ground with a cocked and ready-to-fire R4. He got them to crawl towards the troops' tents, where I don't know what he intended to do. When Warwick was told he didn't look up from his magazine. "Hy kan hulle fokken doodmaak, ek sê. Sê my net wanneer die skietery klaar is." (*He can fucking kill them, I say. Just tell me when the shooting's over.*) In the dark some escaped among the tents and one of them, a Tiffie sergeant, came up behind him and knocked him flat with a spade. With a bloody bandage round his head he spent a few days in RSM Killer Smit's kas, or holding cell, a cage of welded steel re-bars in the open sand in the middle of Omuthiya, burning dark brown in the sun and growing a wild stubble, and we called "Jy, jou poes," as we walked past him to the mess at meal times, and he glared at us from his patch of sand like a chained baboon.

On my very last day at Omuthiya we performed a battalion exercise in hot sun, and afterwards I got into an argument with our gunner, Van Schalkwyk, over my duty to help clean the 20mm barrel. After cleaning the hard carbon from my patmor tube, it felt too strenuous and lengthy a task, as the 20mm's carbon is very hard compressed, and the barrel is heavy, and I refused to do it as I was supposed to. I was just being a lazy shit, if I remember correctly. Without much introductory discussion we fought, but he was a stronger man, and before I knew it my nose was broken in a crunch of cartilage and bone, lying sideways and pulpy across my face with the hot blood gushing down my shirt, and I was begging his poised fist not to strike again.

Late that same night I was on a C130 from Grootfontein to Pretoria for a visit to 1 Mil, the military hospital there. I never saw Omuthiya again.

At 1 Mil my nose was straightened in a quick operation. Blowing great clouds of cocaine up my nostrils with a puffer, the ENT stuck two stainless steel rods deep up my nostrils, held my head tight and in one gristly wrench bent my nose straight. He had a big Merck tin of cocaine on his shelf, so one can only imagine this good-looking young army doctor's life. Once again there was a shower of blood but this time I was giggling through a flood of tears. I had a free run of the hospital, which was modern and big, many storeys high. I wandered around. There seemed to be an incestuous set-up with the male medics who were National Servicemen and the young female nurses, but I was very unfortunately not able to derive any benefit from it, because I looked and sounded like an elephant seal. I was in any case bossies with dark grease-calloused hands. Instead I discovered that Johan Cruywagen, the gunner wounded in the ambush near Tsintsabis in April, was still in the hospital. I located him and had a sad and awkward visit. He couldn't move or speak, and was pale and covered in bedsores, but his ward friends got him to open his eyes. Once as blue as the summer sky, they were now the colour of grey slate and I doubt if there was recognition or focus. He had been so healthy and positive.

I visited family in Johannesburg and then caught a train to Bloemfontein, to rejoin Alpha Company who had returned there, to 1 SAI. They felt like a mob of strangers, and I an alien. There were still tangible conflicts and I kept to myself or my small group of trusted friends as much as possible. In my absence from Omuthiya, all my kit had been stolen, by those closest to me, I suppose. I needed it back to hand in when we klaared out, or I would be forced to pay for it, more than I possessed. So I resorted to cat burglary, for which counterinsurgency training had apparently given me an aptitude. It took bold, patient courage. In a well-planned operation, I leopard-crawled down the smooth floors of the bungalows of the new intake after midnight, and took trommels from beneath the beds, and webbing hanging from the foot of the beds of sleeping rowers. Needing rifle magazines I crept into the guard bungalow between change-times and took all I needed from the webbings of sleeping off-duty guards. Twice the guard commander came in and several times a guard got up to pee. I lay still on the floor amongst the sleeping bodies on mattresses, in the light of a bulb coming through the door to the next room, and was not seen. But the next day the shit hit the fan. Big time. Several troops had gone on similar sprees, and in fact I had met some of them between our forays, and we had pooled our haul and swapped items in a building site where we had cut open the trommel locks with the wire-cutters on our rifles. The Military Police were called and they organised a search of Alpha Company's kit, in an uitpakinspeksie. At the same time we started handing in at the QM stores. We stood at attention in units to be searched, but handed in alphabetically, so there was an organisational flaw in the search. With the MPs already in our bungalow, in growing terror I called softly to my platoon commander 2nd Lt De Jager and explained my motives. He sidled over to the company 2IC, Lt Buys, and quietly described the crisis to him. And he in turn sidled across to the CSM, Staff-Sergeant Koen. By this time the MPs were getting dangerously close, with a group of those rowers who had been robbed, to identify their too-clearly marked things. Watching from a distance at the door Staff-Sergeant Koen, with a stroke of genius, called out prematurely, "Al die Cs en Ds, vat nou julle goed en KM toe met julle, oppie looppas! BEWEEG!" (*All the Cs and Ds, take your stuff now and off to the QM, at the double! Move!*) Audacity and initiative are key requirements for successful soldiers. With seconds to spare and with the MPs nearly standing over me I quickly packed and escaped a year in DB with a pounding heart. So the team still held, and it made me feel great.

The next day the company was to dissolve. There was a final tragic sense of solidarity. We swapped addresses and phone numbers, and I filled pages with them. I believe I only wrote one letter after this, to Peter Barry, but I never received a reply. Michael Eriksen and myself came together for rock concerts and parties, and are still friends.

The day after we trudged through the gate, our opsbalkies pinned on clothes worn, torn, faded and proud. And we scattered like blown leaves … anonymous.

Epilogue

The conquest of the fear of death is the recovery of life's joy.
—Joseph Campbell

My 2014 trip with my son, along the D3001 visiting Tsintsabis and Omuthiya, was no mere fatherly reminiscence. I also searched for and found a Bushman community at Tsintsabis, for which the central feature of their oral history is the 15 April 1982 ambush. It is repeatedly retold because they lost an elder leader with the first RPG-7 fired that day. The Border War, with this one dominating local event, is the main backdrop to their worldview. Thirty-three years after, I experienced surges of gooseflesh as the immediacy of their story flared up. Everyone knew two living members of the community who had been present that day as young trackers. I met one of them and he agreed to guide me to the Bravo cutline and attempt to find the ambush site.

Everything had changed, but not beyond recognition. The cutline still exists but is overgrown. It has a central game fence now with low fences on either side, with two tracks within the fences. It's important to start off on the correct track. They are heavily corrugated and the sand is soft – you need 4x4 all the way. With two Bushmen in the car, the older man and a youngster, our road trip had become surreal. Our 60-year-old ex-SADF tracker assured us that none of the trees were the same as they had been. We went on and on, slowly, bumping rhythmically. There were no distinguishing features, and the cutline went on into infinity, but after 20km he announced our arrival. Though I had given him no prompting, as a test of his truth, what then followed confirmed every physical detail of my story as received from my interviews of Platoon 2 members in June 1982.

There was a derelict gate in the fence on the north side, like many other gates. There was a track, barely. It was overgrown and nothing had used it for years. I had to negotiate dry thorn branches, go around trees in the track, and was forced to scratch my vehicle. No turning back now. The track led straight north at right angles from Bravo. We crawled on and on. Suddenly after a kilometre, light appeared in the dense bush ahead. Practically a kilometre wide itself, dramatically, lay a wide-open pan with dark grey dried mud, surrounded by trees, under an eternal sun. There were no elephant spoor. No track led across it, so still in 4x4 we forged our own deep grooves.

As we went, he became excited, animatedly waving his hands and leaning out his window as he talked. "Ooo, daar was GROOT oorlog daai dag," (*Oh, there was big war that day*) he exclaimed, pointing to remembered helicopter gunships in the sky. At the far side, we couldn't find where the track continued into the bush, so we got out. He demonstrated in the black mud, drawing a diagram of a horseshoe-shaped ambush with the Ratel at its centre, where "baas Danie, en ou Jan" had met their end. He repeated how the trees had changed, that it was "moeilik" (*difficult*) and he first walked up and down the edge of the trees, getting his bearings. Then we plunged in, he walking fast just ahead of me, snapping thorn branches that might have whipped me. He zig-zagged this way and that, never too far from the shona. It had happened close to the edge, he said. There was no 'small clearing' now. Everything was thickly overgrown. My girlfriend, who was also with us, discomforted by the thorns, the dryness and the dense vegetation, commented that she had had no idea we had been in such a harsh environment. That meant a lot to me, that validation at last of what we had never been able to express, that I hadn't been just faking it all along.

It was late afternoon and I was starting to worry that we should have come in the morning. We had no time for this the next day, as we wanted to drive to Rundu. During the searching, the younger Bushman was wandering around with my son, showing him veldkos (*food in the wild*). My son was barefoot on the unfriendly surface, and I think the Bushmen liked that. Suddenly they stood before us with something in their hands. "What is this?" they asked. It was a corroded RPG-7 tail. And then, suddenly, we found everything. With it came a wave of gooseflesh and tears, and camaraderie with the older man.

So why had I made this journey? 1983 was the first of difficult years after the army. It was expected of homecoming National Servicemen that they should act a little strangely, and therefore should be humoured and given a bit of space. They had experienced a delusion, and were labouring under a misapprehension. They had been deceived, and needed to find themselves again. Their experience was not to be questioned, analysed or discussed. Instead, it should be countered blankly, without recognition, with the least amount of talk, in short, ignored as if it didn't exist. And so the whole trauma became deeply internalised. My trip, and this book, are not a quest for closure, but validation. We don't want closure, like it never happened. We want openness, and continuity, the past with the present, and into the future. This is what we seek, this is what was denied.

When Zulu warriors came home from war (according to Credo Mutwa), they were delayed from rejoining society until they each had gone through rites of purification. Even if a man had not killed, the evil presences at the battlefield were deemed powerful enough to follow him home and infect society. Furthermore, the first child conceived of an uncleansed warrior was thought to exhibit unnatural tendencies, such as a destructive nature, or psychopathy. Therefore the warriors were taken into the care of qualified matriarchs, often widows, older women, who dealt with their spiritual, mental, and perhaps also physical, needs. They affirmed their heroism, but at the same time severed the battlefield and warlike thinking off from the normal life they were expected to resume. When they were ready, they could return home calm and whole men. This may have been superstitious tradition, but reading about it got me thinking that at least that society felt the issue was important enough to allocate it some effort. I have given much thought to what happened with us. In our case, we were left in limbo, to deal with all the jangling memories and emotions by ourselves. We were encouraged to go about life pretending it never happened. And then I also got to reading and thinking about rites of passage, which all traditional societies, in all times, have considered essential to turn boys into men. Perhaps it *is* essential, and we should be asking *why* Western society has so many problems with young adults. These rites of passage were performed regardless of whether war was involved, although war *could* be treated as a rite of passage, and in some societies was, deliberately. A rite of passage took teenage boys from their mothers, and handed them over to the men, changed and charged with new responsibilities. Typically, boys would be captured, taken terrified and disorientated to a secret location, made to suffer an ordeal while being instructed on values and traditions, and given a profound sense of duty to society, and of co-belonging with the adult men. After this, they were brought home to joyful welcoming and celebration by the community. Often, their childhood things were publically sacrificed and they were handed new, adult, possessions. The local Xhosa rite of *ulwaluko* is in no way unique in the world. After ritual circumcision, the initiates live in isolation for up to several weeks, often in the mountains. During the process of healing they smear white clay on their bodies and observe numerous taboos. It is traumatic, yes, but trauma is necessary for the experience to be felt deeply and have the desired profound effect. Other traditions may involve other forms of mutilation, hunting a dangerous animal, suffering a lonely trial of survival in the wilderness, or head-hunting.

Our National Service went some way to mirror an initiation ritual. Initially, we were forced to discard our childhood and upbringing, along with all their norms and social mechanisms. This was done in six months of physical and mental fatigue, brought on by insufficient sleep, and intrusion into the sanctum of our personalities. At the same time, selfish thoughts or actions resulted in failure. Our individual self image and self worth was challenged, and capitulated, making our personalities hollow and open to influence. Instruction was enforced by repetition and suffering. The eventual appearance of a fatherly authority figure, a combat leader, was often messianic. We were enthralled by the sense of belonging, after being deprived of kindness, and clung to the spiritual dimension that was provided in the new relationship. It was from this spiritual connection that an esprit de corps became possible. We proved and affirmed ourselves in the eyes of this leader – new, proud personalities were formed.

I'm not saying that any of this was wrong. It was right! But there was *one major omission* or flaw. In an initiation rite, youths are forced to undergo a period of deprivation and emotional uncertainty in order to clarify the distinction between childhood and adulthood, and to begin to put that distinction into practice. Then, instruction by elders is performed, and the youths are at this stage receptive and impressionable, perhaps even scared. All inputs are understood by the youths to be 'necessary'. They are psychologically cleansed, so that their future roles are contextualised not only in society but in the cosmos. There is usually a terrifying test *in extremis*, which confers status and responsibility. Failure is unthinkable. Then the newly created young men are received back into society with ceremony, and they are affirmed by society. *This important last bit didn't happen with us.* Marching proudly into your home town to be greeted by cheering crowds is important for homecoming warriors.

We came home from Angola, or at least National Service, needing affirmation, and there was the opposite. It was the same for the Vietnam War veterans in the United States. If people actually knew about the Angolan conflict, it was with distaste. I have lived for years with unfinished business inside my head. My great rite of passage was a flop and I felt cheated – I think a sense of otherness has followed me ever since. This is why so many of us have flocked to be part of veterans' associations today, because we are still searching for affirmation. And indeed, how could society be expected to affirm their new, modified young men, in the circumstances? Going off to war can be a full and satisfying rite of passage, but it depends on the rightness of the war as well as the confidence placed in the combatants by society. We went to a war nobody understood. And our new set of values didn't fit in. We were, returning, adult soldiers as opposed to mothers' sons, perhaps still immature at the age of 20, but adults. And there was no comedown, or transition from war mode to civilian mode. We just landed with a bump and had to get on with it.

Returning from the war, I wandered around for years looking for enemies, for how else to justify my existence? It would be easy to flip into 'kill mode', with blank, penetrating eyes and empty mind. I knew that in certain circumstances I would not be blamed if I killed. I looked out for such circumstances and entertained vivid fantasies, like standing in a bank queue hoping a hold-up would take place, so that Walter Mitty could heroically save the day. Some people at that time would have us believe there were enemies everywhere among us. Happily, I didn't kill any, and my sleep is peaceful now, though it has taken a long time. But sometimes I still see against a mist of smoke and luminous green leaves the front end of an RPG rotating slowly clockwise.

Appendix I
A Brief History of the Border War and the War in Angola

The war for independence in Angola began in 1961. South Africa supported the Portuguese against the resistance movements. The main resistance, the Movimento Popular de Libertação de Angola (MPLA), sided with the Soviet Union. The other resistance movements – Frente Nacional para a Libertação de Angola (FNLA) and União Nacional para a Independência Total de Angola (UNITA) – had originally also sided with the Soviet Union. Even before Portugal had withdrawn from the territory, friction between the movements had resulted in them fighting one another. The resistance leaders met with Portuguese authorities and agreed to end their armed conflict. In January 1975 they signed an agreement granting Angola its independence on 11 November 1975, and established a transitional government. This agreement was short-lived. Fighting between the three movements escalated quickly, and the FNLA and UNITA requested support from the West. At the request of the United States, South Africa sided with the FNLA and UNITA to put a non-communist government in power when colonial rule came to an end in November 1975. But the MPLA seized Luanda and formed a one-party state government, and developed further ties with the Soviet Union and other communist states. Cuba sent troops and technical advisors to Angola. The civil war, however, continued to rage. In early 1976 the South African Defence Force (SADF) left Angola and the FNLA disintegrated, while UNITA continued the struggle against the MPLA government. The SADF continued to support UNITA logistically as part of the South African government's Cold War strategy. The SADF gathered the remnants of the FNLA in southeastern Angola, where they were trained and formed into what became known as Bravo Group, which was tasked with fighting the South West Africa People's Organisation (SWAPO). SWAPO had been waging an insurgency war in South West Africa since 1961, infiltrating from bases in Angola. In 1976 Bravo Group became 32 Battalion, which would fight SWAPO not only in South West Africa, but also clandestinely in Angola.

The South African Border War started in 1966, when the first shots between SWAPO and the SADF were fired. SWAPO was founded as a Marxist liberation movement in 1960. Its purpose was independence from South Africa, which clung to a mandate to rule South West Africa, granted by The League of Nations after the First World War. Pressured by revolutionary activity at home and in South West Africa, South Africa sponsored a democratic process to rid itself of the liabilities of the territory. South Africa hoped with this to ensure a peaceful transition to democracy, and prevent communism from taking root in its neighbour. This was the Turnhalle Constitutional Conference held between 1975 and 1977, tasked with the development of a constitution for a self-governed Namibia. The conference was in defiance of the 1972 United Nations General Assembly decision to recognise SWAPO as the 'sole legitimate representative' of Namibia's people. Consequently SWAPO did not participate, and the UN rejected the conference. However SWAPO was not the only representative of South West Africans, and furthermore was committed to a violent Marxist takeover and a one-party state. It was inferred that SWAPO's rejection of the Turnhalle process was in reality a rejection of democracy as a whole. This is why black South West African volunteers fought SWAPO alongside the SADF. SWAPO remained a legal political party in South West Africa and had offices in the territory. However its armed wing aimed at destabilisation and violent revolution, and was treated as an enemy by South Africa. SADF strategy was governed by the requirement to maintain a condition of peace and order in which the democratic process could proceed. South Africa's Border War succeeded in as much as it maintained peace and order within the territory, and forced SWAPO to participate in the democratic process.

The MPLA offered SWAPO bases in Angola in March 1976. Almost all the fighting between the SADF and SWAPO took place in Ovamboland, because 25 percent of the population of South West Africa lived in that area and it bordered Angola. With Russian and Cuban help, by the middle of 1978 the MPLA had reorganised in line with Soviet doctrine. It now had motorised infantry brigades equipped with artillery, tanks and anti-aircraft systems to deploy in conventional warfare, and light infantry brigades to deploy in counter-guerrilla operations. South African aid to UNITA escalated following the MPLA's reorganisation.

The first objective of the SADF was to channel SWAPO's attack, by eliminating insurgency into the other border provinces of Kaokoland, Kavango and Caprivi. By doing this, the main effort (to clear Ovamboland) could be achieved through the concentration of resources. Once SWAPO infiltrations had been limited to Ovamboland, it became SADF strategy to deny them the use of the adjacent region of Angola. This was done through clandestine SADF operations against SWAPO, and through operations against the MPLA by UNITA. However it proved difficult to attack SWAPO in areas where the MPLA was consolidating control. With its well-defended bases and lines of supply, The MPLA supported SWAPO. UNITA became incapable of preventing this as support for the MPLA by Russia and Cuba grew. In 1981 the SADF launched Operation Protea, in which it not only destroyed SWAPO bases but also cleared the MPLA from a large part of southern Angola. This became known as 'The Area in Dispute'. SWAPO bases were now forced to locate an inconvenient 200+km north of the border, beyond the reach of the permanent SADF presence. Periodic raids were conducted to locate and destroy these bases (as in Operation Meebos in 1982). MPLA forces attempting to reoccupy The Area in Dispute or aid SWAPO also occasionally came under fire, although this was an uncomfortable necessity rather than desired policy.

Dialogue between the Angolan and South African governments was possible from an early stage and increasingly affected the strategic situation. South Africa wanted to link a ceasefire, and independence for South West Africa, to a complete withdrawal of Cuban and other foreign military allies from Angola. Negotiations proceeded in fits and starts, until unsustainable military commitment on both sides provided the goad for meaningful compromise.

UNITA controlled the southeast corner of Angola. From 1981 onwards, the MPLA attempted to capture UNITA strongholds and destroy the movement. The invasions kicked off in central Angola and advanced southeastwards. Each time, SADF support for UNITA helped to halt and reverse the MPLA probes. The 1987 invasion of UNITA territory with Cuban and Soviet material support was directed by Soviet officers. A massive import of Soviet equipment gave the MPLA air superiority over the SADF and a considerable superiority in numbers. Starting with the usual SADF deployment of 32 Battalion, additional fighting units were committed incrementally. In Operation Modular, an MPLA armoured brigade was destroyed by the SADF, and several other brigades were badly mauled, with the remnants retreating to Cuito Cuanavale.

There the MPLA dug in, and the episode identified by its enemies as the South African 'defeat' now took place as the Angolans reinforced the position. For several months the MPLA resisted an SADF siege by inferior numbers. On the brink of an escalation to costly total warfare, both sides approached the negotiating table with a sincere desire to end hostilities. South Africa agreed to withdraw the SADF from Angola and allow the immediate independence of South West Africa, under United Nations supervision. The Angolans agreed to send the Cubans home, and keep all forces – including SWAPO, which was to be confined to bases – a distance from the border. The Soviets at this time were in any case reducing foreign military commitments of their own accord.

But in 1988, as the SADF was reducing its forces, Cuba was secretly sending powerful reinforcements into Angola. A Cuban tank army was deployed to southwest Angola, threatening an invasion of South West Africa in a dramatic reversal of the strategic balance. While the SADF began assembling massive reserve forces, a hurried SADF redeployment into Angola led to a clash that convinced Cuba that further conflict would be self-destructive. Both South Africa and Cuba now withdrew their forces from Angola, setting up the conditions necessary for the independence of South West Africa.

In 1989, when most SADF units had been withdrawn from South West Africa and the remainder were confined to bases, SWAPO left its bases in Angola and invaded South West Africa. The last contact of the Border War took place as some SADF units were called out under United Nations supervision, and killed a large number of SWAPO fighters. South West Africa became independent in 1990 as the democratic state of Namibia.

Appendix II
The 15 April 1982 Ambush in Operation Yahoo!

The following account is taken from Major General (Retired) Roland de Vries, *Eye of the Firestorm* (Naledi, 2013):

The SWAPO deep infiltrations should be viewed as a holistic sequel to their decisive defeats during all previous such operations, which had a marked effect on the infiltrators' operational conduct during Yahoo. This time the SWAPO planners had done their homework thoroughly and had clearly studied our tactics; in 1982 they came back better prepared and more dedicated and ferocious than ever before, so much so that it would take the security forces close on two months to run them into the ground.

The Special Unit comprised well-trained insurgents, and by 1982 had an active strength of about 400 combatants who were, theoretically at least, devoted to the political ideals of SWAPO (I say "theoretically", bearing in mind the 16 prisoners who did not hesitate to change sides, and at least one subgroup which retreated to Angola very early on). Their command cadre had undergone rigorous training in Eastern Bloc countries and China, and new recruits were carefully selected for these deep raids.

Their legendary commander was the charismatic Danger Ashipalo, whose staff consisted of his second-in-command, Kapoko, a political commissar named High Court and an engineer commander, Kandove. Many battle names like these became legendary during the border war (I met a few of them subsequently over a beer or two ... nice people, really).

Volcano, their operational base, was located about 35km southwest of Lubango and was home to 10 platoons of between 35 and 45 men, each commanded by seasoned leaders like Kilimandjaro; Amin; Mandume; Nangobe; Castro; Ndowishi; Kayofa; Shikongo; and Kaunda. Before the insurgents left Lubango for the Death Triangle they were briefed and motivated by the senior cadre of SWAPO, including Sam Nujoma in person, supported by Martin Shalli (the Senior Staff Officer PLAN, who, incidentally, I met in

October 2010) and Danger. Secrecy was so strict that they did not receive their final instructions until just before their departure. Their main mission was to infiltrate the designated target areas and fight until those areas were liberated, because 1982, they were told, was "the Year of SWAPO". Specifically they were to lay ambushes and mines; kill white farmers; sabotage infrastructure; shoot at vehicles; attack and raid shops on farms; attack the towns; conduct progressive political actions to boost the cause of SWAPO; reconnoitre enemy bases and plot targets of opportunity; and establish and develop underground networks to support future infiltrations to follow … It is interesting to note that the Special Unit men were planning to infiltrate as far southwards on foot as we had raided northwards by vehicle and parachute during Operation Daisy in November 1981 …

They set off on their infiltration notwithstanding the fact that after Operation Protea the SADF/SWATF had turned all of south-central Angola into their personal hunting ground, or that Daisy had disrupted their operations, or that there were constant counterinsurgency operations on the go not just in Ovamboland but also in southern Angola, across the transit route to the border …

The 52-strong Western Group under Kilimandjaro travelled by vehicle from Lubango to Cahama, from where they walked to the border and crossed over near Ruacana on 7 [March], then bombshelled into three smaller groups. A few of the groups made contact with the security forces in Sector 10; some infiltrators became disheartened and decided to return to Angola. Those who were left unscathed (and unintimidated) continued their stealthy southward trek, and on 29 March the first group to be reported to the security forces was spotted on the farm Welkom, in the district of Kamanjab.

The seven Eastern Groups aimed at the Death Triangle and the Mangetti Block left Lubango in Ural trucks at the beginning of April, bound for the Techamutete-Cassinga area via Matala, their jumping-off point. They were commanded by Nangobe, Castro, Ndowishi, Kayofa, Kalulu, Shikongo and Kaunda. They marched southwards for about 370km, crossed the border and set off for Tsumeb, about 240km further on. In the process several of these groups were involved in contacts with the security forces in Ovamboland, but in each case their tracks were lost.

On 10 April the tracks of a significant number of infiltrators – about 150 of them – were located near Nkongo. A hot pursuit followed, but somehow this group also managed to evade their pursuers. They soon made their presence felt, however: at 19:00 on 11 April a patrolling Sector 10 Buffel MPV stood on a mine along the Charlie cutline, 30km due north of Tsinstabis. A 20-strong group was later detected to the east, but the follow-up failed when their tracks vanished.

[These were] ... the specific taskings five of the seven groups had received before leaving Volcano (those of Nangobe and Castro were never ascertained by us). Kayofa and Kalulu had been tasked to activate the Mangetti Block and lay an ambush for the security forces on the Bravo cutline for deception purposes; Ndowishi was ordered to commit acts of terrorism in the vicinity of Mount Aukas, near Grootfontein; Kaunda was instructed to infiltrate and subsequently activate the Tsumeb, Otavi and Kombat districts; Shikongo was tasked to infiltrate further south to Omaruru and Otjowarongo.

Intelligence management ... spent countless hours with our captives, so as to extract information from them (and found that most of the involuntary guests spilt the beans within 30 minutes of being captured ...). Another extremely important source of intelligence was the captured enemy documents yielded up by both the living and the dead ...

I was confident that [61 Mech's] Alpha Company could handle anything the enemy might throw at it. [Captain Jan] Malan was a vibrant commander, one of the new breed of mechanised infantrymen, and had shown himself to be an astute tactician. His second-in-command, Lieutenant Hubrecht van Dalsen, had had his baptism of fire in a short but fierce action at Môngua during Operation Protea; the acting Company Sergeant Major, Staff-Sergeant E. Koen, was an experienced man – all in all, a young, enthusiastic and committed command team. Their national service rank and file were of equal quality, 150 lively, well-trained troops who would be going into action for the first time in their young lives and were looking forward to it ...

Alpha Company ... left Omuthiya for Tsumeb on 14 April, the intention being to attend a concert at the Etosha High School that evening and then deploy directly to Tsintsabis; the rest of 61 Mech would come from Omuthiya in Samil-100 trucks and join them at Tsumeb for the concert. The concert was staged by the SADF's Entertainment Group, and was one of the recreational outings we regularly organised for our soldiers ... all went well at first, and by 21:30 the concert was in full swing, when I was called to the radio room at our rear HQ, and was informed ... that there had been a massive influx of insurgents over the Bravo cutline during the course of the evening ... With great regret I went back to the school and summarily stopped the concert. The civilian entertainers watched wide-eyed as their audience evaporated ... I had already instructed my second-in-command, Major Thys Rall, to activate our contingency plan. It all swung into motion quite smoothly, since it was all SOP.

I ordered Jan Malan to deploy Alpha Company into a suitable stopper position to the north of the Bravo cutline and close to Tsintsabis until we knew more about what was happening, then told Giel Reineke to join me in my command Ratel for the trip to Tsintsabis ... The super-efficient Malan was wasting no time: he had crammed his entire leadership group into his command Ratel, and under the dim cabin lights they were already assessing the scanty information at hand and working out tentative plans and orders as they bucketed through the night towards Tsintsabis ... By 01:00 on 15 April Jan Malan reported that he was deployed north of Tsintsabis and was ready for anything, be it vigil or action or both ... . I contacted Daan van der Westhuizen – veteran master tracker and fieldcraft expert *par excellence* – at his farm Koedoesvlei, 15km west of Tsintsabis, explained what was happening and said we needed his renowned tracker team to report soonest to the Tac HQ. Without hesitation he said he was on his way.

In due course the team arrived at Tsintsabis in Daan's cut-down drab brown Land Rover – tall, imposing Daan himself; his son-in-law, farmer-rifleman Hendrik Potgieter, who was married to his daughter Olivia; his friend and long-time Bushman employee, Jan Kouswab (widely known as "Jan Kaka"); and two other Bushman trackers. Back at Koedoesvlei, Daan's wife, the legendary "Tannie Pompie", was on all-night at the radio relay station which had been installed in her kitchen ...

The surreal friendliness of full daylight at last reached Tsintsabis on the morning of 15 April ... I instructed Jan Malan to go and investigate [the tracks on the Bravo cutline] with one of his platoons and Daan van der Westhuizen's seasoned tracker team. By now the Pumas and the two Alouette gunships squatted at Tsintsabis ...

I personally debriefed the platoon concerned soon after the ambush, and my story is one that I have reconstructed from what they told me. I also have Jan Malan's personal account, which I asked him to write for me when we were both serving at the Army Battle School at Lohatla in 1983:

> On my arrival at Tsintsabis I met the tracker team of Lieutenant Daan van der Westhuizen for the first time. After a quick marrying-up and a motivational talk to my platoon, we left for the area where the enemy tracks

had been found. Just before we left Tsintsabis, Hendrik Potgieter still remarked how joyful it was to work with such motivated and dedicated men.

The trackers travelled with us, mounted on our Ratels. As we moved westwards along the cutline the Bushmen maintained a close watch for signs and tracks of the enemy. Arriving at the crossing site, we observed numerous sheets of white paper strewn about. I instructed my men to dismount and we approached the suspect area on foot in open formation. Closer inspection revealed typical SWAPO propaganda pamphlets.

The next moment one of the Bushman trackers came to an abrupt halt and pointed to a suspect area in the sand. I halted our search and marked the suspect area with a mine marker I had on me. I then tasked the trackers to do an all-round search of the area. Three enemy tracks were leading in a southerly direction. We found shallow trenches of the enemy along the northern edge of the cutline. The signs on the ground clearly indicated they had evacuated their positions hastily the previous night.

We found a clear path of approximately 20 tracks leading in a northwesterly direction. After a brief discussion with Van der Westhuizen and Potgieter, we decided to do a 360° search of the whole area. All of us were in agreement that the enemy teams would most likely swing back and cross the cutline on a southerly track. It was now about 10:45 and the trackers indicated that the tracks were approximately 12 hours old.

At this stage I gave feedback by radio to Commandant Roland de Vries at Tsintsabis. My suggestion was to carry on with the search, and he agreed with me. The plan was now for one infantry section to move to the south of the cutline and search for enemy tracks for 200m in a westerly direction. At the same time Lieutenant Daan van der Westhuizen, with the remainder of the trackers and another infantry section, continued with the search to the north in a westerly direction for 200m.

The terrain alongside the cutline in both directions was extremely dense. From the moment Ratel 12A with van der Westhuizen on board left they were out of my sight. Daan van der Westhuizen, apparently occupying the Ratel turret, reported that the enemy tracks were leading west. The next moment there were maddening explosions and rippling small arms fire coming from their receding Ratel's direction.

I immediately recognised that the fire was not from the Ratel's 20mm quick-firing gun. I tried to call the section on the radio but there was no answer. I immediately deployed the remainder of the platoon and started moving in the direction where the fire was coming from. The bush was dense and our movement was slowed down considerably.

At one o' clock from our position in front of us we observed two 300m signal flares bursting in the sky. By now the fire had ceased. I instantly reported our dilemma to my battalion commander at Tsintsabis and requested the gunships. Without delay the Alouette gunships were airborne and flying towards us.

We then sighted the burning Ratel. My troops dismounted into an open formation as we moved forward. We did not fire for fear of hitting our own people in front of us. At the same moment two of our soldiers came running anxiously towards us from our left flank. They were streaked with blood and totally shocked. The two soldiers reported to me that they had driven right into an ambush. They said to me that many of their section members had been killed.

Massive black clouds and flames erupted from the Ratel. I deployed two of our sections and moved to the other side of the inferno, and we took up a defensive position. There was no sign of enemy nearby. I quickly moved towards the burning Ratel, accompanied by the platoon commander. We peered inside; it was obvious that nobody was alive. At this stage the ammunition inside the Ratel started exploding and the roof hatches were blown sky-high.

All around the burning Ratel I found our remaining soldiers ... They were all wounded and shocked. The medical orderly, company HQ and platoon HQ personnel removed the wounded to a safer area, and rendered first aid ... At that moment the Alouette gunships arrived. I indicated to them the assumed direction in which the enemy had retreated. Approximately one kilometre further west of our position we heard the gunships firing at the ground.

In the meantime I had requested the HQ at Tsintsabis to dispatch the two Pumas for casualty evacuation. The Pumas were on their way immediately. By now we had adopted an all-round defence. We started preparing a helicopter landing zone. The Ratel was still burning profusely. The tyres were sending up columns of black smoke and explosions ripped large pieces off the hull.

The Pumas landed and our dead and wounded were taken on board and flown south to Grootfontein. The gunships were still firing into the bushes to the west of us, where three terrorists had been killed. One of the gunships evaded a SAM-7 fired in retaliation from the ground. I then followed up with two sections in the direction of the contact. We found the three bodies as well as the SAM-7. One of the dead terrorists was identified as a section leader.

I had lost a total of eight men killed in this one ambush. Five mines were later lifted by our engineers in the area where the ambush had been sprung. The enemy had left a clear trail for us to follow. The ambush had been cleverly planned and carefully set up. It was in the form of a horseshoe. It was located in a thicker part of the forest, on the verge of a more open area. The enemy had prepared shallow trenches for their RPG-7s, SKS rifle grenades and machine guns. We found the position for the SAM-7 and a 60mm mortar as well.

Our Ratel was allowed to approach to within 15-20 metres before the enemy opened fire. It was later found that the Ratel had been penetrated by seven RPG-7 rockets and rifle grenades. The enemy platoon returned to Angola after they had completed their mission.

Appendix III
The 4 August 1982 Ambush in Operation Meebos

The following account is taken from Major General (Retired) Roland de Vries, *Eye of the Firestorm* (Naledi, 2013):

FAPLA was effectively neutralised in the Area In Dispute from mid-1981 [Operation Protea] until mid-1984 ... This favourable situation soon changed after the 11th Brigade of FAPLA was destroyed by 61 Mech at Cuvelai during Operation Askari in January 1984 under the command of Commandant Epp van Lill. After Askari the peace talks between South Africa and Angola once again flared up in all seriousness. This allowed FAPLA to filter back into [the Area in Dispute] ... In between Protea and Askari the SADF and SWATF had to contend with operations such as Makro and Meebos ... From September 1981 onwards a tactical headquarters (Tac HQ) and forward operational base was established at Ondjiva as an extension of Oshakati. Adequate counterinsurgency forces were allocated for operations on a rotational basis by the SADF as well as SWATF ... This included units on a more permanent footing such as 32 Battalion; 201 Battalion (Bushmen); 1 Parachute Battalion; and 2 Parachute Battalion (citizen force). From Ondjiva Alouette gunships and Puma helicopter troop carriers could be employed at leisure wherever the SADF chose to strike.

Battle Design for Operation Meebos

Colonel Jan Pieterse, an accomplished anti-aircraft gunner from army HQ in Pretoria, was appointed as the operational commander at Ondjiva. The SAAF established a forward air force command post, which at this level was referred to as a mobile air operations team (MAOT). Special Forces as well as UNITA provided liaison staffs for these operations. Reconnaissance teams from Special Forces as well as 32 Battalion and 201 Battalion supported these external operations on a continual footing. The famous scout from 32 Battalion, Captain Willem Ratte, was deployed in theatre virtually throughout ... The overarching operation was nicknamed Meebos and consisted of two subsidiary operations, namely Handsak (Handbag) to the east and Makro to the west. The boundary between these two operations was an imaginary north-south line drawn through Môngua on a map ...

Meebos II [13 July 1982-30 August 1982] consisted of a number of deceptive moves followed by sequential ground and air attacks in the form of Puma heliborne assaults supported by Alouette gunships ... Attacks were preceded by the gathering of near real-time intelligence through high altitude aerial reconnaissance, enemy radio intercepts and information gathered from the local population. The final work of fixing the enemy and gathering real-time intelligence was left in the capable hands of the reconnaissance teams of Captain Willem Ratte of 32 Battalion. To facilitate guaranteed communications between the scouts and the Tac HQ an Impala jet fighter roved the skies high above to act as a relay station at critical moments. Two companies from 32 Battalion and one from 1 Parachute Battalion operated as the main striking capability – our own guerrilla force.

This operation had a mechanised flavour, one in which the extrapolative deterrent value of 61 Mech increased the success rate ... significantly as the mobile reserve of the force. At least the initiative and freedom of action so desperately required could be maintained by curbing FAPLA. 61 Mech was sanctioned to strike hard at FAPLA if they dared to intervene with the operation on the ground ...

The first objective was codenamed "Smelling Rat" and was located on 30 July by Willem Ratte on the southern bank of the fast flowing Calonga River. Ratte had infiltrated for more than 25-30km on foot, wearing captured enemy boots with soles which had been reversed. He followed comprehensive counter-tracking procedures. He eventually lurked well-hidden and camouflaged inside the enemy base. From this extremely dangerous position he dispatched bits of information to the Tac HQ via an Impala aircraft which flew high above and to the side out of hearing range. Every so often Ratte needed to stop sending scraps of information as some enemy passed close to him. He truly lived on the edge for hours on end.

Following on Ratte's scouting missions a number of minor as well as more significant contacts were ... made with SWAPO ... The elusive headquarters of the enemy were however never found. Many times the crafty reconnaissance teams of 32 Battalion would find the enemy, only to be rewarded with an empty lair once the ground assault went in. The enemy was extremely sensitive to strange moves in their immediate environs ...

On 31 July we heard on radio intercepts our revered FAPLA brigade at Cuvelai screaming for help against the background thunder of their useless and wasteful artillery barrage – it was actually funny. *"We need more artillery ammunition … ! We have fired all our artillery ammunition at the enemy! Our situation is abnormal! We are surrounded by the South Africans! We are going to be attacked at any moment … !"* From the enemy's sporadic and frantic staccato cries two things became crystal clear. The commander of 11 Brigade was trapped for the moment at Techamutete during one of his liaison visits there and the brigade at Cuvelai was absolutely sure that they were on the priority list to be attacked next … The consequence was absolute terror and prolonged agony for 11 Brigade … The humorous part was that the FAPLA brigade commander informed Cuvelai by radio that there was enough artillery ammunition left in one of the warehouses. "Yes," the reply came, *"the man who has the key has fled, because of all the excitement"* …

On the afternoon of 3 August we received extremely valuable intelligence about the enemy's predicament through another radio intercept. FAPLA was going to dispatch a large logistics convoy from Techamutete that same night to replenish 11 Brigade along the treacherous 60km route … Time was too short and the distance too great to respond with the whole of 61 Mech in an ambush of the enemy relief column alongside the road. Our unit was still laagered approximately eight kilometres away from the HAA next to the Cuvelai River. The distance from the laager position to the road was close on 20km through immensely dense bush. I was also apprehensive about losing the element of surprise by closing in on a prospective ambush position with a noisy mechanised force in the dark.

My plan was simple: 61 Mech would ambush the enemy column with a single platoon and then pounce on the disrupted enemy with the Alouette gunships at first light. I would accompany Neall Ellis in the command aircraft to coordinate the ground action … Time was of the essence and 61 Mech had to respond rapidly as dusk was approaching. I therefore immediately requested the Alouette gunships of Neall Ellis to remain in the HAA for the night. I also requested the Pumas to undertake one more sortie before they left for the safety of Ondangwa – to drop one of my platoons (35 men) near a possible ambush position close to the Techamutete-Cuvelai gravel road. I subsequently requested a sortie of Mirages to fly a combat air patrol over the Cuvelai-Techamutete road the next morning as soon as it was light. Captain Neall Ellis would act as the on-board forward air controller.

I was now on my way with my Ratel driving swiftly towards 61 Mech. My choice for the ambush commander was the tactically astute enthusiastic young mechanised infantry Captain Jan Malan, the commander of Alpha Company. Travelling with me was Captain Willem Ratte, scout supreme. I had asked him to brief my troops on enemy convoy tactics and counter-ambush drills ... I gave quick radio orders to Captain Malan on the move and requested him to hastily prepare a platoon for the ambush. He was to personally command the minute force and was to take some 60mm mortars with the 35-man fighting contingent. When I arrived at 61 Mech's position, Malan and his platoon were ready – excited, armed to the teeth and suitably camouflaged ... Malan had already completed his appreciation of the mission and had selected a suitable ambush position on the map. He was ready to brief the commander of the lead Puma ... The platoon duly emplaned and flew off to the west ... We would occupy some high ground nearby to maintain first-class communications with the ambush party of Captain Jan Malan ...

At stages during the night we encountered some problems with our radio communication and those bedevilling skip distances. However, close to first light Jan Malan reported, his voice crystal clear and calm: He could hear the far-off drone of the enemy's approaching vehicles ... The platoon-sized force of 61 Mech stopped the FAPLA column of more than 22 enemy vehicles dead in their tracks ... approximately 13km north of Cuvelai. It was a remarkably successful ambush ... Here is [Jan Malan's] story:

> My ambush party comprised my command element; three infantry sections; two sappers from the Field Engineer troop attached to 61 Mech; my company signaller; one medical orderly. I instructed the two sappers to take five tank mines ... We arrived at our ambushing position selected with precious minutes daylight to spare. This was time enough for a final reconnaissance and to determine our exact deployments for the night. This was followed by final orders for the impending action. I decided to keep the ambushing platoon reasonably closely grouped for the night.
>
> There were huge trees alongside the road and dense under cover. I therefore deployed the killing group reasonably close to the road, approximately 20 to 25 metres from the killing area selected. The ambush was set up as follows: Two infantry sections with two RPG-7 rocket launchers and three light machine guns were deployed in an extended formation parallel to the road; my HQ position was selected

in the centre of the formation with the platoon commander acting as my second-in-command; the 60mm mortar was positioned close to my HQ position under control of the platoon sergeant; the third infantry section deployed in a half-moon formation behind us to ensure all-round defence; alternative positions were selected for the depth section on the northern flank to thwart a possible enemy counter-attack on our position, if it came to that. There was no time to dig into the ground, so each member of the ambush party filled two sandbags each with loose sand and placed it in front of them for cover against possible enemy fire. The platoon sergeant and the two sappers were now instructed to plant the tank mines as well as Claymore shrapnel mines in front of us on the road. In addition a few trip flares (illumination) were placed in the tree line on the other side of the road.

Within 30 minutes of returning the sappers reported to me that with all the excitement they had forgotten to arm the mines. Somewhat disappointed I decided to leave the mines where they were. In retrospect this was a divine intervention as we would have been too close to its explosions if activated by the enemy. The sign to unleash hell on the enemy would be the activation of the trip flares and the illumination of the killing area with 300m illumination flares. By now the 60mm patrol mortar had found a suitable position to fire northwards over the trees towards the rear of the expected enemy convoy. We now established communications with the combat group HQ with a B25 radio and a dipole antennae and the waiting began.

At times through the night the troops in the killing area dozed off. They were kept awake by means of jerks on a communications rope, which we had strung from one to the other. At about 04:00 we lost communications for a while with the combat group HQ. We felt very lonely out there in front of the total darkness and vastness of Africa. At about 05:30 we heard the subtle engine drone of the enemy convoy approaching our position from the north. All in the ambushing party were wide awake by now, nerves on end, excitements were stirring among us, adrenaline surging.

We reported to the combat group HQ that contact was imminent. I told the signaller to dismantle the B25 radio. He said quietly to me that the oncoming vehicles sounded to him like Bedfords. I now deployed the depth section to our northern flank. The section knew that they had to protect our northern flank from a possible enemy counter-attack as soon as our party started withdrawing from the killing area. All the troops by then had packed their kit and were carrying it in rucksacks on their backs. At about 05:45 the first two enemy vehicles entered the killing area right in front of us. We could hear from the exchanging of gears further back that the enemy convoy was slowing down one by one, as they caught up with the next vehicle on the rise. The first two vehicles were extremely close to each other and were now in the centre of our killing area – they looked like Russian Ural cargo tucks. The enemy was driving with all their vehicle lights switched off.

At this moment I gave the command to open fire on the two enemy vehicles in front of us. The troops immediately adopted firing positions standing up and started firing short bursts into the killing area. The light machine guns and the RPG-7 rocket launcher fire added to the mayhem right in front of us. The two Claymore mines were set off at the same moment. The remains of the exploding enemy vehicles were clearly silhouetted by the blazing trip flares on the other side of the road. It was not necessary to fire the illumination flares, as the whole area was lit up in front of us. Massive explosions rippled as the trucks had obviously been loaded with mortar and artillery ammunition. It was astonishing that none of us were killed or maimed by the shrapnel flying all around. The 60mm patrol mortar started firing speculatively on the enemy convoy further to the north.

There was instant chaos amongst the enemy's ranks. We could hear vehicles turning around, people shouting frantically, gears gnashing in panic and metal tearing as some of the vehicles crashed into each other. The convoy to the rear was trying to escape northwards back towards Techamutete, away from the pandemonium. After a short while I gave the killing group the order to cease fire and to make ready to withdraw at my command. The section on the northern flank was now given the command to open fire to cover our withdrawal.

All our actions unfolded calmly as if we were busy with a drill exercise on a parade ground. The killing group started to withdraw orderly along our south-easterly withdrawal route to a prearranged checkpoint. I looked at my watch and observed the hour-hand closing in on 15 minutes before first light. Our ambushing party withdrew for a distance of approximately 3km and then doubled back to lay in ambush on our tracks. The welcoming pleasantness of first light arrived and we could start discerning dirty smiling features all round. Our camaraderie was protected by the denseness of the African bush against any hostiles, which may lurk in our immediate environs.

We established communications with the combat group HQ and gave then the good news and a brief Sitrep (situation report). There was happiness for our safety and success and congratulations were duly expressed. Commandant Roland de Vries informed me that two Mirages were on their way from Ondangwa to patrol the road between Cuvelai and Techamutete. He confirmed he was on his way with the Alouette gunships. Our ambush party was furthermore tasked to sweep the ambush site as soon as the gunships arrived at the scene, which would provide close air support.

We prepared for the next mission. We were extremely tired, although we felt confident and highly satisfied by the extraordinary outcomes of the night. More so, we were fired up, ready to undertake the mopping-up operation with enthusiasm. As we formed into a sweep line to patrol back towards the killing area the gunships arrived. I established communications with the command Alouette of Captain Neall Ellis and with Commandant Roland de Vries …

The platoon came across two Urals that were left completely intact by FAPLA … The gunships commenced with [their] sweep along the road in a northerly direction towards Techamutete. I was watching closely for dust clouds from the approximate positions of Cuvelai in the south and Techamutete in the north … The avenging gunships kept on firing at clusters of enemy on the ground … There was the calm chatter coming from the microphone and headset, the drone of the aircraft's engine, now and then the stutter of the machine gun from next to you … We flew for approximately 20km northwards and found another eleven vehicles that had been rushed away by the enemy during the night and early morning hours. Many were left abandoned, haphazardly driven into bushes beside the road; a few had overturned.

It was almost macabre to see a gunship hovering, placing few accurate 20mm cannon shells into a Ural and, as flames erupted from the truck, drifting over to the next vehicle to repeat the treatment … . A complete convoy of 20 FAPLA vehicles had been annihilated and two captured.